Canada
Under Free Trade

The University League for Social Reform was launched in the sixties as an interdisciplinary group dedicated to bringing provocative thinking to a general readership.

It has sponsored substantial books on important national, social and political issues. Earlier publications include:

Stephen Clarkson, editor, *An Independent Foreign Policy for Canada*

Alkis Kontos, editor, *Domination*

William Leiss, editor, *Ecology versus Politics in Canada*
——— *The Limits to Satisfaction: An Essay on the Problem of Needs and Commodities*

Trevor Lloyd and Jack McLeod, editors, *Agenda 1970: Proposals for a Creative Process*

Ian Lumsden, editor, *Close the 49th Parallel Etc.: The Americanization of Canada*

Alan Powell, editor, *The City: Attacking Modern Myths*

Abraham Rotstein, editor, *The Prospect of Change: Proposals for Canada's Future*

Peter Russell, editor, *Nationalism in Canada*

David P. Shugarman, editor, *Thinking About Change*

Mel Watkins, editor, *Dene Nation: The Colony Within*

The University League for Social Reform

Canada
Under Free Trade

Edited by Duncan Cameron
and Mel Watkins

James Lorimer & Company, Publishers
Toronto, 1993

James Lorimer & Company Ltd. acknowledges with thanks the support of the Canada Council, the Ontario Arts Council and the Ontario Publishing Centre in the development of writing and publishing in Canada.

Canadian Cataloguing in Publication Data

Main entry under title:

Canada under free trade

Includes index.
ISBN 1-55028-379-0 (bound) ISBN 1-55028-377-4 (pbk.)

1. Canada - Economic conditions - 1991-   .*
2. Canada - Economic conditions - 1971-1991.*
3. Canada - Social conditions - 1971-   .*
4. Canada - Politics and government - 1984-   .*
5. Free trade - Canada. 6. Free trade - United States.
7. Canada - Relations - United States. 8. United States - Relations - Canada. I. Cameron, Duncan, 1944-   . II. Watkins, Mel.

FC630.C35 1992   971.064'7   C92-093760-8
F1034.2.C35 1992

James Lorimer & Company Ltd., Publishers
Egerton Ryerson Memorial Building
35 Britain Street
Toronto, Ontario M5A 1R7

Printed and bound in Canada

Contents

Acknowledgements

The idea for this book came from its publisher, Jim Lorimer. The co-editors wish to thank Stephen Clarkson and Daniel Drache for their assistance in the conception of the project. Much of the text benefited from the editorial assistance of Ed Finn, Research Associate at the Canadian Centre for Policy Alternatives. The Centre and the Common Frontiers Project in Toronto got many of the authors involved in analysis of the NAFTA text, and this book draws on the work done for the Centre publication entitled *Which Way for the Americas*. We are grateful to Jane Fredeman for copyediting the manuscript. Many thanks to Ginette Rozon, Manon Leclerc, and Francine D'Amour of the Faculty of Social Sciences at the University of Ottawa who provided assistance in preparing the manuscript for publication. Duncan Cameron wishes to acknowledge the assistance provided by the University of Ottawa through a sabbatical leave. This book is supported by the University League for Social Reform, and the co-editors welcome this association.

Introduction

Duncan Cameron

Rarely, if ever, has Canada seen a debate like that over the free trade agreement with the United States. From September 1985, when the Macdonald Royal Commission proposed a bilateral deal, until the 1988 election, proponents and adversaries argued over what was at stake and organized support and opposition for their positions. While the nationally televised leaders' debate during the election dramatized the confrontation, free trade was more than just a media event. In articles and books, studies and reports, models and impact assessments, specialists analyzed the meaning of the deal for the Canadian economy, for Canada's relationship with the U.S., and for Canada's place in the world economy. The Canadian public joined the debate; free trade became a kitchen table subject, a coffee shop issue. Indeed, the free trade debate ranged between an occasion for old enemies to trade insults to a national seminar on the nature of Canadian society and the workings of democracy.[1]

Though the election of a Conservative majority government ensured that the free trade agreement (FTA) would go ahead, it did not end political debate on the issue. The federal New Democratic Party favours abrogation of the FTA, the Liberals want the pact renegotiated, and the Conservative government has expanded its free trade agenda through negotiation of a North American Free Trade Agreement (NAFTA), a trilateral deal to include Mexico and, eventually, other Latin American nations. NAFTA is slated to come into effect in 1994, after the federal election. As drafted, NAFTA will override the existing bilateral accord, which, however, remains in force in case NAFTA fails to be implemented or is abrogated at some future date.

The purpose of this book is to examine the impact of free trade on Canada. Is Canada better off as a result of the FTA? To what extent has the recession of 1990–92 been caused by the FTA? What, if anything, can Canada do differently? These are the questions addressed in the contributions to this volume. They assess the arguments over the accord on the basis of more than four years of evidence. The book brings together expert analysis of how the deal has worked for various sectors of the economy and assessments of what changes are in store under NAFTA. It looks at how Canada's relationships with the U.S., Mexico, and the rest of the hemisphere are evolving as the free trade agenda broadens. The intent of the book is to help inform discussion about Canada's future.

Canada has long enjoyed an expanding trading relationship with the U.S. Cross-border trade had been governed by a multilateral agreement, the General Agreement on Tariffs and Trade, commonly known as the GATT. Under its rules, trade between the U.S. and Canada became the world's largest between any two trading nations. In effect, with the FTA, Canada now has two trading agreements with the U.S. Setting the FTA in context requires a comparison of the dynamic at work in the operation of the two accords.

Strategic Bargaining

Canada initiated free trade talks with the U.S. But it was President Ronald Reagan who signalled American intentions when, in his inaugural address in 1980, he called for a North American accord that would include both Canada and Mexico. U.S. negotiators clearly came to the bilateral table with important strategic objectives as well as with the blessing of the president to pursue them. The U.S. bargaining agenda included gaining greater access to Canadian resources and energy; protecting American investment; achieving new rights for services, agriculture, and entertainment industries; and bringing intellectual property under trade rules, as well as other trade-specific items. Most, but not all, American objectives were attained in the bilateral accord; others, notably those related to intellectual property, were achieved under NAFTA. In many instances, U.S. positions were not confined to bilateral matters between Canada and the U.S. They were a part of an overall trade strategy designed to establish precedents for multilateral talks. The U.S. was also showing it was prepared to negotiate with its trading partners one by one if it could not accomplish its strategic objective through the Uruguay Round of GATT talks. Since most U.S. trade is with countries other than Canada, the significance of the GATT round obviously weighed on the U.S. negotiators. The final text of the bilateral accord is unusual because it contains multiple references to the GATT round. To include references to an ongoing negotiation in a text designed as a basic document to be used for years to come surely attests to the importance the Americans attached to getting Canada to co-operate in GATT. For the U.S. to link Canada with the American negotiating stance in GATT on investment and intellectual property is no small feat. Canada is a major host country for foreign investment and a major importer of intellectual property, while the U.S. seeks to protect its investments abroad and exports intellectual property.

The basic negotiating structure of GATT provides for bilateral negotiations between major trading partners on tariff concessions and so-called non-tariff barriers to trade. In the past, this structure has consistently worked to Canada's advantage in gaining concessions from the U.S. Within the context of GATT negotiations, items are subject to bilateral Canada–U.S. talks, in which each side makes mutual concessions. Most granting of concessions by Canada is limited to what it gives up directly to the U.S. in return for U.S. concessions to Canada. This is the case because so much Canadian trade, about 80 per cent of exports, is with the U.S. In the meantime, however, the U.S. is involved in major concession bargaining with the partners that represent the 70 per cent of U.S. trade that is non-Canadian. Because the basic operating principle of GATT is the most favoured nation clause — what is conceded to one nation is conceded to all — Canada gains from the GATT talks all the concessions the U.S. grants to others. In effect, these U.S. concessions amount to unilateral gains by Canada from the GATT process. Often they are more important to Canada than what Canada can gain directly from negotiations with the U.S. The "injury test" that must be applied before countervailing duties may be assessed is one example. It was negotiated between the European Community and the U.S. under the Tokyo Round (1973–79), and it then became available to all other GATT countries.

Security of access means freedom from trade harassment. The U.S., like other countries, is able to bring accusations of unfair trading practices before domestic tribunals. Importers face anti-dumping laws, countervailing duties legislation, or safeguard actions. Such measures have the sanction of the GATT. When issues arise about the application of national laws and their conformity to GATT practices, GATT provides for dispute settlement by a panel drawn from member countries. Proponents of the FTA argued that Canada–U.S. trade was too important to be entrusted to the uncertain outcome of the GATT Uruguay Round. Canada needed a bilateral pact to secure access to the U.S. market in the face of U.S. protectionist threats. In addition, Canada would benefit sooner from increased access to the U.S. market through a more rapid reduction of remaining tariff barriers than would occur through awaiting the outcome of the GATT process. As a result, Canada changed its basic trading approach from multilateral negotiation to bilateral bargaining.

The Canada–U.S. trade deal falls under the GATT exemption for free trade areas. Under the GATT rules, Canada was entitled to eliminate the aplication of countervailing and anti-dumping duties within the free trade area. No such exemption was achieved in negotiations. Instead, the bilateral deal provided for judicial review in each country to be replaced by binational dispute panels that would assess whether an unfair trade law has been properly applied according to the law of the country initiating the action. In other words, Canada is still subject to U.S. trade actions despite the FTA, and, indeed, the number of trade actions against Canada has increased significantly since the FTA came into effect. Major cases have been brought against Canadian exports of steel, wheat, sugar, Honda motor vehicles, and softwood lumber. The dispute-settlement mechanism has not shielded Canada from trade harassment.

The agreement was also sold in Canada on the basis that economic benefits would flow from staged elimination of tariffs. But it is not primarily a tariff agreement. Canadian exporters faced an average tariff of only 1 per cent on all exports before the deal was negotiated and an average of 4 per cent on exports on which duties were levied. Fully 85 per cent of exports were duty free before the FTA. Clearly, its central goal is economic integration — between a superpower and a medium-size country. Flows of investment are liberalized, and corporations get national treatment (i.e., citizenship) in each other's market. However, restrictions on immigration remain. Both the FTA and NAFTA are partial common markets arrangements; they exclude the free movement of people and lack a common external tariff but provide for capital mobility and, eventually, tariff-free trade in goods and services. When each country says it will treat the other's companies exactly the same as its own, these national treatment provisions eliminate the ability of Canadian governments to legislate in favour of Canadian enterprise. Any laws passed in the U.S. to promote industrial goals put pressure on Canadian legislators to provide a business climate as favourable as that prevailing in the U.S. quickly or risk losing business investment.

The government's own attitude to the free trade deal, now that it is a reality, has changed considerably. In January 1988, the Department of Finance was indicating that "The economic benefits from the Free Trade Agreement will start to be realized shortly after the implementation of the agreement, January 1, 1989."[2] But the government has been unwilling to lay out the benefits in regular economic assessments, though if such information were available, it is hard to imagine government ministers would have kept it secret. Instead, after the deal had been in operation for one year, the government released a report by Infometrica, an Ottawa firm that has consistently supported the accord, on how the benefits might be measured. Yet, there has still not been a study on the economic impact of free trade by the government or an examination of the workings of the agreement by the House of Commons. The government did mail a brochure to households extolling the benefits of free trade and the advantages of NAFTA. But analysis of the special data package done by Statistics Canada for purposes of preparing the brochure reveals a different picture. (These figures were obtained under access to information legislation and are presented in Section II of this volume.)

Throughout the recession of the 1990s, the government rejected evidence of the destructive impact of the deal on Canada. By the spring of 1993, Trade Minister Michael Wilson began to point to a recovery in exports as evidence that the deal was working. In short, the government denied any causal link between Canada's economic performance and the trade deal while the economy performed poorly; but when the economy picked up somewhat, it credited the agreement for the improved results.

Evaluating the FTA

Few can doubt that the free trade agreement is important enough for Canada to merit analysis based on available evidence. The task is to see to what extent the agreement and the forces it set in motion have contributed to changes in the economy and in political approaches to national issues. In the chapters that follow, the agreement is assessed against its objectives as stated by the parties to the accord and as set out in the text of the accord. No assessment can be the final word, but distinct trends can be identified: the promise of free trade has not been realized, and economic integration with the U.S. is closing off options on trade, investment, industrial, social, cultural, and fiscal policy. For Canadians, the way in which the free trade model of economic development has worked so far raises the question of whether it is worth pursuing the NAFTA project and keeping the FTA.

What is most important in examining the implementation and workings of the bilateral accord, and in assessing its economic costs and benefits, is how it has served each country. From a Canadian perspective, initial conclusions are sobering. Section I shows that the FTA has imposed severe constraints on Canada. A new framework, akin to a constitution, is shaping Canada's integration with the U.S. economy. The FTA limits Canada's options, especially when its terms are compared to the multilateral trade rules of the GATT. Overall, while the major corporations that dominate cross-border trade have gained additional freedom to pursue their objectives, Canadians have not benefited from the new continental economics.

Section II details why the arguments advanced about the economic benefits to Canada of the agreement cannot be substantiated at this time. Indeed, the Canadian manufacturing sector went into recession in 1989, shortly after the trade deal went into effect and before the recession officially began in April of 1990. Both opponents and supporters agreed that economic restructuring brought about by the deal would bring dislocation for workers and their communities. But these so-called adjustment effects have been more swift and severe than was expected. Four years after the deal was concluded, there were about 500,000 fewer Canadians holding full-time jobs than before the deal. The promise of enhanced, secure, preferential access to the U.S. market was that new investment in Canada would promote new industries and expand existing operations. But the evidence shows that existing industry has been weakened considerably by free trade and that industrial expansion has failed to materialize to anything like the degree needed to offset job losses. Many Canadian firms have taken advantage of the investment protection available under the FTA and relocated to the U.S.

The governments of Ontario and Quebec identified the industries at risk under free trade, and job losses have occurred in those industries. That this has happened so swiftly is probably the result of the impact of tight money on the Canadian economy. High interest rates hurt Canadian companies as did the rising value of the Canadian dollar. A made-in-Canada recession was the result of free trade adjustment and the zealous pursuit of zero inflation. The dramatic increases achieved by American exporters in the Canadian market were not matched by Canadian companies in the U.S. market. These U.S. gains at the expense of Canadian production occurred in a slumping Canadian market. Canadian job losses were four times greater per capita than U.S. job losses.

Normally, imports fall during a recession, but this was no ordinary recession. Contrary to the case in the 1982 recession, job losses tended to be permanent rather than temporary. According to the Ontario Ministry of Labour, which is the only agency to keep this type of statistics, permanent losses increased from less than 25 per cent of the total in the 1982 recession to above 60 per cent in the recession of the early 1990s. The issue is whether Canada has experienced a one-time adjustment to the new market conditions or whether a trend has been identified towards continued weakness because of the incentive for Canadians to invest in the U.S. and the advantages for American-owned companies to service the Canadian market from the U.S. In the language of economists, if the marginal cost of production in the U.S. is less than the average cost of production in Canada, in an open market for investment there is a clear advantage to producing in the U.S. rather than Canada. In plain language, if it costs less to produce an extra amount for the Canadian market in the U.S. than it does to produce the product in Canada, production will shift to the U.S. from Canada, and new investments will be undertaken in the U.S. These production shifts have taken place (see Appendix I). NAFTA adds even lower-cost production from Mexico to the equation. Overall, business investment in Canada has declined. Those industries that have experienced growth account for a small share of production and jobs.

Section III of the book examines the issues that arise from the impact of free trade plus NAFTA. Looking at the most significant aspects of free trade suggests that hopes are being quashed and fears realized. The prospect that investment decisions will benefit Canada is dim. Concerns about the adverse aspects for the environment, culture, financial services, and public services are very real. For instance, the pressures on Canada to reduce its social policies to the American level are being borne out. Under NAFTA, the introduction of intellectual property rights creates a new protectionist regime for mainly American corporations. And the constitutional authority of the provinces to manage agriculture, energy, and other resources is constrained.

Section IV explores the broader issues of the free trade era: the extension of free trade to Mexico, the Enterprise of the Americas initiative, the fate of trading blocs, and the question of whether or not the agreements should be renegotiated or cancelled by the next Canadian government. In NAFTA, intellectual property rights and transportation are covered for the first time, there is a significant change in the way services are treated by the agreement, and new rules on industrial trade raise doubts about whose interests are being served by North American integration. In effect, NAFTA reflects a major renegotiation of the FTA, and Canada's preferential access to the U.S. market, much vaunted by supporters of the FTA, is downgraded.

In evaluating the FTA and NAFTA, it is important to distinguish what is meant by free trade, trade, and trade agreements; otherwise, important differences are obscured. In its technical sense, free trade means trade free of tariffs. In the case of the Canada–U.S. deal, tariffs are being phased out over ten years. But the agreement does not mean that people can move goods freely across the border. Customs declarations and border inspection of goods continue, whether it be for travellers returning from abroad or for importers of merchandise. Domestic sales taxes are levied on imports. In the FTA and NAFTA texts there are explicit rules of origin to determine whether or not goods have sufficient North American content to qualify for tariff reduction. And, of course, goods from outside North America are still subject to duty. Safety and health regulations must be met before imports can be accepted for domestic consumption. Concerns over the smuggling of illicit goods mean that border restrictions will always remain.

The words "free trade" have a strong ideological content. They are often used as a slogan to persuade people of the attractiveness of a point of view. People who rally to the call of free trade usually see it as corresponding to their free market convictions. As an ideology, free trade has important implications for democracy and the role of public policy, and the free trade agreements need to be examined in this light as well. As a slogan, free trade serves to mystify the complexity of the modern world economy.

What the Macdonald Commission, the Economic Council, and even the Department of Finance did not figure into their calculations of the benefits from free trade was the impact of exchange rate changes on the agreement. Indeed, modern trade theory, however sophisticated, does not deal with flows of capital, interest rate adjustments, and exchange rate changes when it models the effects of tariff changes on the economy. Instead of seeing monetary policy as central to economic performance, trade models treat it as something to be added in later. This method may simplify the task for analysts, but the results are misleading for anyone who takes their projections of economic benefits from free trade seriously. The increase in the value of the Canadian dollar that accompanied the negotiation and the implementation of the deal upset all projections of benefits to Canada from free trade (see appendix II). In effect, an increase in the exchange rate of 15 per cent is equivalent to imposing a tax on all exports of 15 per cent and removing a 15 per cent tariff on imports. Under these circumstances, the phased tariff reductions under the agreement pale into insignificance.

Critics of free trade were concerned that the agreement would lead to a downward harmonization of Canadian standards in social policy to levels prevailing in the U.S. The argument was straightforward. Since Canadian social programmes were more expensive than American social programmes, there would be increased pressure, under more open competition, to curb social spending. Ministers denied it. Business leaders denied it. But spending cuts occurred in the first budget after the agreement was implemented. More cuts were to come. The Canadian prime minister promised those whose lost jobs as a result of free trade the best adjustment packages in the world. Now, in Sweden, they spend more on job training than they do on national defence. And they spend, proportionate to GDP, more on national defence than we do. So, are we now bringing our adjustment programmes up to the Swedish level? Well, in fact, no. Instead of an adjustment programme, in 1989 we cut about 150,000 people off of U.I. benefits and reduced benefits for the rest. In 1992, access to the programme was reduced again.

In debating the merits of the FTA and NAFTA, proponents often fail to distinguish between opposition to a trade agreement and opposition to trade itself. While it may be useful in attempting to convince an audience of the value of the FTA to paint your adversary as being against trade, this rhetorical gambit avoids the fundamentals of international commerce. In order to trade, you need a product, a client, and, eventually, a contract setting out the details of the transaction. For Canada, the important trading issue is how to develop companies that can produce products for the international marketplace. Since the FTA and NAFTA rule out many common practices of industrial policy, they can be understood to reduce Canada's capacity to trade internationally rather than to enhance it. Arguments put forward in the abstract about the benefits of free trade need to be set against the terms of the FTA/NAFTA, not treated as if the agreements themselves are of little account and the only issue is that some people want trade and others do not.

Both Canada and the United States had national objectives in mind when they negotiated the bilateral free trade agreement. Some of these objectives were complementary. Others, very clearly, were not. Classical political science suggests that the workings of the agreement should be measured against the national objectives and interests of the parties to the accord. After more than four years of free trade, it is clear that the American government's principal negotiating objectives are being met. The same cannot be said for the Canadian government's objectives.

In negotiations on investment, the Americans wanted enhanced access to Canadian assets. They got much of what they wanted before the negotiations began through the transformation of the Foreign Investment Review Agency into Investment Canada. The upshot of the negotiations was that to all intents and purposes a continental capital market was established. Expanded merger and acquisition activities were the result. The takeover value of Canadian companies has been bid up to reflect American investor interest. Venture Economics reported that foreign takeovers amounted to $12.6 billion in the first three quarters of 1989 alone and pointed out that buyouts of minority Canadian shareholders in foreign subsidiaries are "directly attributable" to the trade deal.[3] Of course, overall, the inflow of capital pushed up the value of the Canadian dollar.

American objectives on investment were shared by Canadian business groups that supported free trade. Individual companies that wish to sell out have the advantage of higher prices created by greater freedom for American companies to purchase Canadian companies. In addition, Canadian companies get national treatment for investment in the U.S. With continued concern over security of access to the U.S. market for Canadian-based exporters, the new investment rules served to attract new Canadian investment to the U.S. In the meantime, there has been a decline in the annual growth of business capital expenditures in Canada, from 16.6 per cent in 1988 to 10.6 per cent in 1989 to -0.4 per cent in 1990, to -6.1 per cent in 1991 and to -1.5 per cent in 1992.

The American economy is a great consumer of resources. Security of supply has been an explicit objective of U.S. governments since the Paley Report assessed U.S. strategic needs after World War II. Officially, the trade deal only raises the threshold for the review of new investments. In fact, by enshrining national treatment for American investors and by prohibiting export taxes and performance requirements for American companies, the deal does much more. It integrates Canadian resources into a North American market model for economic development. At a time when environmental concerns should be given greater importance, the scope for further resource exploitation has increased.

The Canada–U.S. free trade agreement enshrined continental market rules for energy. Specific aspects of the agreement affect both energy pricing and security of supply. It is difficult to overstate the importance of energy in economic life. Energy consumption underlies every economic act. The cost structure of an industrial economy is built upon energy prices, and prices depend on assured access to supplies. The American objectives in negotiating with Canada were clear. They wanted unrestricted access to Canadian energy resources. As negotiated, the agreement guarantees the Americans access to whatever proportion of energy resources they receive from Canada even if Canada is running short of energy itself. In this proportional-sharing scenario, Canada gives up security of future supply in return for energy sales in the U.S. market. Under NAFTA, Mexico negotiated an exemption from the proportional-sharing provisions. In the first year of free trade, U.S. buyers moved swiftly to tie up future sources of energy from Canada. An incredible 90 per cent of Canada's proven Arctic gas reserves are now destined for the American market. In total, some 58 per cent of Canada's total gas reserves are now committed to the U.S.

Unlike the GATT, the free trade deal prohibits export taxes. It explicitly denies the government the right to establish higher prices for exports, leaving the marketplace to determine prices. Over time, the operations of the market should raise Canadian prices to the higher levels prevailing in the U.S. The only way Canadians can recover security of supply is to bid up the domestic price to the point where no Americans want to buy. Yet, in order to be competitive in the U.S. market, we need low-cost energy.

Canadian government policy offers public subsidies and tax advantages for oil and gas exploration. In a major departure from what is allowed for other goods elsewhere in the agreement, these subsidies are guaranteed by the deal. Though the subsidies are paid for by Canadian taxpayers, the prohibition of export taxes and differential pricing means that there is no way of recouping the cost of Canadian subsidies from American consumers. Therefore, Americans are guaranteed the same price as Canadians for Canadian energy.

In return for giving the U.S. the right to buy forever a proportionate share of our publicly subsidized energy, at our prices, Canada did not get security of access to the U.S. market for energy. In the spring of 1989, the Maine Public Utilities Commission cancelled a $5.3-billion export contract signed by Premier Robert Bourassa on behalf of Quebec Hydro. A regulatory body in California has yet to decide whether a Canadian gas consortium can supply the lucrative southern market in that state.

So, for energy, the Americans got the right to buy resources developed in Canada on a non-discriminatory basis, but we did not get the right to sell on a non-discriminatory basis. It is no exaggeration to state that the U.S. was able to ensure by treaty that Canadian energy resources should be part of its energy future and that developments would be paid for by Canadian taxpayers through subsidization of American oil companies that rate amongst the richest companies in the world.

This chapter of the agreement is so important that it is difficult to imagine that it will not be the subject of future controversy in Canada when energy supplies become tight, as they periodically do. What is at issue here is non-renewable resources. Energy that cannot be replaced is being shipped or contracted to U.S. consumers. Canada has given up rights to protect security of supply to its own gas reserves. The historical effect of instability in the Middle East on oil prices points to the dangers of the agreement for Canada.

One America

George Bush hailed the North American Free Trade Agreement as part of his dream for One America. His views can be dismissed as the musings of a lame-duck president indulging in the usual American fondness for hyperbole, or they can be seen as a statement of policy with serious consequences for Canada. The evidence points to the latter interpretation. American foreign policy in the post-war world has been bipartisan. It is worked out carefully in collaboration with business interests. Presidents don't speak off the cuff for themselves alone. They speak for a foreign policy coalition that has shaped the post-war world. And nowhere is this more true than on economic issues.

Taking a long view, and actively pursuing American interests, led successive American governments to act to make the world safe for American business. From the Marshall Plan to the Gulf War, the U.S. has been prepared to act unilaterally to promote its vision, with Canada usually following along. A network of transnational corporations grew out of liberalization of markets in Europe and the dismantling of colonial empires. The giant American-controlled corporations today dominate American foreign policy. They don't have the global economy to themselves, far from it. Both the influence of the U.S. government and the power of U.S. business are in decline on the world stage. The economic resurgence of Europe and Japan gave George Bush all the more reason to update the Monroe Doctrine.

Consolidating the U.S. economic domination of the Americas is the foreign policy objective behind NAFTA and the wider "enterprise for the Americas" initiative. Calling it free trade conceals the intention: keeping Europe and Japan out. NAFTA is a trading bloc. It is designed to fit Canada and Mexico into the American model of development, on terms amenable to American corporations. There is no willingness to share political power, as in the European Community. In fact, the idea is to use American power to enforce NAFTA rules directly.

As an international treaty, NAFTA becomes the law of the land for Canada and Mexico, but not for the U.S., although this fact is usually overlooked. The U.S. negotiated NAFTA, as it did the Canada–U.S. trade deal, under the so-called fast track authority. This allows the president to enact NAFTA as an executive agreement with Canada and Mexico if a simple majority of both the Senate and the House of Representatives agree to pass enabling legislation. An international treaty requires two-thirds support in the Senate and becomes the law of the land, standing above domestic legislation. Under an executive agreement, it is the enabling legislation that gives the treaty effect, and it is subject to the general legislative practice of Congress, meaning it can be overridden by any subsequent law passed by Congress.

Like the Canada–U.S. free trade agreement, NAFTA reflects the arguments of lawyers who favour a trading relationship governed by rules as well as the views of economists that are based on the theoretical case for free trade. While all three parties had important negotiating objectives, the wide disparity in bargaining power is reflected in the agreement. In reopening the FTA, it was improbable that the U.S. would have been obliged to give Canada any concessions at the expense of major U.S. interests. Yet, the U.S. was able to secure new gains from Canada. If, in the ongoing operations of NAFTA, Canada or Mexico did come out ahead, the U.S. would be able to force a renegotiation of the terms. This capacity was shown by the ease with which American negotiators were able to require Canada and Mexico to negotiate parallel accords on labour standards and the environment. International agreements between partners of disproportionate size cannot be expected to favour the smaller partners when they are bilateral or trilateral undertakings. The rule of law is always subject to power of negotiation. Even a superpower needs multilateral treaties like the GATT, though the superpower has much less control over the outcome of the negotiations and the workings of the treaty than it does in bilateral arrangements. It follows that for countries the size of Canada, multilateral treaties, where smaller countries can combine to negotiate common positions, are superior to bilateral treaties.

In a world where so-called knowledge-based industries represent the future, there is a tremendous advantage to be had from ensuring that new technologies, products, and processes can be patented and sold around the world. Property rights no longer mean just owning land, buildings, factories, and equipment: they also mean the commercial exploitation of scientific discovery. When it is recognized that a small group of huge companies control the process of turning ideas into products, the terms under which these intellectual property rights become available to the rest of humankind become a central political issue, subject to power relations and translatable into law.

In NAFTA, Canada gives U.S. owners of intellectual property the rights they have been seeking for years in international trade negotiations. For a country that — like almost all countries in the world — uses more intellectual property than it generates, this is a concession of major proportions with far-reaching consequences. In effect, we have accepted that rights accorded producers under American law will extend to Canada.

A large country with a small population needs a different transportation system than a large country with a large population does. By opening up the transportation sector to so-called free trade, Canada gives up the policy tools required to ensure basic East-West transportation services. Economic integration accelerates North-South trade flows, weakening the national rail, air, bus, and trucking industries. The NAFTA text builds on U.S. open market rules for transport.

Under the Canada–U.S. deal, a list of services was included for national treatment rules. NAFTA covers all services except for those specifically exempted. In North America, services industries employ more people and account for more domestic product than elsewhere. In Canada, this sector accounts for about 60 to 70 per cent of employment and product. Making most services subject to NAFTA rules means following American legislative prerogatives. Opening up the Canadian telecommunications market puts at risk a sector where Canada has enjoyed some important successes.

The *Wall Street Journal* has editorialized that NAFTA is about creating "Fortress North America." The Canada–U.S. deal included strict rules of origin designed to keep out products substantially manufactured outside North America. But for Canadian manufacturing, NAFTA is worse than the FTA. The new rules of origin are designed to favour higher levels of U.S. content. Canadian clothing made from European fabrics is subject to quotas in the U.S. NAFTA also removes incentives for major auto investments in Canada, and the auto parts industry that has not already shifted production south will have even greater reason to do so.

A lot of surprised people read in the government brochure, delivered to the door, that free trade has been great for Canada and that extending it to Mexico is going to make it even better. But if Canada wants an economic strategy to reverse the current decline, NAFTA is not the answer, and the costs of terminating the FTA must be faced. The alternative is another half a million jobs lost and industrial destruction. When President Franklin Roosevelt was questioned about his plans for fighting the Depression, he used to answer: "We'll try something, and if it doesn't work, we'll try something else." On free trade with the U.S., now to include Mexico as well, Michael Wilson and Brian Mulroney put a new twist on Roosevelt's approach. They try something, and if it doesn't work, they say it did. Then they do it again.

Section I
An Overview

Chapter 1

Constitutionalizing the Canadian-American Relationship

Stephen Clarkson

The Canada–U.S. free trade agreement is much more than a trade deal. Indeed, it can be best understood in the words of Ronald Reagan as "a new economic constitution for North America."

In this chapter, Stephen Clarkson shows how the bilateral relationship has been "constitutionalized" through setting new limits to government, defining new rights, and introducing new enforcement mechanisms, ratification procedures, and amendment procedures. In the new trilateral agreement, as under the bilateral deal, the principal point is that while Canada and now Mexico will be strictly bound by its terms, the U.S. retains the bulk of its sovereignty. Whether such an asymmetrical balance can be viewed for very long as desirable by the junior partners remains to be seen.

Constitutions and International Change

The world of the 1990s is marked by conflict and confusion: conflict within and between states; confusion about the characteristics that the resulting new political and economic forms are assuming. Great analytical uncertainty accompanies this geopolitical chaos: new realities no longer fit categories such as nation state that have been used to describe and explain them in the past.

One established concept under strain in the flux of late-twentieth-century political economy is that of "constitution." Over the past three centuries, when the global system comprised a set of largely autonomous states, the notion of constitution denoted the formal documents and unwritten conventions that determined and reflected the balance of social, ethnic, or regional forces within a political regime. Whether enshrined in written prose or established by legal custom, constitutions demonstrated six basic attributes:

   i) they described common policy-making institutions that had authority over the whole system;

   ii) they defined powers and set limits to what political institutions can do;

   iii) they established rights for citizens of the state;

   iv) they were enforced by mechanisms, whether formal or informal;

   v) they were legitimized by some method of ratification; and

   vi) they could be amended only according to specific formulae.

Constitutional analysts confined the scope of their interest to the internal workings of states for the good reason that — with the exception of imperial systems — interstate relations were too anarchic to be comprehended by a paradigm premised on the rule of enforceable law.

One consequence of military, technological, economic, and cultural globalization has been a loss of autonomy by the nation state, which has taken on increasing obligations to international regimes. The internalization of international constraints can be seen in its most articulated form in the members of the European Community, which accepted new disciplines on their behaviour in exchange for participation in the continent's supranational structures. The treaties and acts that have created the new Europe since World War II can readily be seen to be constitutional because they set up a supranational policy-making apparatus, imposed new limits on the actions of the individual nation states, defined rights for their members, worked out enforcement and amendment mechanisms, and achieved legitimacy through each participatory government's ratification process.

In sharp contrast with Europe, North America's gradual evolution over the past century as a continental state has been driven until the late 1980s more by forces of economic, social, and cultural integration than by clear political goals articulated by national élites. The recent trade agreements negotiated between Canada, Mexico, and the United States constitute a shift towards the formalization of the previously informal processes of continentalization. They reflect a strategic response by the U.S. to its changing global position and have dramatic implications for the political position of its two neighbours.

In the immediate post-war decades, when the U.S. was enjoying the dominant and benevolent phase of its world hegemony, Congress was loath to abandon any of its sovereign power to a supranational trade body. Accordingly, the General Agreement on Tariffs and Trade (GATT) was born weak and tied the hands of its smaller members as loosely as it did those of capitalism's superpower. In the overarching context of the Cold War, the United States dealt generously with its allies; it acted as first among equals in the various international bodies that handled the industrialized world's interrelations.

After 1970, when the United States found its economic primacy challenged and entered the second, predatory phase of its hegemonic trajectory,[1] it started to shift its diplomatic energy from ideological Cold War imperatives towards more commercial "Cold Peace" objectives. Washington came to believe that its competitors in Europe and Asia were using their governments' policies to create unfair advantages for their exporters while protecting their own markets in ways that improperly excluded American products. U.S. trade doctrine assumed that American transnational corporations could still triumph in world markets if only they faced a "level playing field." The task of U.S. trade diplomacy was to level the international field.

The Tokyo Round of the GATT's trade liberalization marked a transition by moving beyond simple tariff reductions to the knotty problem of non-tariff barriers, such as countervail and anti-dumping actions against competitors. At the Organization for Economic Co-operation and Development (OECD), a code of investment behaviour was worked out, defining "national treatment," the principle that policies developed for national firms should be applied to foreign corporations without discrimination.

As a result of the new trade agenda, the economic defences of smaller countries in the OECD and the Third World came under increasing pressure from outside at the very time that the formulae for the Keynesian welfare state and import substitution industrialization were failing to assure prosperity and high employment. Rather than protecting its national society against predators from the outside world, the nation state was increasingly having to respond to the demands of a globalizing market that required its own political system to reduce its economic defences. The state was becoming "internationalized" as part of a global decision-making system.[2] The price of membership in the world's trading institutions was to accept increasingly intrusive demands for conformity to internationally defined standards for social, industrial, and even environmental policy.

Although trade negotiators spoke the language of tariffs and non-tariff barriers, the United States kept adding other phrases to the international agenda in its attempt to reach a globally harmonized policy environment: intellectual property (corporations' right to profit from their patents and technology in other countries); free flow of information (the transmission of all kinds of data without political hindrance); services (financial, professional, touristic, and administrative activities that do not involve the exchange of commodities but account for huge financial transactions). In these new areas involving high technology and telecommunications, Washington was convinced that American transnationals enjoyed a significant comparative advantage whose exploitation would do much to restore the U.S.'s faltering global standing well into the twenty-first century.

In this period, the United States's attitude became much more demanding towards its trading partners. With the Soviet-bloc countries on their knees, it no longer felt it had to acquiesce to its partners' economic priorities in order to gain their military collaboration. For the United States a properly multilateralized world was one whose policy practices were uniform and modelled on its own. Accordingly, Washington's policy-makers started paying careful attention to the "unfair" practices of its smaller trading partners, whether rich or poor.

For Canada, the impact of the United States's international economic agenda went one step further, and the political price turned out to be considerably higher.

Canada and the Continental Economy

Canada's post-war experience in constructing a Keynesian welfare state under a centre-right Liberal Party yielded a high standard of living for three decades, but the experiment was built on weak premises. In the Cold War period Canada's great wealth derived from a series of traditional staple-based, low-value-added, high-volume, export-led industries whose main market was the downstream operations of integrated transnational corporations in the United States. Economic rents from the resource sector were redistributed by a moderately interventionist state to create a considerable degree of social equity for the country's less-developed regions and to support a somewhat inefficient, high-wage, import-substitution "Fordism" that relied largely on a tariff wall and branch plants that were continental extensions of other U.S. transnationals.[3]

Under these conditions, many sectors of Canada's political economy became continentally integrated. Independent production of complete warplane systems was abandoned in 1958, and the country's military-industrial complex became formally integrated with that of the United States in the Defence Production Sharing Arrangement of 1959, just one year after Canada's air defence was strategically absorbed within the North American Air Defence Command. Automobile production, almost completely controlled by four American companies, was rationalized on the continental level following the signing of the Auto Pact in 1965.

Even beyond such formal agreements, many sectors of Canadian life became completely absorbed by those of the United States. Mass culture industries (entertainment television, movies, advertising, sports) had little national content unless determined by government regulation or produced in the public sector. Canada was being continentalized by stealth. The federal state played an ambivalent role, sometimes as facilitator of Americanization and sometimes as defender of a certain minimal level of Canadian autonomy. One institution, for example, the Canadian Radio-Television and Telecommunications Commission, could in the same year both approve the introduction of cable TV, which effectively moved the U.S.'s cultural border three hundred kilometres to the north, and legislate Canadian content rules that created a reserved programming space for Canadian artistic production on the air waves.

Although the process of Canada's integration in North America was not formalized by an overarching document or institution, there were clear signs that a continental state was developing with a constitution based on convention.

i) *Common Policy-making Institutions*. Beyond the military sphere created by NORAD, policy-making at a continental level took place mainly within transnational corporations.

ii) *Limits to Government*. Washington accepted limits to the exercise of its superior power over Canada provided that Ottawa supported American anti-communist foreign policy abroad and refrained from interfering with American capital at home.

iii) *Rights for Citizens*. Individuals had no continental rights. The right of access for American corporate citizens to Canadian resources and the Canadian market was taken as given; Canada was treated to certain fruits of the American system, such as special access to bidding for Pentagon contracts.

iv) *Enforcement.* Enforcement of the rules of this intuitively understood game was assured by the high level of trust and co-operation that had developed among the relevant decision-makers of both political systems.

v) *Ratification.* The conventions of North America's continentalism were periodically legitimized by ritualized statements made by the national leaders, who, in uttering comforting clichés about the "world's longest undefended border," would confirm the "special relationship" between Ottawa and Washington with its emphasis on complementarity, not competition, between their economies.

vi) *Amendment.* Significant alterations in the continentalist system were generally made after extensive consultation. Since changes made by Washington to its macro-economic policy or its military strategy affected Canada as directly as if it were an American territory, Canadian politicians regularly requested — and just as regularly received — exemptions from particularly damaging measures.

This comfortable continental constitution was disrupted in the early 1970s when, experiencing the inflationary and commercial consequences of its disastrous venture in Asian warfare, the United States realized its global hegemony was being challenged by the emerging economic blocs in west Europe and east Asia. Washington decided it would have to get tough with friend and foe, partner and competitor. In August 1971, the shock of the protectionist measures known as Nixonomics jolted Liberal Ottawa out of its complacency. Overnight, Richard Nixon had changed the continental constitution. Suddenly, Canadian politicians discovered that Washington no longer felt itself limited by a gentlemanly code in what it could do to Canada: instead of communicating through quiet diplomacy, it leaked its demands to the press. Washington wanted to expand the obligations of the Canadian government in responding to U.S. demands and to enlarge the rights of its corporate citizens: domestic international sales corporations (DISC) were invented to promote the home-country operations of American transnational corporations at the expense of their foreign branch plants. Washington was enforcing these new policies by compulsion not by consensus: Canada could no longer count on Washington giving it privileged consideration in its policy-making. The American government was amending the conventions of the Canadian-American relationship unilaterally, not by consultation: American leaders stressed competition, not complementarity, in their discourse, thereby delegitimizing the special relationship. Had Nixon not thrown the American presidency into a turmoil that would take a decade to resolve, Canada might have had to bend to Washington's will much sooner.

As it was, Ottawa tried — under Pierre Trudeau's half-hearted leadership — to reduce its vulnerability to American economic nationalism and chart for itself a more national course of development that resembled the social democratic approaches taken in some north European countries. Although it never developed a comprehensive industrial strategy to move the Canadian economy towards a high-value-added, high-technology, nationally directed model, the federal government did take several steps towards making the Canadian economy less vulnerable and more autonomous. It created a national investment company (Canada Development Corporation), an agency to review foreign takeovers and extract greater benefits from the branch operations of transnational corporations (Foreign Investment Review Agency), and a national oil company (Petro-Canada). These efforts by the federal state to develop a more national mode of regulation were largely ineffectual in the face of the deepening continental regime of Canadian capital accumulation patterns.[4]

By the end of the 1970s, Canada's dual-sector model was running into trouble. The terms of trade turned against raw materials in the staples sector, where exploitation was becoming increasingly capital intensive and uncompetitive as resource supplies dwindled. Foreign ownership was so extensive in the manufacturing and service sectors that they had little of the indigenous innovative capacity in high-technology areas that has been so central to the economic successes of Japan and Sweden. As levels of tariff protection fell, the manufacturing sector lost ground in the home market without being competitive enough to make gains abroad.

In the face of a sullenly unresponsive business community, the Trudeau Liberals took a big gamble. In 1980 they made a bold move to regain national control over the petroleum industry. The National Energy Program (NEP), designed to exploit rising petroleum prices for industrial development, came to symbolize the ambition and the folly of the Liberals' national consolidation strategy. Its ambition was to displace foreign with national ownership of the oil and gas sector; its folly was to attempt this radical action at the very moment that Ronald Reagan came to power in Washington and prices on the world oil market peaked.[5]

Towards Bilateral Treating

In calling for the establishment of a "North American accord" during his 1980 election campaign, Reagan showed an extraordinarily intuitive grasp of the continental requirements of American economic strategy. Multilateral and unilateral trade initiatives could only have limited successes; bilateral action in the Western hemisphere promised the best prospects for restoring America to the saddle in the emerging tripolar world.

Washington was bound to continue its active participation in multilateral negotiations for trade liberalization since gains made at the GATT had global effect and so were potentially the most rewarding in the long term. But the United States's clout was no longer great enough automatically to achieve its goal of breaking down its competitors' economic defences. This realization did not prevent American politicians from taking an aggressive stance in the new Uruguay Round of the GATT negotiations; they demanded an abolition of agricultural subsidies, a new regime for intellectual property rights, the inclusion of services in the trade regime, and the declaration of a code defining what industrial subsidies governments would be allowed to offer their enterprises.

If Washington had least control when working multilaterally at the GATT, it could exert most control unilaterally. Despite the neo-conservatives' rhetorical insistence on trade liberalization, the Reagan years saw a further tightening of Congress's already powerful protectionist legislation. The 1988 Omnibus Trade Act and its infamous "Super 301" gave the U.S. administration powerful new weapons that could be fired at individual trading partners — whether in the First World or the Third — who were deemed to be unfairly subsidizing their entrepreneurs' exports to the U.S. or using their state policies to constrain the scope for American exporters.

Bilateral action, the third dimension of the Reaganites' approach to trade diplomacy, represented a new twist on an old strategy. Ever since President Monroe had enunciated his doctrine of hemispheric supremacy in 1823, the United States had claimed the Americas as its special sphere of influence. Now its prime geopolitical objective was to stem the U.S.'s relative decline in global strength by building a regional base from which to take on its European and Japanese competitors. Enlarging the scope of its transnationals' protected home market and finding them a Third World (maquiladora) labour base within Fortress America would strengthen their competitiveness. Extending tariff and non-tariff barriers against European and Japanese conglomerates would help prevent their competitors from benefiting from the advantages of a single North American market.

The beauty of a bilateral game plan was that it could be executed in parallel with GATT's multilateral negotiations. The successful negotiation of a bilateral trade deal would also signal to the international community that the United States had other arrows in its quiver. Progress made on a bilateral agenda could be applied as precedents at the multilateral level. By signing a bilateral trade treaty with Israel, Washington had already shown that if its global interlocutors were not ready to talk, it had other options for achieving its goals — and they had better be careful lest they find themselves left out in the cold.

By the mid-1980s Canada — the United States's most open and most accommodating partner — was the obvious subject for testing this strategy in the Western hemisphere. Its flirtation with a more autonomous mode of regulation had come to an ignominious end even before Pierre Trudeau resigned as prime minister in 1984. Under his aegis, the Liberal government had shown its interest in expanding the scope of managed trade by tentatively proposing to Washington the negotiation of more free trade sectors on the model of the Auto Pact. Although nothing had come of this probe, it prepared the way for Trudeau's successor, Brian Mulroney, to endorse the notion of continental free trade wholeheartedly.

When Mulroney was first elected prime minister in September 1984, the contradictory label of his party, Progressive Conservative, nicely defined his political position: he claimed to be committed to preserving the social programmes of the welfare state as a "sacred trust," but he was also the spokesman for business interests impatient with the constraints imposed on them by the allegedly interventionist Liberal government. The tensions created by trying to juggle these incompatible positions proved unbearable. Within a year, the prime minister had adopted a mainly neo-conservative agenda, which had been conveniently articulated by a massive public inquiry, the Macdonald Royal Commission. This massive public inquiry, established three years before by the Trudeau government, managed to articulate the Canadian business community's continental interests as theorized by neo-classical economics.[6]

Central to this new agenda for Canada was the achievement of a bilateral free trade agreement with the United States that would, it was argued, gain not just "secure" but "enhanced" access for Canadian manufacturers to the huge American market: *secure* through gaining exemption for Canadian exporters from the application of U.S. protectionist legislation and *enhanced* from a reduction of U.S. tariffs against Canada's manufactured goods. In effect, free trade was to become Canada's alternative to import substitution as an industrial strategy: it would allow Canadian firms to become globally competitive by exploiting the magic of scale economies. Eagerly promoted by a prime minister who had made "super relations" with the United States the cornerstone of his foreign policy, bilateral free trade became a matter of life and death for the government. Mulroney promptly asked Washington to begin negotiations. Pleased to be dealing with a government so eager, even desperate, to reach an agreement, Washington played with its northern friend like a game fish, using its considerable bargaining skills and greater strength to toy unashamedly with its interlocutors and land a deal that created many valuable precedents for American trade policy, making breakthroughs in the fields of government disciplines, access to Canadian resources, investment rights, and services trade.

Washington gave up little and gained much when it signed the Canada–United States Free Trade Agreement (FTA).[7] In exchange for eliminating its tariffs along the Canadian border, it secured the elimination of Canadian tariffs that were on the average twice as high. It maintained intact the sovereignty of Congress to pass new trade measures that could supersede the trade agreement. It avoided negotiating a definition of "subsidy" that might lessen the scope of its countervail actions against Canadian producers or exempt Canadian exporters from the application of its other protectionist laws.

The concessions that Canada made in response to American negotiating demands suggest that what is known as an agreement about "free trade" can be more properly understood as a constitutional document as important for the future of the northern dominion's political system as the Constitution Act of 1982. The FTA took a hesitant step towards creating common policy-making institutions, set new limits to government, defined new rights, introduced new enforcement mechanisms, was brought into force by acts of the signatory states, and laid out amendment procedures.

i) *Policy-making Institutions.* The Canada–United States Trade Commission (CUSTER) was set up on paper but not in practice. With neither supranational secretariat nor permanent address, it consists merely of periodic meetings of the Canadian trade minister and the

United States trade representative plus seconded staff. As an institution CUSTER is a hollow shell.

ii) *Limits to Government.* Those who had read the Macdonald Report had been given the vision of a bilateral agreement that would concentrate on trade barriers and exclude the Auto Pact, agriculture, energy, and culture from its purview. Citizens had heard their prime minister and his negotiators publicly insist that neither the Auto Pact, nor culture, nor energy would be "on the table."

In fact, the FTA constrains governmental action in each of these sectors and in many other ways.

- In the energy sector, Canadian governments are prohibited from using the price system to act in the interest of Canadian consumers or Canadian industry over those of American importers.
- In controlling foreign investment, the powers of the federal agency to impose conditions on foreign capital are greatly restricted.
- The Auto Pact has been altered to make future Japanese transplants unable to use Canada as a base for their North American assembly plants.
- In agriculture, the competence of such institutions as the Canadian Wheat Board is severely curtailed.
- In financial services, the Canadian government is prevented from discriminating against American banks, which are given national treatment.
- Cultural policy, while nominally excluded from the scope of the FTA by section 2011/1, is actually included by the subsequent paragraph, 2011/2, which establishes the United States's right to retaliate by taking "measures of equivalent effect" in any other economic area to compensate for losses that the American entertainment industry might claim because of future cultural policies enacted by Canadian governments.[8] The practical result of this clause is to prevent Canadian governments from taking any action to protect or extend Canadian cultural industries that impinge in any way on Hollywood's ample bottom line.

The FTA shifts power from the provincial to the federal government as Scott Sinclair explains in Chapter 16. While there has been a stormy debate about the implications of these and many other provisions, defenders and opponents of the FTA alike agree that it will make the undertaking of another National Energy Program impossible. In other words, no future Canadian government would be able to mount an interventionist industrial strategy, whether by leaning on the energy sector to serve the national interest at the expense of supplying the American market or by using other policy tools commonly used by industrialized states.

iii) *Rights for Citizens.* The only "citizens" whose rights are extended by FTA are corporate entities. In accepting the principle of national treatment, Canada is prevented from providing any help for Canadian firms that it does not also offer American companies. National treatment, the right of establishment, and the right to bid on government procurement contracts effectively grant American corporations access to important new fields, such as services, and represent major extensions of their sphere of operation in Canada.

iv) *Enforcement.* At first glance, the enforcement provisions of FTA are not impressive. No august supranational chamber has been created to act as the supreme court of North America. CUSTER is fraught with so many ambiguities in the FTA document that it is difficult to foresee how various eventualities will be handled.[9] For instance, the federal government is obliged to have the provinces respect the letter and spirit of FTA even though the courts would not necessarily deem Ottawa's jurisdiction adequate to this policing task.

Nevertheless, a second reading makes it clear that the FTA significantly extends Washington's power to monitor and control Canadian political life. Notification is specified as an obligation for each "party" to give the other "party" advance warning of any intended local or federal government policy that might affect the other side's interests as defined by the FTA. Implicit is the recognition that the United States has the right to know whatever is going on in the Canadian political system that might have some bearing on its interests. Uncle Sam's desire to know has become Cousin Canuck's duty to inform.

A similar emphasis is put on engaging in bilateral consultations as the means to warding off potential conflicts. The other side's right to know becomes extended to the right to satisfaction through negotiations — even before the democratically elected parliaments of the federal or provincial governments have had a chance to act in what they believe to be their public's interest. This significant extension of political interdependence increases Canada's vulnerability, multiplies the possibilities of linkage between bilateral issues, and introduces new ways for the United States legitimately to intervene in Canadian politics and press its demands.

The dispute-settlement mechanism, over which much ink has been spilled, does not comprise a truly supranational institution.[10] Rather the panels that the Canada–United States Trade Commission (CUSTER) can establish under the FTA's Chapter 19 for resolving commercial disputes are bodies set up on an ad hoc basis merely to determine whether one government's trade action is consistent with its *own* trade law. The presence of panelists from both jurisdictions represents a minimal concession to the idea of supranationality, but the agreement clearly leaves the implementation of a panel's ruling up to CUSTER, which is a binational body deciding issues by consensus. Translated into plain American, deciding by consensus means that each country — but, most importantly, the United States — retains a veto power over the actions of the enforcement agency.

As the number of panel settlements grows, a body of precedent is being created. Panel members are not permanent officials, but their experience contributes to a consolidation of American trade-law practice, which directly affects federal and provincial bureaucrats in Canada, who now plan policy so that it will not come up against American contingency protection. In this respect, CUSTER is helping continentalize U.S. trade law, getting it applied at the heart of the Canadian political process.

In the mechanism for settling disputes arising from the implementation of FTA that is described in Chapter 18 of the agreement, a party's ultimate sanction is to take retaliatory action against the other. Given the overwhelming disparity in power between the United States and Canada, the FTA's legitimizing of retaliation means that Washington's right to discipline Canadian governments for not performing in a manner satisfactory to it is accepted explicitly.

v) *Ratification.* The passing of the FTA by both the American Congress and the Canadian Parliament, with the ultimate signature of the document by the American president and the Canadian prime minister on 1 January 1989, indicates the weight of legitimacy given by the ratification process.

vi) *Amendment.* If it takes agreement by both Congress and Parliament to alter it, the constitutional quality of the FTA for Canada needs little further substantiation. For Canada, the tablets are chipped from stone on Capitol Hill.

Constitutional Asymmetry

If the FTA's provisions are so powerful that they can be considered part of Canada's constitutional framework, does it not follow that the

FTA is *ipso facto* part of the United States constitution? On the face of it, there are good reasons to think this to be the case. The FTA is a bilateral agreement made between two formally sovereign states that are committed to its application. In most cases, the clauses apply equally to each "party" to the agreement. Nevertheless, the tenor of the document is not symmetrical, as we can see by estimating the constitutional weight it will bear in the American system.

i *and* ii) *Limits to Government.* While the U.S. may be theoretically bound by the same restrictions on its energy policy as is Canada, the effective limitation is negligible because it imports rather than exports petroleum. The provisions affecting the automobile industry are pertinent only for Canada. It is difficult to see in what way it can be maintained that the FTA puts a crimp on future U.S. policy-making. U.S. implementing legislation explicitly asserted Congress's right unilaterally to pass laws that altered the FTA.

iii) *Rights for Citizens.* The Canadian government — which is only too eager to claim every possible benefit on the FTA's behalf — has not suggested that the application of the national treatment principle will force Washington to make the new Clinton administration's industrial strategy incentives and stimuli available to Canadian firms on the same footing as to its own companies. Where the Canadian negotiators had a strong case for reciprocity — getting the same treatment for Canadian banks in the U.S. as Canada was giving U.S. banks in Canada — they were flatly turned down. If the FTA had really given Canadian firms operating in the United States substantially greater rights, there would be no reason for so many to have closed down and moved to the United States to gain access to the U.S. market — but as American corporate citizens.

iv) *Enforcement.* The frail nature of CUSTER's institutional structure underlines how little the FTA has constrained American sovereignty. In establishing a dispute-settlement mechanism, the United States has simply accepted some Canadian personnel participating in a review process with fixed deadlines that is to provide a means for deciding whether determinations made by its quasi-judicial trade bodies correctly apply U.S. law. While dispute-panel decisions are said to be binding, there is nothing beyond political goodwill that makes them so: the United States need not fear Canadian retaliation in cases of its non-compliance with panel decisions.

v) *and* vi) *Ratification and Amendment.* In a formal sense, the FTA has a constitutional quality for the United States because it can only be ratified and amended with the agreement of the Canadian government. What President Reagan referred to as the continent's economic constitution was ratified by the American president and the Canadian prime minister formally signing the agreement and by the legislature in each country passing legislation to implement the FTA's provisions in domestic law.

While this is true in a legalistic sense, what is far more important is the power Congress has retained for its trade law to take precedence over the FTA. The application of the omnibus trade bill to Canada was not restricted in any way by the FTA. Precedents in the U.S. Supreme Court indicate that provisions of international agreements signed by the U.S. executive do not prevail over subsequent legislation passed by Congress. The FTA accepts in section 1902 that Congress can change its laws affecting trade with Canada so long as such amendments specifically mention Canada. Far from constitutionally tying the hands of Congress, the FTA provides an instrument with which Congress can exert its leverage over Canada by setting up oversight processes that further institutionalize its interest in keeping its competitor to the north under control. In short, the FTA constitutionalizes Canada's continental dependency as a post-national state with barely any limitation on the autonomy of the American hegemon.

From the FTA to NAFTA
Canadians were astonished when they learned that, having just worked out what was meant to be a historic trade agreement with Canada, the United States was already in the throes of bilateral trade talks with countries throughout Latin America. Having exploited Mexico's crisis during the 1980s to pressure the Institutional Revolutionary Party (PRI) government into taking a broad range of liberalization measures, Washington wanted, first of all, to institutionalize the Salinas regime's many measures to deregulate, privatize, and downsize the state. However Washington rationalized its initiative with Mexico — to encourage "democratic values" south of the border; to facilitate employment opportunities there and reduce the pressure of Mexican emigration; to extend the space for American transnationals and secure a cheap labour force for them; to expand the domain of Fortress America and secure it against Japanese competitors — inducting Mexico into a trade agreement would be the next step towards reducing the power of the state throughout Latin America and continuing the World Bank's structural adjustment

programmes that bring market discipline to government economic policy throughout the Third World.

From the point of view of neo-conservative ideologues in Canada, this was good news, but the Canadian government had barely begun to deal with the consequences of the FTA when it had to face the prospect of the United States signing a separate trade deal with Mexico. Canada feared such a deal could jeopardize what it considered to be its privileged position in Washington if it did not participate in the Washington-Mexico negotiations. It needed to resist the extension of a hub-and-spoke system for the hemisphere, in which Washington was the hub and every other country formed a separate spoke linked only through the emerging continental capital.[11]

While the federal government trumpets American gains in NAFTA as if they were good for Canada — far more invasive provisions for intellectual property rights, higher North American content rules that are already driving Japanese investors from Canada, further extensions of the application of national treatment, broadened definitions of services — two characteristics strike a Canadian eye.

In the first place, NAFTA is as significant a constitutional document for Mexico as the FTA was for Canada. With its wide-ranging prescriptions for what the Mexican government must do and cannot do, with the rights of American corporations spelled out in great detail, with the more elaborate dispute-settlement and enforcement mechanisms, with its three-government ratification, and with its difficult amendment process (agreement by the three signatory states), NAFTA introduces a new dimension to Mexico's constitution.

What is more, the new document is almost as institutionally empty as was the FTA. This suggests that as the constitution for an enlarged continental regime, NAFTA will remain a highly asymmetrical power system. The U.S. will retain the bulk of its sovereignty while its growing band of junior partners are strictly bound by NAFTA and, later, WHEFTA (Western Hemisphere free trade) into a new post-national dependency in which one of their governments' chief roles will be to enforce U.S. policies on their territories.

Next Steps

In trying to assess the significance of the FTA and NAFTA for the future of the Canadian political system, it may be helpful to put our crystal ball in a comparative and ideological context. We should first compare the unbalanced, poorly articulated constitutional structure of the emerging North American state with Europe's measured process of continental integration.[12] The European Community's more deliberate, more democratic, more balanced and more gradual process of continentalization has encouraged member states to give up some sovereignty in order to increase their autonomy. The supranational institutions of the European Community (EC) assure its smaller post-national members larger voices in the vital affairs of the continent than they would have as more sovereign nation states.[13]

We also need to consider the question of ideological conjuncture. Entrenching a radically right-wing agenda in Canada and Mexico through trade agreements at the very moment that America's infatuation with neo-conservatism is coming to an abrupt end presents a conundrum. President Clinton's Washington is committed to playing catch-up with Japan and the European Community by promoting the competitive potential of American enterprise. Yet, with NAFTA, Ottawa and Mexico City have agreed to renounce the very kinds of industrial policy that the "new Democratic party" in Washington is busily preparing to adopt. In effect, Clinton will be ignoring NAFTA's disciplines while his junior partners blithely tie their second hands behind their own backs and, more important, those of their successors in power.

The passing of the nation state may well be inevitable, but the kind of continental state in which it is to find a place is not an immutable reality. Constitutions embody ideological values. They express the interests of dominant élites. But an externally enforced constitution like NAFTA, which violates democratic norms (by withdrawing policy power from elected governments) offends popular values (by getting adopted in the face of public opposition) and represents the interests of a generation whose time has come, and almost gone, is unlikely to enjoy a long and happy life.

Political scientists have long affirmed that a constitution can only succeed in directing a state's functioning if it is reasonably attuned to the political and economic forces at play within its boundaries. The new trade agreements that the United States is managing to impose on its neighbours are unlikely to survive in the long term if they awaken the democratic forces they were designed to marginalize.[14] If the new entity created by Washington's trade bilateralism better serves the interests of its corporations than those of its citizens and undermines rather than supports the structures and cultures of its member states, it is hard to foresee it living happily ever after. Driven by remorseless global pressure, the Canadian, like the Mexican, state will not be able to avoid engaging in a continuing process of reforming its external constitution. Although it will continue to be difficult to deal with a beleaguered United States, these countries would do well to seek strength in pressing for a recasting of NAFTA by developing concerted demands based on their common position as territories on the United States's immediate periphery. Canada may not agree with many of the Mexican government's views on environmental and labour rights. Nevertheless, the two countries do share a larger interest either in achieving a more articulated set of continental institutions that provide representation of the peripheral countries at the centre or in dismantling the inherently unstable NAFTA. *E pluribus unum* might not be a bad motto for the countries of the Western hemisphere contemplating trade agreements with the U.S.A.

Chapter 2

Continental Corporate Economics

Bruce Campbell

Continental free trade is about giving more freedom to corporations over investment decisions. Transferring production facilities from country to country or region to region in pursuit of lower wages, easier environmental regulations, less onerous tax regimes, and generally more compliant government policy becomes a real alternative for many companies. This free trade dynamic has important implications for Canada.

In this chapter, Bruce Campbell shows that much of the free trade case has been built on questionable assumptions. Full employment is a given, as is capital immobility. Yet, for Canada, persistent unemployment has been a serious problem in much of the country for years, and international capital mobility is a fact of life. Lowest common denominator competition inhibits environmental protection, weakens the fiscal capacity of government, and attacks wages and labour standards across the continent. Four years of Canadian experience show that free trade has been a multi-purpose device for advancing the deregulation and privatization agenda of the Conservative government.

Despite its name, free trade is firstly about the deregulation of investment and secondly about the removal of government controls or regulations on economic activity that directly or indirectly affect trade. For free trade advocates, any derogation from the ideal of total free or unregulated trade is sub-optimal and, even if necessary under real world conditions, a second-best solution. Regulations or controls are seen as barriers to trade that should be removed. To resist the removal of controls or deregulation is to be labelled (pejoratively) protectionist, on the side of narrow self-interest and inefficiency.

The provisions that deregulate capital are at the core of the FTA/NAFTA. Their social, economic, and environmental impacts on Canada far outweigh, for example, the tariff elimination provisions. A trade agreement whose main aim was to eliminate the 4 per cent average U.S. tariff on dutiable imports from Canada would never have generated the public controversy that the FTA has. Yet, the analysis by free trade advocates almost never emphasizes these features of the agreement. This is particularly interesting because the neo-classical theoretical case for the benefits of free trade and comparative advantage (and likewise the gains projected by computable general equilibrium [CGE] models) is based on several critical assumptions, one of which is that capital is largely immobile across national borders. It is one of the ironies in this debate that many of the proponents of a "borderless world" are basing their case for free trade on a theory that depends critically on the existence of strong borders. Once that assumption is removed, then the reality of capital moving freely in pursuit of absolute cost advantages in the region as a whole, rather than for comparative advantage within national borders, must be addressed.

Another critical assumption of the neo-classical case for free trade is that all national economies are at full employment and that under free trade there is no net job loss but rather a restructuring involving the movement from less-efficient to more-efficient jobs. However, in an economic space dominated by capital mobility and absolute advantage considerations, there is no guarantee that specialization and trade will not harm one or more of the countries (or the majority of the population within each country) in terms of loss of capital and jobs and therewith a loss in aggregate demand and output, even if one were to assume that it would increase overall output in the area.

This is what appears to have happened in Canada during the first four years under the FTA, though it is hotly denied by most free trade proponents. Or consider the case of Mexico. During the 1980s, Mexico, under conditions of extreme financial duress, dramatically opened its economy (with a little help from the International Monetary Fund). It produced a virtual boom in manufacturing exports. Led by the auto and the maquiladora sectors, manufactured exports expanded more than fourfold during the period 1980–88. However, during roughly the same period, aggregate output remained at a standstill, and average real wages fell by 50 per cent.[1]

The FTA/NAFTA has little in common with conventional free trade agreements. The multitude of agreements of this type that have come into being since the Second World War (the European Free Trade Area and the Latin American Free Trade Agreement are examples) have been essentially tariff-reduction agreements on merchandise trade. If FTA/NAFTA were such a deal, there would be relatively little controversy. It is, despite its name, a sweeping economic integration agreement as ambitious in many areas as the integration initiative of the European Community and, indeed, goes beyond it in areas such as resources. Therefore, FTA/NAFTA must be analyzed concretely in terms of its specific provisions and their impacts and not according to some stylized formulation of "free trade" to which it bears little resemblance.

A measure of the inability of neo-classical theory to predict the effects of free trade accurately is evident when the CGE models' employment forecasts for Canada under the FTA are compared with the actual Canadian employment experience. These results are summarized in Table 2–1. The divergence between the expected and the actual is so great that, even taking into account the other factors at play, the claims made as to their scientific authority are largely discredited.

To illustrate the lack of realism of neo-classical assumptions built into CGE models, Jim Stanford outlines an imaginary conversation between an auto worker and a CGE model builder. It bears quoting in its entirety:

> Imagine a conversation between an auto worker in the Midwest and the architect of one of the CGE models reviewed above. The worker fears that her employer [Ford] may transfer the production of, say, Taurus cars to Mexico, hiring workers for less than one-tenth her wage with no independent union; output is exported back to the U.S. She would be laid off — and in a region, with a chronically depressed "Rustbelt" labour market, would be unlikely to find another job with comparable wages.
>
> The CGE modeler quickly reassures the employee. "Don't worry", he says. "In my model, firms cannot move their factories to Mexico (no capital mobility), and the lack of union protection there has no impact on wages (competitive factor markets). At any rate,

the Tauruses produced in Mexico are fundamentally different from those produced at home, and are not preferred by U.S. consumers (Armington assumption). Anything imported from Mexico must be balanced by exported American products (balanced trade). And because you earn above-average wages at Ford, you obviously possess much 'human capital' (competitive factor markets), and thus you will certainly find another job very shortly (full employment) in one of the new export industries, which will probably pay more than your current job. So a NAFTA will be great for you ... at least in my model." We might forgive the Ford employee for being less than convinced by a CGE model that crosses a deep ravine by assuming a bridge.^{2}

The FTA/NAFTA covers trade in services as well as goods, capital mobility as well as labour mobility for professional and business groups, and the activity of corporations as well as the management of resources. These trade agreements establish regimes governing financial, transportation, telecommunications, and agricultural sectors and introduce an intellectual property code and harmonized standards in areas such as professional qualifications, agricultural inspection, and health. Directly or indirectly, little of Canadian economic, social, or environmental policy has been untouched by the FTA.

The FTA/NAFTA codifies, or entrenches in treaty, a continental integration process (and accommodating changes in national regulatory regimes) that has proceeded quite rapidly in the 1980s. Not only has it continentalized these regulatory regimes, but also it has introduced new regimes and stimulated a major new round of economic integration and restructuring. Ultimately, the FTA/NAFTA represents a further shift in power in favour of capital, reinforcing globalization trends, further constraining government policy, and weakening the power of labour and other social groups.

Key provisions of FTA/NAFTA take away a host of policy tools that help to hold transnational corporate decision-making accountable to national or provincial economic priorities. These include: performance requirements to promote domestic value added, technology transfer, and so forth; resource management tools, such as export taxes or quotas, to encourage domestic processing; agricultural supply management tools to balance supply and demand; compulsory licensing of patents to nurture home-grown technology, and many more. Other provisions prevent governments from adopting

Table 2–1
EFFECTS OF U.S.–CANADA FTA ON SECTORAL EMPLOYMENT IN CANADA
Projected Percentage Changes by Selected Studies

	Cox Harris 1986 (1)	Economic Council 1987 SIM2 (2)	Brown Stern 1987 (3)	Brown Stern 1989 (4)	Actual % changes Dec. 1988-Dec. 1992 (5)
Forestry/logging			2.2		-13.1
Mines, quarries, oil wells		4.7	2.2	-1.1	-23.4
Food and beverages	-1.8	2.9			-14.7
Rubber and plastics	6.2	-0.7	2.4	-1.2	-27.4
Leather industries	-6.9	-5.2			-36.3
Textile	72.5	-0.7	-0.4	-35.4	-23.2
Clothing	261.6	2.6	0.8	-6.4	-39.6
Wood	-12.1	5.0	1.1	-6.1	-23.3
Furniture	37.4	2.4	2.4	-2.5	-30.3
Paper and allied	31.7	1.1	0.7	-19.3	-18.1
Printing and publishing	13.5	7.1	-0.9	-3.3	-9.7
Primary metals		3.9			-22.2
Iron and steel	27.9		1.2	28.5	-28.5
Nonferrous metals			3.1	152.4	-12.5
Metal fabricating	-6.6	2.8	-1.6	-7.1	-21.3
Machinery	-33.2	2.8	2.5	-1.2	-28.8
Transportation equip.	62.2	1.6	3.3	0.5	-12.2
Electrical products	-0.5	-2.5	-0.7	-14.2	-22.8
Non-metallic mineral	-0.6	2.8	0.6	-16.8	-27.8
Petroleum and coal	-7.4	1.3	2.5	-11.6	-18.4
Chemicals	-0.2	0.6	-0.8	17.9	-7.8
Construction		6.7	-0.1	1.0	-24.0

Source: Adapted from Ricardo Grinspun, "Are Economic Models Reliable Policy Tools? Forecasting Canadian Gains from Free Trade" (Toronto: York University [work in progress], 1992).
1. D. Cox & R. Harris, "A Quantitative Assessment of the Economic Impact on Canada of Sectoral Free Trade with the US," *Canadian Journal of Economics*, 19 (1986), pp. 377 – 94.
2. Economic Council of Canada, *Venturing Forth: An Assessment of the Canada–US Free Trade Agreement*, p. 22.
3. D. Brown & R. Stern, "A Modeling Perspective," in Stern et al., *Perspectives on US–Canada in Free Trade*, Brookings, 1987.
4. D. Brown & R. Stern, "A Computable General Equilibrium Estimates of the Gains from US–Canadian Trade Liberalization," in D. Greenway et al., (eds.), *Economic Aspects of Regional Trading Agreements* (N.Y. University Press, 1989).
5. Statistics Canada: *Employment, Earnings and Hours*.

policies that favour the development of domestically owned over foreign-owned businesses; still others limit governments' ability to meet policy objectives through public enterprises or procurement policies.

The Ontario Attorney General's 1988 legal analysis captured the magnitude of the free trade agreement in the following passage: "[It] will permanently alter the capacity to make economic and social policy in Canada, sometimes shifting it to the federal government, sometimes abandoning it for all governments. This dramatic change in the ability of governments to respond to the legitimate expectations of their populations amounts to a constitutional change."[3]

If one looks back over the last four years, the FTA can be seen to have been an effective multi-purpose device for securing and advancing the agenda of deregulation and privatization launched by the Conservative government in 1984: it has acted as a *wedge,* providing impetus for major policy initiatives to further entrench or "constitutionalize" the agenda; it has acted as a *ceiling,* hindering or preventing intervention-minded governments from implementing their agendas and thwarting legislation that bends corporate activity to public priorities; it has served as a *vise,* within which the federal government unilaterally continues to deregulate, further compressing the policy space available to future governments; it has been used by the United States in tandem with GATT as a *whipsaw* to further weaken or eliminate interventionist Canadian laws and regulations; and the FTA has served the Conservative government as a *key lever* to facilitate and speed up the implementation of its agenda of continental integration of the Canadian economy and harmonization of Canadian economic, social, and environmental policies.

Deregulating Capital

Provisions in the NAFTA reproduce, expand, and supersede the provisions found in the FTA. They include: national treatment, that is, that U.S.-owned corporations must be treated the same by Canadian governments as domestically owned corporations (e.g., Articles 301, 1102, 1202, 1405, 1703); freedom from government-imposed performance requirements on foreign corporations (Articles 1106, 1107); freedom to repatriate dividends, royalties, and so forth (Article 1109); freedom from discriminatory expropriation and adequate compensation for measures that interfere with their business in a way deemed tantamount to expropriation (Article 1110); freedom to move top management, professional, and technical personnel around at will

(Chapter 16); provisions ensuring compliance by sub-national governments (Article 105) extending into new areas of provincial jurisdiction, such as sanitary, phytosanitary, and technical standards (Chapters 7, 9) and financial services (Chapter 14); entrenchment of their ownership of knowledge through extended periods of monopoly protection of patents and other intellectual property instruments (Chapter 17); freedom from encroachment on their turf by crown corporations (Articles 1502, 1503); powerful enforcement mechanisms ensuring the protection of corporate rights (e.g., Articles 1115–37, 1714–18); and a strengthened general nullification and impairment clause protecting against loss of rights or benefits caused by government measures unanticipated by the terms of this agreement (Annex 2004).

Examples of how NAFTA further expands corporate rights include the following:

NAFTA reproduces the prohibitions on performance requirements that are in the FTA, namely, prohibitions on minimum levels of Canadian ownership, forced divestiture of corporate assets, requirement to export, requirements for import substitution, requirements to purchase from local suppliers or to have minimum levels of Canadian content, restrictions on the repatriation of profits. Exceptions that were grandparented in the FTA, such as forced divestiture of book publishing companies and limitations on the sale of Canadian-owned energy companies, have been unilaterally removed by the federal government and could not be reimposed by a future government. To these are added a further list of prohibitions on performance requirements (Article 1106); technology transfer requirements, assigning world or regional product mandates to transnational corporations' (TNC) subsidiaries, trade balancing requirements (i.e., that foreign corporations balance their exports and imports); and prohibitions on requirements that minimum numbers of Canadians be appointed to senior management positions (Article 1107).

NAFTA contains a comprehensive intellectual property chapter that secures corporate control over knowledge through extended periods of monopoly protection (via patents and other instruments) and by expanding the reach of proprietary knowledge to include plant and animal life forms.

Corporations have obtained an important new dispute process in NAFTA through which they can directly challenge government measures at international arbitration panels. The so-called investor-state dispute mechanism will have a major chilling effect on policies that infringe upon corporate interests.

Whereas the FTA applied only to corporations, NAFTA extends coverage to practically all forms of investment: minority equity investment, debt, interest and dividends, real estate or other property, tangible or intangible.

Whereas the FTA prohibited requirements limiting the corporate repatriation of proceeds from asset sales and dividends, NAFTA extends this prohibition to include requirements limiting management fees, technical assistance fees, royalties, and virtually any corporate financial transfer.

NAFTA places further limits, beyond those already in place under the FTA, on the ability of government to regulate investment through existing or new crown corporations or public enterprises (Article 1502). Any government monopoly must "act solely in accordance with commercial considerations in the purchase or sale of that monopoly good." This provision alone negates the rationale of establishing many crown corporations. Furthermore, it goes beyond the FTA by requiring that all state enterprises accord non-discriminatory treatment to U.S. (and Mexican) investors and abide by the provisions of the investment chapter, including with regard to procurement.

The Canada–U.S. Auto Pact enforcement mechanisms were severely weakened by the FTA, but they are rendered practically inoperative by NAFTA. The proposed rules of origin will apply to the entire continent, not to any one nation. No longer will national content rules guarantee jobs and investment in each country based on its proportional share of production. No longer can a Canadian government negotiate corporate commitments in exchange for market access in this or any other industry.

The financial services chapter of NAFTA goes well beyond the provision in the FTA extending national or non-discriminatory treatment (with limited exceptions) to all U.S. (and Mexican) financial services corporations, including provincially regulated services. The much broader definition of financial services means that a wider range of financial services will come under the terms of the NAFTA than is the case with the FTA. Furthermore, corporations providing financial services will be able under NAFTA to transfer and process information freely for their Canadian activities outside the country, putting Canadian data-processing jobs at risk and threatening privacy laws [see Chapter 15, this volume, ed].

Capital Mobility and Free Trade Benefits

The deregulation of capital (domestic or foreign-owned) allows it to operate throughout an integrated economic space in which tariffs and other border restrictions are being dismantled and standards are being harmonized, enabling it make decisions about how to organize production and where to add value, where to locate new investment, where to close down a facility, where to conduct research and development, advertising, and accounting, where to source supplies, and where to transfer management and other professional personnel much more on the basis of commercial considerations. Governments (provincial and federal) are greatly restricted from active industrial policies that regulate investment in order to influence the sectors or regions of the economy to which it is channelled and ensure that their citizens get a share of the employment and other benefits. Thus, industrial policies to promote balanced economic development — industrial diversification, adding domestic value to resources, regional development, knowledge-intensive production — are severely curtailed.

Under such circumstances, when the ability to shape competitive advantage is limited, there is a tendency to concentrate on absolute advantage, which, in the case of Canada, is resource-based production and exports. This concentration is not consistent with a sustainable development path.

Moreover, corporations have added freedom in which to play government off against government, extracting subsidies and tax breaks in exchange for investment, thereby draining public treasuries and preventing them from making social and environmental expenditures. To the extent that they do it, the added ability of corporations to relocate production constitutes a loss of tax revenue and, to the extent that they threaten to do it, keeps corporate tax rates and, therewith, revenue, down. Tax revenue is also kept down by the enhanced ability to evade taxes through transfer pricing.

The inappropriateness of the assumption of capital immobility is highlighted by the fact that the Mexican government is selling the deal primarily on the grounds that it will attract capital. Ironically, this has also been a selling point of NAFTA for the Canadian government. However, there is mounting empirical evidence that investment has been shifting out of Canada in the last three years under free trade and that it will continue to do so under NAFTA.

Some of this evidence is summarized below:

- Canadian business (non-residential) fixed capital investment growth rate slowed dramatically in the first three years of free trade, from an average annual rate of 9.9 per cent during 1986–88 to 0.6 per cent per year during 1989–91.[4] In fact, after a spurt in 1989, the investment levels actually dropped in both 1990 and 1991. Furthermore, Statistics Canada's survey of business capital expenditures shows major declines. For example, during 1989–91, capital expenditures fell 11.6 per cent in textiles, 17.5 per cent in the machinery sector, and 32.3 per cent in motor vehicle parts. On the other hand, capital expenditures grew 13.9 per cent in the smelting and refining sector.

- Changes in direct investment cross-border flows by U.S. and Canadian companies reveal some interesting patterns. Canadian companies have been investing in the U.S. at twice the rate that U.S. companies have been investing in Canada under free trade. During 1989–91, U.S. net foreign direct investment flows to Canada were $4.9 billion, while Canadian FDI net flows to the U.S. were $8.6 billion. Another indicator of the exodus of Canadian equity capital is that while U.S. investors spent $1.1 billion purchasing Canadian stocks during 1989–91, Canadian investors spent $7.3 billion buying U.S. stocks.[5]

- Although it is difficult to determine trends in U.S. direct investment in Canada conclusively, there appears to be a shift away from Canada. There has not been a significant drop in net inflows of U.S. direct investment for the period as a whole compared to earlier periods. Inflows did drop dramatically in 1988, possibly in anticipation of the election result. There was actually a net outflow of U.S. investment in 1989, despite a capital inflow brought on by a surge in takeovers of Canadian companies. But stronger net inflows resumed in 1990 and 1991.

- However, Canada has been receiving a smaller share of total U.S. direct investment, declining from 18.4 per cent to 16.2 per cent during 1987–1990, which suggests the diversion of U.S. direct investment flows to locations such as Mexico. In fact, U.S. direct investment has surged into Mexico in the last two years, exceeding the total cumulative inflow for the previous ten years. The net inflow of U.S. corporate direct investment to Mexico in 1990 and 1991 was $US4.7 billion, actually greater than the net U.S. direct investment flows into Canada of $US4.4 billion during this period. This change is especially striking in light of the much smaller size of the Mexican economy.[6]

- There is also evidence that aggregate net inflows are masking U.S. *investment diversion*, particularly in the manufacturing sector. Most dramatic has been the dismantling of the U.S.-owned branch-plant sector. For example, the Ontario Ministry of Labour recorded 397 complete plant closures from January 1989 to August 1992; close to half were foreign owned. Complete closures accounted for 65 per cent of layoffs during this period, compared to less than one-quarter during the 1981–82 recession. This is reinforced by data compiled by the Canadian Centre for Policy Alternatives on the relocation of Ontario manufacturing production to locations outside Canada, primarily to the U.S. and Mexico (see Appendix I). Although the data is far from complete, in cases where a relocation to the U.S. occurred and where the state was specified, close to half went to southern states, generally considered to have lower wages, low unionization, and less stringent environmental and health and safety standards.

- This shift of U.S. and Canadian direct investment is supported by much anecdotal and survey evidence. For example, the *Wall Street Journal* reported on 21 August 1992 that "since the free trade treaty went into effect, between 400 and 700 Canadian businesses have set up shop in Buffalo."[7] Moreover, a survey of 455 senior U.S. corporate executives conducted for the *Journal* found that "about one-quarter of U.S. executives say they are likely to make a capital investment in Canada in the next few years — significantly fewer than the — [40 per cent] targeting Mexico."[8] This finding is reinforced by a survey of 190 senior U.S. executives by Cleveland Consulting Associates who believed overwhelmingly (71 per cent) that Mexico would benefit most from NAFTA; 22 per cent felt that the U.S. would benefit most, and just 2 per cent believed that Canada would be the big winner.[9]

- Professor Kimon Valaskakis, in a study for the Montreal Board of Trade, conducted in-depth interviews with 100 CEO's from Canadian- and foreign-owned corporations. He concluded: "Not only are the losers closing their factories in Canada but many of the winners are, too. They are packing their bags and moving to the

United States or Mexico. With the North American Free Trade Agreement, this trend is likely to continue."[10]

- A Conference Board survey (September 1992) of major U.S.- and Canadian-owned manufacturing and resource corporations observed that the FTA was a central factor in changing corporate restructuring practices, and they anticipate that this trend, particularly relocation to the U.S., will intensify under NAFTA. As one respondent from a U.S. subsidiary stated, "The driver in these changes will be free trade and the movement toward a single North American Market."[11] The survey found that Canadian companies are concentrating on investment in the U.S. It also found that U.S.-owned subsidiaries have been shutting down productive capacity in Canada. "In the emerging free trade environment ... there is a continual re-evaluation of the need to stay in Canada."[12] Respondents from Canadian-owned corporations said that the FTA, in forcing them to become more competitive, is drawing investment away from the higher-cost Canadian manufacturing sector to the U.S. market.

- Evidence indicates that Japanese investment in Canada is drying up and the FTA/NAFTA is held to be partially responsible. According to Japanese Ministry of Finance figures, Japanese direct investment in Canada jumped from $700 million in 1987 and 1988 to $1.4 billion in 1989 but declined to $300 million in 1992.[13] One report found that only one new Japanese company began operations in Canada in 1991, compared to seventeen per year in the late 1980s.[14] According to Susumi Eto, president of Mitsubishi, "when Japanese investment rushed into Canada in the late 1980s, there was a general optimism that the free trade agreement would bring real 'free trade' across the border. This illusion burst when it was proved that the one sided protectionist action by the U.S. suddenly changed the basic precondition of business activities here in Canada ..." According to Eto, "there is a growing trend to thinking that Mexico may be the place to invest in North America."[15]

- A report by the U.S. Congressional Office of Technology Assessment found that "NAFTA could precipitate a significant diversion of U.S. investment to Mexico [and] could lead to greater Asian and European investment in Mexico to serve the U.S. market ...

[Consequently] with increased investment in Mexico and a large (over 20 million) and rapidly growing pool of less educated workers there, U.S. employers will gain added leverage in their dealings with less educated U.S. workers ... Increasingly, employers will be able to use the threat of relocation to depress wages here."[16] There is good reason to suppose that the same factors will also result in a shift in investment from Canada.

* A confidential (1991) study for the Federal Department of Finance by Professor David Conklin found that many corporate managers are re-evaluating strategies in the face of the reality of "a single unified North American market ... [where] manufacturing costs in Canada significantly exceed those in certain municipalities in the United States ... Some managers point to the current recession as an additional stimulus to the development of a new North American strategy ... Over the past few months, many executives have come to focus on the possible de-industrialization of Canada."[17] The statement of an executive of EMCO Ltd. is revealing: "There are a lot of things you can do less expensively in the U.S. ... Those things are working against the Canadian economy, and what I look at is lop-sided in regard to investment attractiveness." He continues: "Some manufacturing companies have made a decision fairly easily after free trade to shut down Canadian activity and just use sales in the Canadian territory ... Such a decision wouldn't have been made five years ago. I think this kind of decision will benefit everyone except the Canadian workforce."[18]

* According to a poll of 2,033 senior business executives and company owners across Canada conducted by Dun and Bradstreet Canada for the *Globe and Mail*'s *Report on Business Magazine,* 37.1 per cent of interviewees surveyed thought that NAFTA would have a negative effect on Canada's economy in the 1990s while only 32.9 per cent expected the deal to have a positive effect. Ontario business was even more pessimistic than the national average, with 42.9 per cent of respondents predicting that NAFTA would have a negative economic effect.[19]

Lowest Common Denominator Competition
Once it is understood that FTA/NAFTA is an economic constitution locking in a deregulated trade and investment regime with no agreed-

upon or enforceable social and environmental rules within which competition must take place, then it is quite obvious that what is set in motion is a lowest-common-denominator competitive process where different areas within the continental economic space vie for absolute cost advantages, resulting in a downward spiral of standards, wages, taxes, and so forth. The extent to which potential investment diversion is offset is largely the result of business pressure to cap and reduce these standards, wages, and taxes. *The Wall Street Journal* survey of 455 senior U.S. corporate executives cited earlier found that one-quarter of the respondents openly admitted that they would use NAFTA to bargain down wages. This is what business calls levelling the playing field or what Linda McQuaig, author of *The Quick and the Dead*, calls "the race to the bottom."

The logic of Canadian-based business arguing that it now has to have a level playing field on which to compete has become very compelling; so, too, given its new mobility, are its threats to leave. This is a central aspect of the FTA/NAFTA's importance as an lever. The following not-so-veiled warning to the Ontario government on labour law reform by the president of Ford Canada is illustrative: "Multinational companies such as Ford have many choices to consider before deciding where to assign production of new products. So before they introduce new legislation governments should ask themselves this question: Will it encourage business confidence or is it likely to discourage investment?"[20]

This is not an idle threat. Ford has a state-of-the-art, high-quality plant at Hermosillo, Mexico, that produces 165,000 Escort cars per year for export to the U.S. and Canadian markets. Productivity and up time are both high at this plant, and assembly time is low, below the average for North America. The plant employed 1,665 hourly paid workers in 1989. Total compensation per production worker per hour was $US2.00, compared to $US30.00 in the United States (slightly less in Canada). This alone represents a labour-cost saving of $US672 per vehicle, which for 165,000 cars is $US111 million. This does not include major cost savings accruing from the much lower wages paid to its 370 salaried employees.[21]

Under FTA/NAFTA, the penalties to Ford for not complying with the Canadian content conditions of the Auto Pact have almost completely disappeared. The Ontario government can offer incentives, but it is playing a game with other jurisdictions that have deep pockets and have other regulatory cost advantages over Ontario. Ford is in a powerful bargaining position.

To adjust to this new reality, Canadian governments of all stripes, whether they want to or not, are under pressure to phase out many features that make the Canadian economy "uncompetitive." Aligning cost and regulatory structures often means lowering wages, weakening unions, watering down labour and environmental standards, lowering taxes, and squeezing social programme spending.

Professor Donald MacCharles, a strong free trade advocate, describes what this means for unions: "the threat of job loss due to increased competition may make union-management relations more co-operative ... With some luck governments will also respond and adapt their labour codes to allow for right-to-work laws and other measures which will reduce the high degree of rigidity in Canadian labour markets."[22]

Under the NAFTA conditions described above, corporate decisions about where to locate can focus almost exclusively on an array of cost factors: environmental laws and standards, workplace health and safety standards, wages and benefits (especially in relation to productivity), labour laws and standards, education levels, labour turnover, physical infrastructure, proximity to major markets, vulnerability to trade harassment, taxes, government incentives, real capital costs, and political stability (which in the case of Mexico is perceived to be enhanced under NAFTA), and so forth.

Environmental Impact

To the extent that environmental laws and regulations constitute a cost for corporations that produce in a given jurisdiction, especially if these co-exist as part of a cluster of adverse cost factors, and to the extent that it becomes much easier under FTA/NAFTA for a given corporation to move production or shift new investment to a jurisdiction on the continent where environmental compliance costs are lower and sell back into that market with impunity, environmental costs are an important component of the overall decision-making about where to locate investment.

World Bank economists Herman Daly and Robert Goodlord, have observed: "A country which internalizes environmental costs into its prices will be at a disadvantage, at least in the short term, in unregulated trade with a country that does not internalize environmental costs."[23] Environmental dumping occurs when a company brings products into the Canadian market from a country that permits production practices that do not meet internationally recognized minimum standards or practices that cause grossly excessive levels of pollution. Many contend that international law (GATT) should recognize that these practices constitute illegal government subsidies to exporters and that, as such, they should be subject to countervailing tariff action by the importing country.

There is much evidence that jurisdictions with lax environmental standards or enforcement are a magnet for certain companies and industries that want to avoid the cost of compliance with tougher regulation. This is particularly true where these conditions exist jointly with a cluster of other "competitive advantages," such as low wages, low labour standards, and so forth. It is also more evident in regions where various national economies are becoming more highly integrated, such as the European Community and North America. Interestingly, there is much controversy surrounding this issue. Many trade economists who believe that any environmental measure is a barrier to trade and a cover for protectionism deny any significant causal relationship between lax environmental standards or enforcement and the location of certain production facilities.

A recent Conference Board study acknowledged the existence of the relationship but added that its importance varies from industry to industry:

> Stricter regulation, if it implies substantial compliance costs, may lead to market share losses in domestic markets [to imports] as well as in world markets. On the other hand, weak rules, the failure to regulate, can be considered the equivalent of providing a subsidy to domestic firms because they can adopt processes drawing more heavily on the natural environment ... Potentially, such competitiveness impacts could be significant enough to affect investment decisions and induce relocation of production facilities to more permissive jurisdictions. The importance of this effect has been very industry-specific so far: it has been more prevalent in the forestry and manufacturing sectors than in the mining industry, for example.[24]

In the European Community, there is a greater realism in the discussion of this issue, both in acknowledging its importance and in policy responses. The reaction, for example, of the Federal Association of German Industry to the fact that "the advent of the Single European Market will lower the cost of moving factors and of trading goods such that differences in production costs due to environmental policies will increase the pressure to relocate firms or to lose market shares otherwise has been to advocate a harmonization of environmental standards throughout the EC in order to eliminate these competitive disadvantages. It also favours giving more regulatory power to the EC in environmental matters in the hope that this will also harmonize environmental standards." This view is shared by most German labour unions and environmentalists.[25]

A 1991 report of the United Nations Conference on Trade and Development (UNCTAD) warned that changing patterns of industrialization between developed and developing countries could result in a process where the latter are encouraged to specialize in "dirty industries" and suggested that this might already be happening in mineral and metal sectors.[26] Low found that a group of 48 Mexican goods exported to the United States identified as "dirty industries" increased at an average rate of 9 per cent per year during the 1980s, compared with 3 per cent per year for all commodities.[27] Low concludes: "The trade data show that Mexico's export earnings are not overly dependent on pollution-intensive products, which account for a little over one-tenth of total exports. On the other hand, pollution-intensive exports have grown considerably faster than total exports during this period."[28]

Surveys by Professor Roberto Sanchez of the Colegio de la Frontera Norte in the maquiladora city of Mexicali indicate that weak environmental regulation or lax enforcement was an important factor for 26 per cent of U.S. companies that decided to move there. According to Sanchez, "Ten percent of surveyed maquiladoras in Mexicali considered environmental regulations to be among the main factors in the decision to leave the United States, and 17 percent considered it a factor of importance. On the selection of Mexicali almost 13 percent of the maquiladoras considered weaker environmental legislation in Mexico a main factor for relocation and another 13 percent considered it a factor of importance."[29]

It should also be said that whether or not a significant measurable link can be established between costly environmental regulation and shifting of corporate investment, industry lobbyists often argue against the imposition of new legislation or for the reduction of existing regulations in terms of cost competitiveness and the threat of relocation, and legislators often respond accordingly to these appeals. It begs the question why so many corporate resources are devoted to stopping environmental regulations if these regulations have such a negligible effect on decisions to relocate.

The hands-off Mexican government approach to environmental protection and worker health and safety has long been a magnet for U.S. business. The Texas Economic Commission, for example, has used this fact as a selling point to attract industry to the maquiladora. "Government control is minimal; for example, there are no stiff prohibitions such as in the United States with respect to air quality, etc."[30] A 1983 U.S.–Mexico treaty required that all companies that import chemicals into Mexico ship the resulting hazardous wastes back to the United States for disposal. But the U.S. Environmental Protection Agency records showed that in 1988 only 20 of 1,600 maquiladoras actually returned their waste.[31]

NAFTA Article 1114 purports to deal with the so-called pollution haven problem. It states: "It is inappropriate to encourage investment by relaxing domestic health, safety or environmental measures." But this provision has no enforcement capability. It is not a prohibition. It has no sanctions for violators. Violations do not trigger a formal dispute resolution process but only a consultation. Furthermore, it does not address the most pressing problem — the lax enforcement of existing standards. Nor does it provide any protection to a jurisdiction that, by tightening its standards relative to other jurisdictions, puts itself at a competitive disadvantage.

William Riley, head of the U.S. Environmental Protection Agency, in testimony before the House Ways and Means Committee on 15 September 1992, admitted that the remedies for violation of Article 1114 were only consultative. This position is in stark contrast to the strong investor rights enforcement mechanisms in the agreement. Similarly, former Canadian Environmental Minister Jean Charest admitted that the most effective environmental enforcement tool in NAFTA was public opinion.

Fiscal Capacity

The impact of FTA/NAFTA on fiscal capacity is largely indirect. The enhanced ability of large corporations (foreign- and domestically owned) to shift investment or transfer production facilities, to transfer profits through intra-corporate transfer pricing, interest, retained earnings, dividends, and so forth, within the continental economic space imposes ceilings on corporate taxation and generates more pressure on governments to keep them in line with the lowest-common-denominator regime in the region.

The FTA/NAFTA provisions on services reinforce global trends towards increased tradeability of services and the larger role of information as a cost of production. These factors portend more external sourcing and intra-corporate trade. Such developments increase the opportunities for tax avoidance and investment shifts and put additional pressure on provincial tax regimes to be more sensitive to other jurisdictions on the continent. NAFTA lifts restrictions on cross-border information flows for financial service providers and prevents similar restrictions in other industries.

Furthermore, FTA/NAFTA gives corporations increased power to play one jurisdiction off against another to obtain generous tax incentives as a condition for locating new production or maintaining existing production. Granting such incentives could constitute a significant additional drain on provincial and federal resources. And, under NAFTA, there is no longer the possibility of negotiating a common code of allowable and prohibited subsidies that might constrain the competition for TNC investment.

On the other hand, new tax incentives to stimulate the provincial economy must respect the national treatment provisions — that is, they must not (with limited exceptions) discriminate against foreign-owned companies. Such tax incentives are less effective since foreign-controlled corporations have a lower employment-creating propensity, higher import propensity, and weaker linkages to the rest of the economy. More domination by foreign-controlled corporations simply compounds the difficulty.

The temporary entry provisions of the FTA/NAFTA give new freedom to knowledge workers (entrepreneurs, executives, professionals, and certain technicians) to move across borders to sell their services and perhaps to emigrate. This freedom of movement puts downward pressure on the upper personal income tax rates, although probably not nearly as great as on corporate taxes.

It is also likely that, given the pressure on labour at the bargaining table, certain forms of corporate taxes (such as payroll taxes) will be passed on in the form of lower wages.

The FTA/NAFTA reinforces globalization trends weakening labour power: it reinforces low-wage corporate competitiveness strategies that polarize wages, skew income-distribution patterns, and diminish both consumption and income tax bases obtainable from the bottom half or more of income earners whose mobility is not enhanced under the FTA/NAFTA.

Thus, even if the FTA/NAFTA increases economic growth, it does not follow, as free trade advocates argue, that the increase in financial resources will translate into increased fiscal capacity. On the contrary, it will likely decrease fiscal capacity.

Chapter 3

Canadian State Powers: Comparing the FTA and GATT

Mel Clark

International trade negotiations require that national powers be limited by agreement. Negotiators must pay close attention to the powers that are being constrained or foregone.

In this chapter, Canada's former deputy negotiator during the Tokyo Round of GATT, Mel Clark, judges the provisions of the Canada–U.S. agreement harshly. He finds that in areas of vital national concern, Canadian state power has been modified or given up altogether. He evaluates the differences between the powers ceded under the FTA and the restrictions placed on Canada because of its membership in the GATT. He concludes that Canada is better off with only one trade agreement with the U.S. — the GATT.

Trade between Canada and the United States has been conducted under rules established by the GATT. Under any international agreement, national sovereignty is constrained. But when the GATT and the FTA are compared, it is clear that the FTA cedes to the U.S. and the private sector the right to shape many of Canada's economic, social, environmental, and cultural policies. The FTA stripped the federal government of many powers it possessed — and used — both to build a nation state with a distinctive and humane way of life and to develop among Canadians a sense of belonging to a nation that was greater than a collection of provinces. With the federal government weakened, there is a legitimate fear the FTA will integrate the economic, social, environmental, and cultural systems of Canada with those of the U.S. and pull apart current Canadian policies, institutions, programmes, and traditions, including many that bind the country together.

If one assumes the Mulroney government was guided by even normal regard for the national interest, the FTA defies understanding. It makes sense, however, when one recalls that the Business Council on National Issues (BCNI) sought the FTA as a means to place in cement the right-wing policies of the Mulroney government and, as Eric Kierans observed, "to smooth the path of Canadian corporate wealth into the American market and citizenship."

Vital federal government powers ceded to the U.S. and private sector under the FTA include the following: U.S. national treatment rights to Canada's exports (Article 105); tariff free entry for U.S.-processed dairy, poultry, and egg products and motor vehicles and parts (Article 401); relinquishment of Canada's right to use minimum export price requirements (Articles 407.2, 902.2); relinquishment of Canada's right to levy export taxes (Articles 408, 903); U.S. rights to a proportion of the total Canadian supply of any exported good even if Canadians must go short (Articles 409, 904); "harmonization" of Canadian standards and related procedures for agricultural food and beverages with American standards (Article 708) on the basis that "harmonization means identical" (Article 711); U.S. national treatment rights in Canada regarding the ownership, production, distribution, sale, marketing, and delivery of a wide range of services (Chapter 14, especially Articles 1401, 1402, and Annex 1408); national treatment in Canada for U.S. investors in the establishment, acquisition, operation, and sale of all business enterprises except transportation services, government procurement, and certain financial services (Articles 1601, 1602); the legality of U.S. anti-dumping (AD) and countervailing duties (CVD) to be judged on the basis of U.S. law instead of GATT laws (Article 1902.1), the U.S. right to change such laws without Canada's agreement (Article 1902.2), and the U.S. right to provide Canada with least-favoured-nation treatment regarding alleged subsidized exports (Section 409 "Subsidies" of U.S. Implementation Act); the right to retaliate against any Canadian cultural measure "inconsistent" with the FTA without invoking dispute-settlement provisions (Article 2005.2).

Pierre Trudeau summarized the situation when he wrote, "Worse still" [i.e., worse than Meech Lake] "the commendable goal of promoting freer trade has led to a monstrous swindle, under which the Canadian government has ceded to the United States of America a large slice of the country's sovereignty over its economy and natural resources in exchange for advantages we already had, or were going to obtain in a few years anyway through the normal operation of the GATT." In what follows, the limits on national sovereignty imposed by the FTA are compared with the relevant provisions of GATT. It is evident that while vital national powers are protected under GATT, the same can not be said of the FTA.

FTA and
A Cost/Benefit Assessment of Provisions

Note: The assessment is based on FTA provisions and GATT Tokyo and Uruguay Round (Dunkel draft) provisions with Uruguay provisions indicated by an asterisk.

PART I. ACCESS TO THE U.S.

FTA

I. TARIFFS	Remaining tariffs on goods contained in the US Schedule (Article 401.2) eliminated over ten-year period 1989–98.
II. SUBSIDIES AND COUNTERVAIL	
A. The Law	The legality of U.S. countervail is determined on the basis of U.S. law (Article 1902.1).
B. Amending U.S. Law	The U.S. can amend its countervail laws without Canada's agreement (Article 1902.2) and has done so at least twice. One amendment facilitates countervail action only against Canada (Section 409 of U.S. Implementation Act). Another amendment makes generally available subsidies countervailable (e.g., medicare and U.I. [Section 1312 B of U.S.Omnibus and Competitiveness Act of 1988]).
C. Subsidies	
1. Definition	U.S. law.
2. Prohibited	U.S. law.
3. Countervailable	Virtually any measure that U.S. officials determine to be a subsidy under U.S. law.
4. Non-Countervailable	Insofar as is known, U.S. law does not exclude any subsidies from U.S. countervail.

;ATT:
rhat Especially Impinge on Canada's Interest

he substance of the identified FTA provision is in NAFTA. Where feasible, FTA and
!ATT article numbers are in brackets or otherwise given.

'OR CANADA'S EXPORTS

GATT
By 1987, about 95 per cent of Canada's industrial exports entered the U.S. at duties of 5 per cent or less, and 80 per cent entered duty free. U.S. tariffs provided substantial protection for only a few industries (e.g., rapid transit and railroad equipment, resins, textiles, apparel, footwear, certain ceramics). In 1934, the U.S. tariff averaged 50 per cent. In 1987, the industrial tariff averaged 1 per cent on all goods and 4 per cent on dutiable goods.

The legality of U.S. countervail is judged on the basis of GATT law.

GATT law can only be changed by agreement among countries that negotiated it, which normally includes Canada.

GATT does not contain any such provisions, and a U.S. (Section 409) action would be illegal under GATT.

Only subsidies that are specific to an enterprise or industry or groups of enterprises or industries are countervailable. (Medicare and U.I. are not countervailable [Section 1].)

Explicitly defines a subsidy (Section 1).

Subsidies contingent upon export performance or the use of domestic over imported goods are prohibited (Section 1).

Only measures that fall within the definition and adversely affect the interests of another signatory a) cause injury to an industry, b) nullify or impair a benefit, or c) cause "serious prejudice" to its interests (Section 1).

Subsidies that are not specific or specific subsidies for research and disadvantaged regions that meet certain conditions are not countervailable (Section 1).

FTA

D. Countervail	
1. Initiation and Conduct of Investigation	U.S. law
2. Calculation of Subsidy	U.S. law.
3. Determination of Injury	U.S. law.
4. Definition of Industry	U.S. law.
5. Levying Duties	U.S. law.
6. Provisional Duties and Retroactivity	U.S. law.
7. Undertakings (i.e., managed market arrangements)	U.S. law.

III. DISPUTE SETTLEMENT

A. *Law*	Panels must judge U.S. countervail and dumping actions on the basis of U.S. law and are limited to deciding whether the U.S. government has correctly applied U.S. law (Articles 1904.2, 1904.3).
B. *U.S. Countervail and Dumping Action*	From 1 January 1989 to 16 August 1993 Canada requested twenty-two panels to examine U.S. countervail and dumping duties and results have been as follows: two findings in favour of Canada, eight findings in favour of the U.S., two split decisions, six out-of-court settlements and four decisions pending (details are set out in Addendum D). U.S. has levied countervail and dumping duties on magnesium (i.e., Quebec policy to attract power-intensive industries); lumber (provincial royalties and export restrictions); steel, steel rails, pilling and other steel products; iron casting, oil tubular goods; parts for paving equipment; salted coldfish; raspberries; and swine and pork.

GATT

Two pages of precise obligations covering such investigations (Section 1).

Precise rules regarding government provision of equity capital, loans, loan guarantees, and goods and services (Section 1).

Specific rules regarding essential elements of determining injury, such as the volume of exports, their effect on prices, imports from more than one country, and their impact on industry (Section 1).

A "domestic industry," except for carefully defined exceptions, means the producers as a whole whose output constitute the major portion of total domestic production (Section 1).

One page of obligations (Section 1).

One and a half pages of obligations (Section 1).

One and a half pages of obligations (Section 1).

Panels judge U.S. countervail and dumping action on the basis of GATT law and determine whether the U.S. action is consistent with its GATT obligations.

During the six-year period 1978 to 1983, there were only thirteen petitions requesting countervail, and only one resulted in the levying of duties (i.e., optic sensing systems). Canada did not request a panel to examine any of the thirteen petitions.

FTA

C. Time

For reasons summarized below under "Cost of Lawyers," it can require, at a minimum, nearly two years to obtain a panel decision from the time a countervail or dumping action is initiated but, unless there is an out-of-court settlement, it can and has taken much longer. Canada cannot request a panel until the Department of Commerce and International Trade Commission have made final decisions approximately one year after a U.S. action was initiated (Articles 1904.2, 1904.4). In addition, U.S. law permits a panel to refer issues back to the Department of Commerce and/or the International Trade Commission and parties to the dispute to request Administrative Reviews which are mini countervail or dumping actions.

D. Cost of Lawyers

Lawyer costs can be prohibitive for many Canadian companies that fight actions; for example, Canadian lumber producers spent ten million dollars to fight countervail in 1986, and the case was aborted in less than a year. Lawyer costs can and do include the following:

a) opposing a countervail and/or dumping petition when it is being examined by the Department of Commerce and International Trade Commission (up to one year or possibly longer);

b) attempting to persuade a panel or panels to cancel an adverse Commerce or Trade Commission decision (approximately one year if there are no referrals back to either agency);

c) trying to persuade Commerce and/or the Trade Commission to reverse or mitigate earlier decisions when a panel refers issues to them which panels frequently do in fact, as often as three times and each agency can take up to three months to reply and sometimes they request extensions (about six months or longer);

d) unless Commerce or the Trade Commission reverse their initial findings, lawyers again attempt to persuade a panel or panels to cancel such findings and panels have up to six months to reach a decision (or longer);

e) any party to the dispute can recycle it by initiating an Administrative Review which is a mini countervail or dumping action and can take

GATT

For several years, panels have normally reported about eleven or twelve months after a request that one be established. Canada requested a panel twenty days after the U.S. Commerce Department received a lumber countervailed application in 1985 and would have obtained a panel finding about the time the U.S. levied duties if the Conservative government had not aborted the panel. GATT panels do not refer issues back to the U.S. Department of Commerce and International Trade Commission, and there are no Administrative Reviews.

Limited to the salaries of civil servants.

FTA

many months to complete (say a minimum of six months);

   f) a party can then continue the recycling by requesting that a panel or panels examine the Commerce and/or Trade Commission decisions that emerged from the Administrative Review and panels can again refer issues back to Commerce and the Trade Commission, etc.

E. Composition of Panels	Normally three or five persons, with Canada appointing one, two, or three members and the U.S. appointing the others. The panels comprise nationals of Canada and the U.S. and frequently include trade consultants and trade lawyers. This practice is analogous to appointing a lawyer a judge for one case and risks real as well as apparent conflicts of interests.
F. U.S. Officials	Since the FTA requires U.S. officials to only apply U.S. law correctly, the officials are highly vulnerable to the full force of American trade politics.
G. Are Panel Decisions Binding?	Yes (Article 1904.9). But, to repeat, the decisions are based on U.S. law, which the U.S. can amend without Canada's agreement and are limited to whether U.S. officials have correctly applied U.S. law.

H. Other Considerations

GATT

Normally three or five persons appointed by the director-general. With rare exceptions, panel members are not citizens of countries parties to the dispute, and great care is exercised to avoid even the appearance of a conflict of interest.

The Uruguay Round text states "Citizens" of "governments ... parties to the dispute shall not be members of the panel ... unless the parties ... agree otherwise" (Section 5).

When Canada's exports were covered by GATT, U.S. officials considered whether countervail petitions were consistent with GATT law, which restrained them from acting only in the interests of American petitioners and their political allies.

No. But a very large percentage of GATT panel recommendations have been implemented, and most of the outstanding recommendations relate to agriculture subsidies. Uruguay Round proposals substantially increase the probability that the already high level of acceptance of panel recommendations will be virtually 100 per cent, including cases involving agriculture subsidies. In contrast to the FTA, the GATT decisions are based on GATT law, which can only be amended by the parties that negotiated it.

By 1992, GATT had dealt with more than 150 disputes. An examination of these disputes establishes that the GATT system normally results in an equitable and expeditious settlement and that smaller countries can obtain such results in disputes with more powerful countries providing they have a good case and present it professionally.

There have been forty-five GATT complaints against U.S. measures, and the work of two panels has been suspended and reports from four are pending. Of the remaining thirty-nine complaints, all have been resolved except one, and the U.S. has undertaken to implement the panel's recommendations on the successful conclusion of the Uruguay Round. To comply with panel decisions, the U.S. has made many adjustments in its trade practices, and on at least three occasions Congress amended laws, including an export subsidy law. In a case where the U.S. did not comply with GATT, the GATT authorized retaliation, which the U.S. accepted without counterretaliation.

CONCLUSIONS

1. Total access to the U.S. for Canada's exports (i.e., the composite of tariffs, non-tariff measures, and dispute settlement) was substantially better under GATT than it now is under the FTA. The protection provided Americans by FTA countervail and dumping provisions is far greater than the eliminated U.S. tariffs. The GATT dispute settlement system was an effective constraint on U.S. protectionism, whereas the FTA system encourages such protectionism. A dispute-settlement system cannot provide equitable decisions if the law it is interpreting is stacked in favour of one party, and FTA law is U.S. law, which the U.S. can change without Canada's agreement.

2. The FTA replaces the GATT rule of law for subsidies, countervail, and dumping with U.S. trade politics. The FTA, in effect, gives U.S. interests the right to countervail and dumping actions on demand and virtually assures them that such an action will result in increased protection in one form or another.

3. Understandably, U.S. interests are taking advantage of this right. They have not only increased the number of actions against Canada's exports but also obtained increased protection against some of Canada's major industries.

4. A corollary consequence is that the FTA will result in corporations — Canadian as well as foreign — locating production in the U.S. Since such decisions are made in secret, Canadians will never know their cost.

PART II. ACCESS TO THE U.S. FO▶
FTA

POST-TOKYO ROUND

GATT

Canada has requested, co-sponsored requests, or presented evidence to eighteen panels to examine complaints against the European Community, Japan and the U.S. Thirteen panels have submitted reports, another report is pending, three were settled out of court and the work of one has been suspended. Of the panels that reported, ten found in Canada's favour. Eight of the reporting panels adjudicated Canadian complaints against U.S. measures, and all but two found in Canada's favour. We subsequently won one when the case was retried. The U.S. implemented these panel findings — lifting an embargo, removing a discriminatory tax, and reducing customs user fees.

5. Worse still, there is no hope of changing this situation as long as Canada trades under the FTA or NAFTA. If an American company loses a case under Chapter Nineteen, it has the option of invoking Section 409 or amending U.S. law. Even the most competitive and aggressive Canadian exporters will grow weary of paying the business and lawyer costs that are inevitable when a U.S. competitor initiates a countervail or dumping action and either move production to the U.S. or do what is required to accommodate its American competitor.

6. FTA countervail and dumping provisions have forced both the Federal and Provincial governments to make important policy changes — e.g. a de facto suspension of the Employment Support Act, terminating contributions to Unemployment Insurance, increasing forest royalty fees and renegotiating a contract with Norsk Hydro to eliminate a subsidy thereby crippling Quebec's policy of using two-price power for industrial development.

7.The U.S. is the only country that frequently uses countervail and the only country to countervail a Canadian export. This is an important reason why GATT provides much better protection than the FTA against the misuse of U.S. countervail laws.

ANADA'S FOREST PRODUCTS
GATT

After the GATT Tokyo Round agreements were implemented, more than 90 per cent of Canada's lumber exports to the U.S. entered duty free, with only a few duties above 5 per cent (e.g., plywood, 20 per cent, and prefabricated buildings, 5.1 per cent), and all such duties were bound against increase except those applying to shakes and shingles. In addition, most U.S. tariffs on bulk paper products in sheets, rolls, and so forth were duty free with the remaining 5 per cent or less (e.g., test and container board, duty free, wrapping paper, and writing paper duty free and 2 to 2.5 per cent). Relatively few U.S. tariffs on cut-to-size products of interest to Canada were above 3 per cent.

FTA

1983	
1986	In 1986, after FTA negotiations were initiated, U.S. lumber producers again petitioned for countervail (Lumber II) and again alleged provincial royalties granted a subsidy. This time, U.S. officials decided the royalties granted a 15 per cent subsidy and were countervailable despite the fact the general availability principle was still law. U.S. officials apparently judged there was only a minimal risk of the Mulroney government pressing a GATT appeal to a conclusion, and the government sustained this judgement by aborting a GATT panel about a month before its report would have been tabled and accepting the Lumber Agreement.
1987	The Lumber Agreement increased the cost of Canadian exports to the U.S. by 15 per cent (Paragraph 4b) and ceded to the U.S. substantial control over Canada forest policies (Paragraphs 6, 7). The amount of control ceded is described in detail in a letter dated 30 December 1986 from the U.S. Secretary of Commerce and Trade Representative to the chairman, Coalition of Fair Lumber Exports.
	B.C. invoked the Agreement's "Replacement Measures" provisions (Paragraph 5) to convert the 15 per cent export tax to increased royalties, which increased the production cost of most forest products by a commensurate amount in Canadian and overseas markets as well as in the U.S. Quebec converted twelve percentage points of the tax to royalties with similar result.

GATT

U.S. lumber producers submitted their first countervail petition in 1982 (Lumber I) when such duties were still covered by GATT. The petition alleged that provincial royalties (i.e. stumpage) granted subsidies to Canadian lumber companies. U.S. officials, however, decided the alleged subsidies, even if they existed, were "generally available" and not countervailable under U.S. law. Another restraining consideration was that U.S. officials were apprehensive the Trudeau government would challenge the legality of countervail under GATT and win. Officials, like judges, do not enjoy having decisions overturned. Before the Mulroney government aborted the GATT panel, the prevailing view in Geneva was that it would find in Canada's favour.

FTA

1988	Section 1312 b of the U.S. Omnibus Trade and Competitiveness Act of 1988 states: "nominal general availability ... is not a basis for determining that the bounty, grant or subsidy is not, or has not been, in fact provided to a specific enterprise or industry, or group thereof." Before this section was enacted (U.S. law contained a "general availability" principle, and, to repeat, in Lumber I the U.S. applied it by deciding that the alleged provincial stumpage subsidies, even if they existed, were generally available and therefore not countervailable. But, when the same case arose in 1986, the U.S. levied countervailing duties even though the general availability principle was still law. Section 1312b now provides a legal basis for the 1986 lumber decision and supports allegations that generally available government financed assistance should be countervailed.
1991	The Mulroney government cancelled the Lumber Agreement, and the U.S. government initiated a countervail action that alleged log export restrictions as well as royalties granted subsidies (Lumber III). The U.S. now levies a countervail duty of 6.5 per cent. The 1982 and 1986 petitions were initiated by lumber producers and were limited to royalties.
	Canada requested two panels: one to examine whether royalties and export restrictions granted subsidies and the other to ascertain if injury has occurred or is threatened. One panel has decided that both the royalties and export restrictions grant subsidies and the injury panel is expected to announce its decision shortly.

CONCLUSIONS

1. The forest products sector illustrates how U.S. companies have used the FTA to convert GATT free entry or duties of 5 per cent or less to countervail protection of 21.5 per cent (B.C.), 18.5 per cent (Que.), and 6.5 per cent (Ont., Man., Sask., and Alta.) plus substantial control over Canada forest policies during the life of the Lumber Agreement.

2. *Under the FTA:* B.C. and Quebec are stuck with the increased royalties of 15 and 12 per cent because a reduction would run a high risk of initiating another U.S. countervail action; Canadian producers from Quebec to B.C. are highly vulnerable to more harassing and protectionist actions; another attempt to negotiate a sector agreement for lumber or forest products will result in

GATT

Article 1.2 of the agreement on subsidies and countervailing duties provides that a subsidy as defined "shall be subject to the provisions of Part II (Prohibited subsidies) or Part III (Actionable subsidies) or Part V (Countervailing measures) ... only if such a subsidy is specific in accordance with the provisions of Article 2 below" (sec. I).

Article 2.2 provides that "it is understood that the setting or change of generally applicable tax rates by all levels of government entitled to do so shall not be deemed to be a specific subsidy" (Section 1).

Canada asked GATT to establish a panel to examine certain aspects of the U.S. countervail action; the panel has submitted its report, but the report has not yet been made public.

something like the 1986 Lumber Agreement and be inimical to Canada's interests; use of the Employment Support Act, as long as our trade is under the FTA, would eventually result in the U.S. jacking up countervail to offset assistance to Canadian producers.

3. *Under GATT:* the odds are high that we could lift U.S. countervail, restore the integrity of the Tokyo Round access, and probably obtain even better access in the Uruguay Round; reduce substantially the risk of further countervail actions; return to B.C. and Quebec control over their royalties; regain the power to use the Employment Support Act again .

PART III. U.S. ACCESS TO
FTA

I. RESOURCES: WATER, OIL AND GAS, COAL, URANIUM, ELECTRICITY, AND ALL OTHER NATURAL RESOURCES	Canada has undertaken the following obligations regarding all natural resources except logs: to accord the U.S. national treatment on exports as well as imports (Article 105); not to use "minimum export requirements" to maintain prices in Canada that are lower than the U.S. sales price (Articles 407.2, 902.2); not to levy a tax on exports to the U.S. (Articles 408, 903); when goods are in short supply, to maintain the proportion previously exported to the U.S. even if Canadians go short and not to impose a higher price on exports (Articles 409.1 a and b, and 904 a and b); to ensure that provincial governments also honour the above obligations (Article 103).
II. INVESTMENT	Americans have the same rights as Canadians to establish, acquire, and operate any resource company with virtually no conditions attached (Articles 1602, 1603).

CONCLUSIONS

1. Under GATT, the Canadian government had virtually complete control of our resources, including the power to pursue a policy of self-sufficiency for Canadian resources; ensure Canadians are supplied with such resources before foreigners; implement two-price systems for resources; and prohibit or limit foreign ownership and establish conditions for the exploitation of resources. The FTA has stripped Canada of these powers.

The fatal strategic consequences of moving from GATT to the FTA can be illustrated by reference to water and energy.

The Pearse Inquiry, established by the Trudeau government, concluded that water is the "most valuable liquid asset" Canada possess and recommended that the government "provide for a federal water policy that will ensure Cana-

ANADA'S NATURAL RESOURCES

GATT

National treatment is limited to imports, and Canada has no obligation to accord the U.S. such treatment on exports. There are no GATT obligations relating to two-price systems for exports, and Canada has a right to use such systems. Canada can levy an export tax on any good at any level for any period. Export taxes are the only legal means to control or prohibit exports permanently (Article XI.I). There are no obligations regarding the quantity or price of exports affected by export taxes. If Canada imposes export restrictions to acquire products in short supply, it has an obligation to apply them consistent with the principle that "all contracting parties are entitled to an equitable share of the international supply" (Article XX(8)). Since Canada has no obligation relating to national treatment on exports and two-price systems, the question of them being honoured by provincial governments does not arise.

Neither the U.S. nor any other country has any rights, let alone national treatment rights, to establish, acquire, and operate Canadian resource companies, and Canada has the right to establish a range of conditions relating to foreign investment. A panel examined a U.S. complaint regarding the Foreign Investment Review Agency (FIRA) and concluded that GATT "does not prevent Canada from exercising its sovereign right to regulate foreign direct investment." The panel therefore examined the U.S. complaint regarding FIRA purchase and export undertakings "solely in the light of Canada's trade obligation under the General Agreement" and found its purchase undertakings illegal and the export requirements legal.

dians sufficient safe water to sustain their physical, economic and social well-being, for all time." Under GATT, Canada had the powers to implement such a policy, but the FTA has stripped it of such powers.

2. Marc Lalonde accurately and succinctly described the consequences of the FTA for energy when he observed that these provisions "put us exactly in the same boat as the Americans" and "hand over to the Americans our current and future oil and gas reserves ... by guaranteeing them access to the reserves equal to that of Canadians." The key FTA provisions that apply to energy apply to water and all other natural resources except logs. Under GATT, Canada had the exclusive right to develop its energy and other resources to serve Canadians.

I. FISH (B.C.)	
1908 to 1987	
1987	
1989	Since Canada could not levy an export tax, it replaced the export restrictions with a requirement that unprocessed fish be landed at a designated station for counting prior to export. The U.S. complained that the landing requirement conflicted with the FTA; and a panel found the requirement was a legitimate conservation measure but suggested Canada allow 10 to 20 per cent of the catch to be exported directly from its fishing grounds. Canada agreed. Media reports indicate the B.C. processing industry has been decimated.
II. FISH (ATLANTIC PROVINCES AND QUEBEC)	FTA Article 1203c exempts from the agreement the fish-processing laws of the Atlantic provinces and Quebec. But Article 1205 provides that "The Parties retain their rights and obligations under GATT" with respect to matters exempt under Article 1203. Article 1205, therefore, sets the stage for a replay of the developments that have brought about the removal of the export restrictions on unprocessed Pacific salmon and herring. The U.S. can invoke the article to obtain a GATT panel finding that provincial export controls on unprocessed fish are illegal; FTA Article 408 prevents Canada from replacing the export controls with an export tax; and Article 103 requires the provincial governments to lift the controls.

) CANADA'S EXPORTS

GATT

Canada restricted exports of unprocessed salmon and herring caught in its Pacific Ocean waters from 1908 to April 1989 primarily to provide an assured supply to processing plants. From 1970 to April 1987 exports of sockeye and pink salmon and herring were restricted. These species supplied the dominant share of the fish processed in B.C. and provided jobs for about five-sixths of the six to eight thousand workers employed by the industry.

In April 1987, GATT established a panel to examine a U.S. complaint that Canada's export restriction conflicted with GATT obligations, and about six months later the panel reported that Canada's restrictions were illegal.

Under GATT, Canada could have replaced the illegal export restrictions with an export tax, but it did not do so because, in the FTA negotiations, it had either ceded its right or intended to cede it.

FTA

If Canada invoked FTA Article 1205 in an attempt to regain Canada's GATT right to levy a tax on exports of unprocessed Atlantic fish, the U.S. could counter by invoking Article 104.2, which provides that the FTA prevails in the event of any inconsistency between it and GATT — that is, FTA Article 408 prohibiting export taxes would apply.

III. POWER-INTENSIVE INDUSTRIES

1947 TO 1991

1992

The U.S. levied countervailing and dumping duties totalling 53 per cent on imports of magnesium from Norsk Hydro's Quebec plant — 21.6 per cent to offset a Quebec Hydro subsidy and a $34-million government grant for anti-pollution equipment and 31.33 per cent to offset dumping. These duties have created uncertainty in the boardrooms of companies that use or are examining the use of power and will adversely affect decisions regarding exports to the U.S., production levels, expansion, and employment. The *Gazette* reported that Michele Jacques, responsible for aluminum investments of the Société Générale de Financement, which is a partner in the ABI smelter at Bécancour, said, "It does influence business decisions" and warned that aluminum companies could be targets of U.S. trade actions; Hugo Cimmermans, president of Hoogovens Aluminium Quebec, which is a partner in the Alouette smelter at Sept Iles, said, "It makes it not very attractive for investment in Quebec;" "the duty would further delay the resumption to full production for the $500 million [Norsk Hydro] factory, which laid off 136 people last fall and slashed production in half to about twenty thousand tonnes annually." The *Gazette* has also reported that "Norsk ended up renegotiating its power contract to satisfy U.S. authorities."

Power-intensive industries have an alterna-tive: they can locate plants in the U.S. to avoid

GATT

Certain provincial governments (e.g. Quebec, Ontario, and Manitoba) have used two-price power to attract power-intensive industries. Indeed, two-price power appears to have been the basis of Quebec's industrial strategy. Two-price power has never been challenged in GATT, and, in my view, it is legal.

FTA

FTA
FTA countervail and dumping actions and invoke FTA Articles 902.2, 903, and 904 to obtain assured supplies of Quebec's electricity at a price that is competitive with the Quebec price. Moreover, it seems that these FTA articles increase the leverage of U.S. customers in negotiations with Quebec Hydro.

CONCLUSIONS

1. GATT permitted Canada to use export taxes to process fish prior to export, but the FTA has decimated the B.C. processing industry and aborted the East Coast processing industry when fish return.

2. Two-price power policies are legal under GATT, but for practical purposes, the FTA has made them illegal.

3. A combination of FTA provisions enable power-intensive industries to locate in the U.S., obtain assured supplies of Canada electricity at a price that

PART V. AGRICULTURE, SUPPL

FTA
1947 to 1988
1989 to 1992 The FTA permitted the continued use of quantitative restrictions legal under GATT (Article 710) but provided for the elimination of tariffs. The elimination of tariffs has decimated Canada's food-processing industry (Agriculture Canada acknowledges that sixty-seven plants have closed; but other knowledgeable persons such as the Hon. Ralph Ferguson, M.P. and former minister of agriculture, estimate there have been about one hundred closures) and inevitably will phase out supply management for dairy, poultry, and eggs.)
1993 Under FTA Article 401 it appears the converted GATT tariffs established to replace quantitative restrictions would be eliminated.

GATT
_____

_____

is competitive with the Canadian price, and avoid countervail and dumping duties.

4. The FTA provisions that encourage power-intensive industries to locate in the U.S. instead of Canada also apply to all other resources except logs.

5. The FTA not only aborts the Trudeau government policy directed to adding value to resource exports but also will result in increasing such exports in their raw or initially processed forms.
_____

1ANAGEMENT, AND FOOD PROCESSING
GATT
_____

GATT permitted tariffs to protect food processing and products grown by farmers (Articles XI. 1 and 2) plus quantitative restrictions to protect the production of farmers who operated under marketing boards (Article XI. 2c). With this protection, Canada maintained viable supply management for dairy, poultry, and eggs as well as the Canadian food-processing industry.
_____

The Uruguay Round proposal is to convert the Article XI. 2c restrictions to tariffs and then to reduce the tariffs by 15 to 28 per cent. The converted tariff for butter would be 300 per cent and reduced to figure between 255 and 216 per cent, and it is understood the converted tariffs for all other products except one would consist of three digits. There is no obligation to cut the converted tariffs further. If the government retains effective tariff protection for processed foods, supply management should be viable.

CONCLUSIONS

1. The FTA/GATT situation can be summarized as follows: If the GATT Dunkel proposal is cancelled and the FTA retained, supply management will be phased out and food-processing further reduced; if, on the other hand, the FTA is cancelled and the Dunkel proposal implemented, both supply manage-

---

PART VI. AGRICULTURE, FOOD AND FTA

1947 to 1988

1989 to 1992

The FTA requires Canada to "harmonize ... technical regulatory requirements and inspection procedures" with the U.S. or, where harmonization is not feasible, to "make equivalent their respective regulatory requirements and inspection procedures" (Article 708.1a). The agreement states: "harmonization means making 'identical'" (Article 711). Since the U.S. has much greater negotiating power than Canada, we will adopt U.S. standards even when they conflict with Canada's interests.

There is substantial evidence that the Reagan and Bush administrations deregulated the inspection of food plants and the food companies sped up their processing lines. These developments have resulted in the lowering of sanitary standards to a level where U.S. government inspectors are placing the seal of approval on millions of contaminated chickens every week.[1] It would be prudent to assume that many of the diseased birds are entering Canada and that millions more will enter as Canada adopts standards "identical" to U.S. standards.

CONCLUSIONS

1. For all practical purposes, the FTA has transferred Canada's control of its agriculture, food, and beverage standards, technical regulations, and inspection from Ottawa to Washington.

ment farmers and food processing will receive tariff protection and should be viable providing the government, in the Uruguay Round, retains effective tariff protection for processed foods.

EVERAGE STANDARDS

GATT

GATT permits Canada to establish standards to serve the interests of Canada, to apply them at the border, and to prohibit the entry of foreign products that do not conform with them, provided that the Canadian standards do not "afford protection to domestic productions" (Article III). For example, Canada could apply its standards at the U.S. border and embargo the entry of any diseased American chickens and beef.

PART VII

FTA

1965 to 1988

1989	The FTA requires Canada to eliminate the suspended tariffs on vehicles and parts imported from the U.S. The FTA also modified the Auto Pact content provisions, which resulted in U.S. customs officials harassing the Canada Honda Company by accusing it of failing to meet such provisions and threatening to levy import duties. In so far as is known, U.S. customs did not accuse any company that did not meet Auto Pact content provisions prior to the FTA.

1992

CONCLUSIONS

Under GATT the Auto Pact was a viable and legal instrument of Canadian policy. The FTA requirement that Canada eliminate its tariffs on vehicles and parts renders the Pact, for practical purposes, inoperative.

Patrick Lavelle, fromer Ontario Deputy minister of Industry and Trade and Executive director of the Canadian Auto Parts manufacturer Association, recently made the comments below which were published in the *Toronto Star*.

a) "Without recourse" to the tariff eliminated by the FTA, "the Auto Pact ceases to exist." Since 1988 at least 50 Canadian parts firms have moved to the southern U.S. and Mexico.

MOTOR VEHICLES

GATT

The Auto Pact gave foreign companies a choice: They could meet certain content provisions and import vehicles and original parts tariff free, or they could pay the tariff and sell vehicles in Canada regardless of content. The key instrument was the tariff; in 1965 it was 17.5 per cent, reduced to 15 per cent in the Kennedy Round and to 9.2 per cent in the Tokyo Round. The pact does not contain provisions regarding non-tariff measures and dispute settlement, and both countries reserved their right to act consistent with GATT rights obligations. The pact does not require companies selling vehicles in Canada to produce vehicles and/or parts here.

NAFTA again changed the content provisions, and one result is further discrimination against Canada's Japanese producers in favour of U.S.-owned companies.

   b) The FTA discriminated against Honda and Toyota who have invested hundreds of millions of dollars and created hundreds of high-paying jobs in Canada with the assistance of the Canadian and Ontario governments.
   c) "The net impact" of NAFTA "will see high value-added production gravitate to the U.S. and the companies will source cheaper labour-intensive parts in Mexico leaving Canada largely out of the equation."

	FTA

1947 to 1988

1989 The FTA covers a very large number of services not covered by GATT (e.g., services related to medicare, agriculture, forestry, mining, construction, insurance [including auto insurance], real estate, commercial ventures, computers, investment, telecommunications, and tourism (Annex 1408 and Article 1601). The FTA gives Americans the same rights as Canadians to produce, distribute, sell, market, and deliver a covered service as well as access to and use of Canada distribution systems; to establish a commercial presence to distribute, market, deliver, or facilitate a covered service; and regarding any investment for the provision of a covered service and any activity associated with a covered service (Articles 1401.2, 1402.1 and 2, 1602).

1993

CONCLUSION

1. Under GATT, Canada had virtually complete control of its service industries, and the federal and provincial governments were free to choose and develop policies relating to service industries with very few constraints. The FTA, however, strips the Canadian government of most of this control and freedom to choose policies. Although the Uruguay Round probably will reduce Canada's freedom to act regarding services somewhat, our GATT freedom will still be substantially greater than the freedom we now have under the FTA. At least two-thirds of employed Canadians work for a service industry.

SERVICES

GATT

GATT applies to services embodied in goods (e.g., books, computer tapes, motion picture film, and sound recordings) and certain services that complement traded goods (transportation, insurance, and banking). But GATT does not apply to services that substitute for trade in goods (e.g., franchising and leasing) or services that are traded without a relationship with goods (e.g., banking, life insurance, telecommunications, and travel).

The odds are that the Uruguay Round will include an agreement on services. But, on the basis of the Dunkel text, it will cover only financial services, telecommunications, and air transportation, and national treatment will be limited to "all measures affecting the supply of services," that is, import of the covered services (Annex II).

PART IX

FTA

1947 to 1988

1989

The Canadian Schedule in Annex 1408 contains approximately one hundred Standard Industrial Classification (SIC) numbers, but does not describe the services covered by them. Examination of the SIC, fourth edition, 1980, discloses that seven of these numbers (i.e., 861, 862, 863, 865, 866, 867, and 868) cover forty-two specific health-care facilities, including hospitals, clinics, professional medical offices, nursing homes, and blood banks. The government's published description of the services covered by the seven three-digit numbers occupies eight pages. As mentioned above, a) FTA Articles 1401 and 1402 give Americans national treatment rights in Canada regarding the ownership, production, distribution, sale, marketing, and delivery of the covered health services; and b) Articles 1401.2d and 1602 give U.S. investors national treatment rights regarding the establishment, acquisition, conduct, and operation and sale of these services.

Monique Bégin concluded: "Free Trade is a direct threat to one of the five basic conditions of medicare — non-profit public administration." Ms. Bégin asked the question, "If a hospital is run by an American business for profit, who in the hospital will protect universality, accessibility and comprehensiveness?" And she answered, "Free Trade will ... reinforce the various segments of Canadian society, including some provincial governments, which would prefer to see medicare privatized as much as possible. All too soon, Canadians will have a two class healthcare system: one for those who can afford it, and another for the rest."

EALTH CARE

GATT

Canadian governments have complete freedom under GATT to provide health services, including medicare. And medicare is not countervailable.

In 1984, the Liberal government passed the Canada Health Act which turned the "principles of medicare" into criteria each province was required to meet to obtain federal funds. The principles are: universality, equal access to health care services by all Canadians, a comprehensive range of services, portability and non-profit administration. The Federal government used Established Programs Financing (EPF) to obtain provincial adherence to these principles.

FTA

1987 to 1993	The Canada Health Act prevented U.S. companies from exercising their FTA rights to purchase and operate business enterprises producing and marketing health services. In 1990, the Conservative government enacted Bill C-69 which froze the amount of money transferred to the provinces through Established Programs Financing until 1992 and then fixed the rate of growth for 1993 and future years at GNP minus 3 per cent. Bill C-20 enacted in 1991 accelerates Federal withdrawal from financing medicare. It is estimated that by 1998 several provinces, starting with Quebec in 1996 and then Ontario, will no longer receive federal medicare money. The means to obtain provincial compliance with medicare principles will disappear.

The Conservative government also enacted Bill C-22 in 1987 and Bill C-91 in 1993 to extend drug patents to 20 years. Despite government denial Bill C-22 was de facto a part of the FTA and has increased the cost of drugs by an average of 16 per cent. Bill C-91 implements the NAFTA Chapter Seventeen which will add millions and millions of dollars to provincial health costs. Combined with Bills C-69 and C-20, the increase in drug costs will increase pressure on provinces to privatize medicare.

It was noted above that medicare is counter-vailable (Articles 1902.1, 1902.2 and Section 1312(B) of the 1988 Omnibus Trade and Competitiveness Act).

1993	NAFTA:

a) extends FTA coverage to all Canadian health services (Article 1201.1) and drops FTA Annex 1408;

b) extends Canada's drug patent obligations set out in Bill C-22;

c) contains the FTA national treatment obligations (Article 1202);

d) contains the FTA provisions that make medicare grants countervailable (Article 1902.1).

In NAFTA Annex II "Canada Reserves" in the Social Services sector, "the right to adopt or maintain any measure with respect to the provision of public law enforcement and correctional services, and the following services to the extent

GATT

The Uruguay Round text leaves Canada with complete freedom of action regarding the provision of health care services and confirms that medicare is not countervailable (Annex II and Section 1).

FTA

that they are social services established or maintained for a public purpose: income security or insurance, social security or insurance, social welfare, public education public training, health and child care." The annex states the reservation is from national treatment for services and investment (Articles 1202 and 1102), most-favoured-nation treatment and local presence for services (Articles 1203 and 1205) and senior management and boards of directors regarding investment (Article 1107). The services reservation is pursuant to Article 1206(3) and the investment reservation is pursuant to Article 1108(3).

The question is, does this reservation switch medicare from the FTA privatization track and return control of this national asset to Canadian governments?

The evidence that NAFTA would return control of medicare to Canadian governments is listed in clause d above. No other provisions supporting such a conclusion were identified.

Evidence that NAFTA would also privatize medicare begins with the fact the reservation is from only five articles and other non-reserved articles could work for privatization (e.g. articles relating to drug patents, countervail and insurance).

The reservation is further restricted by the fact it only applies "to the extent medicare programmes are social services established or maintained for a public purpose." The conditional words "social service" and "public purpose" are not defined nor is the purpose of their inclusion in the reservation explained. It is clear, however, the conditions reduce the scope of the reservation.

NAFTA Article 1209(b) states "The Commission shall establish procedures for consultations on reservations ... with a view to further liberalization." Liberalize means to release from control and set free. Canada, therefore, has an obligation to remove measures that do not accord Americans the same rights as Canadians to provide health services — "further liberalization," in this context, means, to progressively dismantle medicare. In addition, the consultation procedures will provide the American health industry with a means to maintain or increase pressure on Can-

GATT

ada to dismantle medicare expeditiously. The Article 1209(b) obligations convert Canada's health reservation to a transitional right which will expire.

NAFTA Article 1201.3(b) provides "nothing in this Chapter shall be construed to ... prevent a Party from providing a service or performing a function such as law enforcement, correctional services, income security or insurance, social security or insurance, social welfare, public education, public training, health, and child care, in a manner that is not inconsistent with this Chapter." The named services are the services covered by Canada's reservation. Under Articles 1202 and 1201 Canada has an obligation to accord Americans all-inclusive national treatment in the provision of health services. But, if the reservation preserves medicare, Canada's health service will not be consistent with Chapter Twelve. Does Canada have an obligation or a reservation?

Any panel worth its salt adjudicating a dispute regarding Canada's reservation would examine it in the context of NAFTA's objectives set out in Chapter One. Article 102.2 states "The Parties shall interpret and apply the provision of the Agreement in the light of its objectives set out in paragraph 1 ... " Especially relevant Paragraph 1 objectives are to "(a) eliminate barriers to trade in and facilitate the cross-border movement of goods and services ...," (b) increase substantially investment opportunities ... " and "(c) provide adequate and effective protection and enforcement of intellectual property rights ..." These objectives are "elaborated more specifically through its principles and rules, including national treatment."

It is suggested these objectives will result in panels limiting the scope of the reservation by narrowly interpreting the conditional words "to the extent" that medicare services "are social services established or maintained for a public purpose" as well as accepting the view that Canada's Article 1209(b) obligations mean the reservation provides only transitional protection and should be progressively dismantled.

Panels will also attempt to learn the intentions of the NAFTA drafters. For example, even Canadian panelists will have difficulty reconciling a

GATT

FTA

---

claim the drafters intended to preserve medicare
with the reservations restricted scope, Articles
1209(b) and 101. In addition, panelists probably
will ask "if the intention was to preserve medicare, why did the drafters not incorporate a comprehensive exception in Chapter Twenty-One
and state that Articles 101, 1201.3 and 1209(b),
Chapter Nineteen (Countervail), Part Six (Intellectual Property) and all insurance provisions do
not apply to Canada's health services?" Without
clear sustaining answers to such questions — and
none are obvious — panels are likely to conclude
the Canadian reservation was intended to be limited in duration as well as scope.

CONCLUSIONS

1. The FTA places medicare on the track to being privatized and American-
ized. In addition, the odds are that sooner or later a U.S. corporation will initiate
a countervail action against Canada's exports by alleging that medicare grants
a subsidy. Such action will probably accelerate the privatization of medicare,
just as the threat of U.S. countervailing duties was one reason — possibly the
dominant reason — why the Mulroney government stopped contributing to
U.I.

The evidence is visible and compelling that NAFTA continues medicare on
the FTA track to privatization and Americanization. The means to achieve this
objective was, however, changed. In the FTA the government attempted to hide

---

PART X

FTA

1947 to 1988

GATT

the inclusion of many health services by wrapping them in a shroud of SIC numbers and then burying them in Annex 1408. In NAFTA, the government included all health services in return for an optical concession — i.e. the Annex II reservation — which it is trying to use as cover for the substantive concessions. This NAFTA tactic was used in the FTA to cover substantive concessions regarding the Auto Pact, culture, marketing boards, East Coast fish processing and monopolies.

The U.S. does not have any GATT rights relating to the purchase, ownership, operation, production, sale, etc. of Canadian health services. Equally important, GATT deems medicare grants to be non-countervailable.

INVESTMENT

GATT

Canada has substantial freedom to act to prohibit, limit, and control foreign investment and to attach certain but not all performance conditions. In 1984, GATT established a panel to examine a U.S. complaint that FIRA impaired U.S. rights by obliging foreign investors to:

a) purchase goods of Canadian origin in preference to imported goods or in specified amounts or proportions or to purchase goods from Canadian sources;

b) manufacture in Canada goods that would be imported otherwise;

c) export specified quantities or proportions of their production.

The panel found in favour of the U.S. regarding a) and b) but in favour of Canada on c). The panel also found that "in view of the fact that the General Agreement does not prevent Canada from exercising its sovereign right to regulate foreign direct investments, the Panel examined the purchase and export undertakings by investors subject to the Foreign Investment Review Act of Canada solely in the light of Canada's trade obligations under the General Agreement." This finding means, for practical purposes, that Canada is free to control foreign investment except for the imposition of certain performance requirements that conflict with GATT.

FTA

| *1989* | In addition to service provisions noted in Parts VIII and IX above, the FTA gives Americans the same rights as Canadians to establish, acquire, operate, and sell any business enterprise except those engaged in transportation, government procurement, and certain financial services (Articles 1601, 1602). |
| *1993* | |

CONCLUSION

GATT leaves Canada with substantial freedom to prohibit, limit, or control foreign investment as well as to establish certain performance standards. But under the FTA, Americans can take over almost all Canadian companies, even high-technology companies, with virtually no conditions attached. American ownership means key decisions about jobs, exports, reinvestment, research, and development will no longer be made in Canada, and most of the profits will no longer go to Canadians.

PART XI. CULTURE (E.G. PUBLISHING,

FTA

| *1947 to 1988* | |
| *1989* | Article 2005.1 states that cultural industries are exempt from the agreement except for tariff elimination, divestiture of an indirect acquisition, and retransmission rights. But Article 2005.2 puts culture back in the FTA by giving the U.S. the right to retaliate against Canada for "actions" the U.S. deems "inconsistent" with the agreement. Moreover, Article 2011.2 gives the U.S. the right to circumvent the dispute-settlement procedures whenever it retaliates. |

GATT

The Uruguay Round text regarding foreign investment is limited to repeating existing rights and obligations (Section IV).

BROADCASTING, FILMS AND RECORDING)
GATT

GATT places no constraints on Canada's freedom to act to sustain its cultural industries other than those relating to tariff concessions.

In addition, GATT Article IV permits Canada to establish screen quotas that "require the exhibition of cinematograph film by national origin." This is a very substantial right. It is a derogation from three of GATT's most important articles; i.e., I, most-favoured national treatment; III, national treatment; and XI, prohibition of restrictions.

Under GATT, the U.S. would have to prove to a panel that a cultural measure conflicted with Canada's GATT obligations before it could retaliate. The panel would judge the U.S. complaint on the basis of GATT law and *not* the vested interests of the U.S. broadcasting, publishing, film, and recording industries.

FTA
of receiving a panel report, Article 1807.9 gives the U.S. the right to retaliate.

Compensation	Article 1605: Expropriation provides for the "payment of prompt adequate and effective compensation at fair market value," if Canada "directly or indirectly nationalizes or expropriates an investment." The *Toronto Star* (17 Sept. 1990) reported that Peter Kormes and Simon Reisman said this provision would not apply to a public auto insurance plan. The *Star* noted "The interpretation by Kormes and Reisman contrast sharply with that of the previous Liberal Government which said public "auto insurance would contravene the free trade deal and force Ontario to pay millions of dollars in compensation."

CONCLUSIONS

1. GATT permits Canadian governments, provincial as well as Federal, to establish monopolies in any area of activity and for any purpose, providing they respect its rights and obligations. insofar as can be recalled during forty-five years, the only Canadian monopolies to breach such obligations have been provincial liquor boards.

2. In sharp contrast, the FTA prevents all Canadian governments from operating new monopolies. Although the FTA gives Canada the right to "designate" a monopoly, Canada accepted obligations that make it impossible to operate a new monopoly. If Canada breaches FTA obligations, the U.S. has the right to be compensated or to retaliate. These FTA obligations appear to have been an important, if not dominant, reason why the Ontario NDP government reneged on its election campaign commitment regarding auto insurance.

GATT

1. Mr. Roy Davidson, for many years Economic Advisor to the Department of Consumer and Corporate Affairs, has identified three significant differences between NAFTA and the Uruguay Round text (Annex III): GATT "Objectives," NAFTA provisions on "trade secrets" and the NAFTA and GATT provisions controlling the anti-competition practices in voluntary licensing. He points out that in "each case the GATT text is more favourable to a heavy importer of technology like Canada."

2. Roy Davidson stated "The most important differences are that there is in NAFTA no equivalent to the GATT provisions on objectives in Article 7" and "if these objectives were used to interpret the rest of the GATT text, particularly Article 31, this would go a long way towards acceptance of the compulsory licensing we have had in Canada since 1969, even though some of our procedures would have to be changed in important ways."

3. Roy Davidson concluded his analysis by stating, "The bottom line ... is that if the Uruguay Round of GATT is successful, drug patents provide another strong argument for abandoning NAFTA and the FTA, and relying instead on the GATT."

4. In addition, Harvey Bale (Senior Vice-President, International Affairs, U.S. Pharmaceutical Manufacturers Association and member of the U.S. GATT Tokyo Round Delegation) has noted certain provisions that, in his view, the Uruguay Round text "falls short of NAFTA." For example, he states that Uruguay text Article 27 "specifically excludes from patentability plants and animals, and essential processes for the production of plants and animals — essentially removing many of the newest technology products from the umbrella of patent protection. The NAFTA agreement, while not perfect, provides broader protection for this cutting edge technology."

5. The considerations below suggest that it would be possible to dilute the GATT patent provisions whereas the probability is the NAFTA provisions will be strengthened.

REGARDING PATENTS

GATT

- GATT's basic purpose is to liberalize trade but the Intellectual Property provisions restrict trade.
- GATT has a history of examining monopolies and cartels for the purpose of liberalizing trade.
- Canada's bargaining power is substantially greater in GATT than in NAFTA because, *inter alia,* many GATT members are substantial importers of technology and, therefore, share Canada's interests.

NAFTA

Chapter Seventeen, "Intellectual Property," is reinforced by Article 102: Objectives. Paragraph 2 states "The Parties shall interpret and apply the provisions of this Agreement in the light of its objectives set out in paragraph ... " Paragraph 1(d) states, "The objectives of this Agreement ... are to ... provide adequate and effective protection and enforcement of intellectual property rights in each Party's territory."

- The objective of the GATT Intellectual Property agreement (Article 7) provide that: "The protection and enforcement of intellectual property rights should contribute to the promotion of technological innovation and to the transfer and dissemination of technology, to the mutual advantage of producers and users of technological knowledge and in a manner conducive to social and economic welfare, and to a balance of rights and obligations."
- NAFTA states (Article 102), "The objectives of this Agreement ... including national treatment are to:

(d) provide adequate and effective protection and enforcement of intellectual property rights in each Party's territory."

Chapter 4

How Trade Deals Work for U.S. Corporations: The Case of Patents and Pharmaceutical Drugs

Linda Diebel

The free trade agenda has been driven by large transnational corporations based in the U.S. In this chapter, Linda Diebel, Washington bureau chief for the Toronto Star, *shows the links between the adoption of new legislation in Canada limiting the rights of Canadian corporations to produce generic copies of U.S. patented drugs and trade lobbying by U.S. pharmaceutical companies. Ironically, the effect of the new Canadian legislation is to entrench monopoly rights, not to promote "free" trade. This chapter is adapted from an article that appeared in the* Toronto Star *(6 December 1992) and is reprinted with permission — The Toronto Star Syndicate.*

The Canadian federal drug bill, which will affect the millions who require prescription drugs, is a precedent: it's the first time that legislation will be passed in Canada, then locked in under free trade. It means that, in future, there will be measures that no Canadian government will be able to provide for its own citizens without violating the North American Free Trade Agreement (NAFTA) with the United States and Mexico. Essentially, that includes made-in-Canada drug legislation.

The U.S. pharmaceutical industry, one of the richest and most powerful sectors in America, has been fighting for these very changes since Canada brought in consumer-friendly drug legislation in 1969. Finally, in this round, they won virtually every demand they made of Trade Minister Michael Wilson in the free trade negotiations. In its simplest interpretation, the drug bill extends patent right protection from the current 10 years to a minimum 20 years. But the law and the trade deal taken together will do far more than that. After the law is passed, it will be entrenched in the NAFTA and virtually impossible to change. And NAFTA basically wipes out the sovereign right of the Canadian Parliament to allow generic drug companies to provide cheaper copies of brand-name drugs to consumers.

In the past, Canada has let generic drug companies, with restrictions, copy drugs that have been developed and marketed by somebody else. They're called no-name, or generic, drugs and they're cheaper because the makers of generics face lower development costs than the big pharmaceutical companies that hold the patents. These brand-name companies are largely foreign owned; indeed, 95 per cent of all patents are owned outside Canada.

Opponents of the new drug legislation say that drug prices will soar, and that provincial drug plans, often the only safety net for the old and the poor, will be devastated. The Conservative government says that price increases will be marginal, and that Canadians will benefit through a wider range of available drugs, a healthier industry, more research and development in Canada and more jobs. But there's always been a fail-safe with this kind of consumer legislation. If it didn't work, the government could simply rewrite, or abolish, the law. Not this time. As justification, Canadians have been told that this drug legislation is necessary to bring Canada into line with other countries. We're encouraged to think that Canada is far behind in providing both patent protection for multinational pharmaceuticals and the means to stop generic knock-offs of big-name brands. But the drug bill, C-91, coupled with NAFTA, will give American multinational drug companies a better deal in Canada than they will have anywhere else in the world, including at home in the United States.

Canada appears to have been the guinea pig. Referring to NAFTA, Harvard University professor Edgar Davis, a former drug company executive, told the *New York Times:* "It shows what an industry that has its act together can do." It's a rich business. The U.S. drug industry's profit margin has topped every other sector in America for the past six years straight. Its foremost lobby is the Pharmaceutical

Manufacturers' Association, and worldwide sales for the association's hundred or so members for this year will top (U.S.) $75 billion.
In Canada, the U.S. drug manufacturers are represented by the Pharmaceutical Manufacturers Association of Canada. Essentially, the
Canadian group is a branch-plant operation of its powerful American
parent. The U.S. drug lobby never pulled its punches about what it
wanted, indeed expected, from Ottawa. But these views have been
relatively unknown to Canadians. In fact, the entire controversy over
changing Canadian drug laws — stretching back six years in the
latest round — has been marked by a difference in impressions on
both sides of the border. For example, there is no sense among
American policy makers that the big pharmaceutical companies have
any intention of ever transferring significant biomedical research to
Canada as the Pharmaceutical Manufacturers Association of Canada
has promised in exchange for new drug laws. "Canada doesn't have
to worry about having a biomedical research industry — they can
make use of ours," Gail Wilensky, a special assistant to former
President George Bush, recently told the U.S. Public Broadcasting
System. "That gives Canada something of a free ride. That's what it
means to be a small country next to a large country."

NAFTA served as a perfect tool for the U.S. drug companies.
Through another of its lobbies, the Intellectual Property Committee,
it sent a letter on Feb. 26, 1992, to U.S. Trade Representative Carla
Hills. It was an aggressive letter, full of verbs like "insist" and replete
with a detailed list, divided into six sections, of what Canada "must"
agree to in NAFTA to satisfy American drug makers. The letter was
signed by Bristol-Myers Squibb, E.I. du Pont de Nemours & Co.,
FMC Corp., General Electric Co., Hewlett-Packard Co., IBM Corp.,
Johnson & Johnson, Merck & Co. Inc., Monsanto Co., Pfizer Inc.,
Procter & Gamble Co., Rockwell International Corp. and Time
Warner Inc. The Intellectual Property Committee represents the computer and information industries, as well as the drug business. That's
because they have all worked to entrench the notion, grandly referred
to as "intellectual property rights," that products, processes, ideas,
plants, animals and even human life forms can and should be protected like your front lawn. It's a relatively new field in which
multinationals are making up the rules as they go along, then seeing
how far they can get in having these rules adopted as international
standards. That's why setting a precedent with Canada was so important. The aim, basically, is to write patent, copyright and trademark law for the world.

"One of the most surprising things about Canada–U.S. trade negotiations in recent years is that the United States somehow managed to persuade Canadians that free trade would be promoted by strengthening private monopoly," according to Roy Davidson, retired deputy director of the Canadian federal bureau of competition policy. [See his contribution to this volume.] "Of course, the U.S. task was made easier because it faced a pliant Canadian government, a naive Canadian press and a far from disinterested Canadian business lobby."

In 1969, Canada introduced a system called compulsory licensing, which allowed generic companies to copy drugs on payment of a royalty to the patent holder. A 1985 royal commission found that, as a result, Canadians had saved money on prescriptions while drug company profits hadn't suffered. Still, under pressure from the multinationals, Prime Minister Brian Mulroney's government began to dismantle the system in 1987 by bringing in 10 years of exclusive patent protection against competition. It wasn't enough. "In clear, straightforward language, NAFTA must require Canada to dismantle its discriminatory compulsory (generic) licensing regime for pharmaceutical products and to suspend the granting of any compulsory (generic) licences from Dec. 20 1991, and onward," said the Feb. 26 industry letter to U.S. Trade Representative Hills. That Dec. 20 date — which the Mulroney government duly wrote into its new drug bill and which retroactively knocks about two dozen generic licences into oblivion — originates with another set of trade talks. On Dec. 20, 1991, Arthur Dunkel, secretary-general of the General Agreement on Tariffs and Trade (GATT), released a set of draft proposals in an effort to break the deadlock in the world trade body's Uruguay Round. But there was softening language in Dunkel's proposals on intellectual property rights that gave governments leeway in changing their laws and offered generous transition periods, and even outs. The U.S. drug industry, which had obtained the section on intellectual property rights in the first place and had worked hard to influence its contents, was far from happy with the result. In its letter to Hills, the Intellectual Property Committee stressed that the Dunkel text "should be considered a floor — not a ceiling — for the level of protection that must be included in NAFTA's section on intellectual property." NAFTA must make it far tougher, said the committee, for generic companies to put their knock-off drugs on the market.

Here's how the NAFTA agreement does just that:

- Big drug companies will be able to protect their "process" as well as their product, making it virtually impossible for generics to import in bulk and manufacture in Canada.
- Patent holders will have to be found guilty of breaking competition law — a formidable task in Canada — before generic licenses will be granted.
- Sweeping new criminal charges will be laid against patent breakers based on the revolutionary notion (for Canada) that they are guilty until proved innocent.
- New rules on trade secrets will make it impossible for generics to duplicate a drug without duplicating all of the clinical testing. That makes it tougher for generics in Canada than in the United States. The United States provides 20 years of patent protection, but it doesn't require generics to repeat the entire testing process for their products. They simply have to prove bio-equivalency.

"Given all the conditions attached, it is highly unlikely that any new generic copies of patented medicines would ever be authorized under this (NAFTA) article," Canadian analyst John Dillon concluded in a NAFTA study for the Toronto-based Ecumenical Coalition for Economic Justice.

Trade Minister Wilson seemed literally to embrace the American demands. As Dillon points out, Canada didn't even bring its own draft text — essential, one would think, in fighting for Canadian consumers — to the bargaining table. Instead, Ottawa relied on the Dunkel proposals for GATT. Not surprisingly, the American drug lobby was pleased with NAFTA. It still wants an end to Canadian cultural protection as applied to their industry. But the first paragraph of the relevant NAFTA section hints at more to come: "A party may implement in its domestic law more extensive protection of intellectual property rights than is required under this agreement, provided that such protection is not inconsistent with this agreement." On Oct. 1, 1992 a follow-up Intellectual Property Committee letter to Hills lauded "major improvements" in NAFTA over what Dunkel had proposed for GATT. It was the best deal they'd ever gotten. Said the letter: "The provisions of the intellectual property chapter of the NAFTA agreement represent a significant advance in the standards of protection and enforcement of intellectual property rights that have been negotiated by the United States to date." "You ... can be justifiably proud of your achievement." Gerald Mossinghoff, president of the Pharmaceutical Manufacturers' Association, recently summed up: "Now, Canada has recognized that their system was not what it should be, and indeed we applaud the efforts of the Canadian government."

For all this, NAFTA doesn't even protect Canada from further U.S. trade sanctions over patent rights. The Intellectual Property Committee has specifically instructed Hills not to give up the sanctions weapon. On Feb. 26, 1992, it wrote that Canada (and Mexico) shouldn't be given a "free ride" which might "dissipate the critical incentives" for the 128 member nations of GATT to do as the United States wanted in those negotiations. Moreover, throughout the entire NAFTA talks, Canada was under threat of trade sanctions over its drug laws. The United States consistently named Canada to what's known as the Special 301 "watch list" of errant countries whose drug laws aren't deemed appropriate by the American drug lobby.

There are still several key questions about the changes to Canada's drug laws:

* Whose interests are really being served by the timing?

Shortly after Dunkel tabled his proposals, Wilson announced that Canada would change its patent law to comply with GATT. But the Dunkel text was non-binding, and may never be implemented. The government tabled the bill in June 1992, and Canadians subsequently found out that it met the requirements, not of the GATT but of a NAFTA deal that was still six weeks away. Now it appears that NAFTA is being used to ratchet up the level of drug industry protection in the GATT negotiations.

* Why further jeopardize a Canadian patent system that has kept drug prices lower than in the United States?

Reports have consistently proved that Canadians pay less than Americans for prescription drugs. But the cost of new drugs in Canada, which since 1987 have 10 years of patent protection, has gone up faster than the rate of inflation. Now they'll get the same 20-years' protection as in the United States. One recent American study found that the top 20 prescription drugs rose in price 82 per cent between 1985 and 1991. A recent study by a government price monitoring agency showed that Canadian drug prices have increased substantially since the 1987 changes.

• How will the federal watchdog agency be able to do its job?

Ottawa argues that the drug bill gives its Patented Medicines Review Board real clout to roll back prices. But the board will have to rely on information that is virtually impossible to obtain from out-of-country parent companies. It will be doubly difficult because real industry costs are shrouded in mystery. A recent report by the Washington-based Families USA Foundation on prescription drug "price-gouging" found that "more than half the drug industries' claimed research spending is nothing more than a bookkeeping trick." The drug companies claim as 'indirect costs' the money they might have made if the law allowed them to sell drugs without waiting for product safety tests."

• How solid are drug industry promises about new research and development in Canada?

The multinationals have promised $400 million over five years toward building a real biomedical research industry in Canada. But they failed to keep their promises after the Mulroney government first changed the drug laws, with Bill C-22, in 1987. During the NAFTA negotiations, Wilson ignored a report from his own government that found there has been limited job gains and little growth in research and development in the wake of Bill C-22. The draft consumer affairs report was obtained by Southam News under access-to-information.

After winning Bill C-22, Judy Erola, president of the Pharmaceutical Manufacturers Association of Canada, promised: "This means the beginning of a new era in Canadian biomedical research."

Four short years later, in 1991, she was telling Canadians that their drug laws weren't up to international snuff. By then, Erola was insisting: "Canada is the odd man out."

Section II
Assessing the Deal

Chapter 5

Manufacturing

Andrew Jackson

This comprehensive examination of the performance of the manufacturing sector makes sobering reading. While sorting out the impact of free trade is not easy, the overall weakness of this sector since the FTA came into force is not in doubt. Contrary to the rosy scenario pointed by free trade advocates, Canadian manufacturing has undergone a structural adjustment bringing job and output losses that are of crisis proportion.

In this chapter, Andrew Jackson shows that the downturn in manufacturing preceded the overall recession by one year. Job losses are largely permanent, not temporary as would be the case if the recession were to blame. Change in the balance of goods and service trade point to 99,000 Canadian jobs lost. Changes in cross-border investment flows point to another 105,000 jobs lost. In the period preceding free trade, few would have predicted, based on an expanding manufacturing sector, the difficulties to come. There is much evidence that the changed relationship between Canada and the U.S. under free trade has worked against Canadian-based manufacturing. The U.S. share of the Canadian market is up dramatically; Canada's merchandise trade balance has weakened; U.S. manufacturing outpaced its Canadian counterpart; and Canadian investment moved to the U.S. while shutdowns and layoffs occurred in Canada. This paper incorporates some material from the CLC submission on NAFTA to the parliamentary Subcommittee on International Trade and from the author's "A Social

> *Democratic Economic Agenda for the 1990s"* Canadian Busi-
> ness Economics *(1, no. 2, Winter 1993).*

In the wake of the implementation of the Canada–U.S. Free Trade
Agreement, the manufacturing sector has been gripped by the worst
crisis of the post-war period. As many as one in five jobs have been
lost, and the evidence shows that, unlike the case in the recession of
1981–82, these losses are in considerable part the result of structural
rather than merely cyclical factors. We face the reality of major,
permanent job losses across industrial Canada, particularly in the
industrial heartland of Ontario and Quebec. This is a loss of jobs and
industrial capacity comparable to that experienced by the U.S. Rust
Belt in the early 1980s or by the U.K. in the first years of the Thatcher
government.

There is no disputing the scale and severity of the manufacturing
crisis. At issue is, first, the extent to which it is attributable to the
FTA and, second, the constraints imposed by the FTA upon the
necessary response in terms of public policy.

The Tories and big business lobby groups would have us accept
the reality of continental (and, imminently, hemispheric) free trade
and turn our attention to remedying the competitive problems of
Canadian industry. They would have us forget the glowing promises
of jobs and prosperity on which the FTA was sold and shift the blame
for the crisis to strong trade unions and social rights and entitlements
we can supposedly no longer afford.

There is, to be sure, no return to the pre-FTA status quo. But it is
worth at least briefly revisiting the arguments about the benefits of
free trade for our manufacturing sector, and it is certainly important
to assess the degree to which the FTA is to blame for our present
ills. Only on that basis can one develop a clear industrial policy
agenda for the 1990s and beyond.

A Flawed Case

The mainstream economic forecasts about the impact of a Canada–
U.S. free trade agreement upon the manufacturing sector were, to say
the least, rosy. It is worth examining the official Department of
Finance assessment of the likely impacts of the deal in some detail
because it cited, echoed, and reinforced the numerous positive
econometric studies produced by private and public agencies and
because it constituted the "official" set of expectations about the
positive economic impacts of the FTA.[1]

In line with neo-classical economic orthodoxy, the department argued that the FTA would improve efficiency by promoting specialization and economies of scale in production. Canadian industry would produce a narrower range of products in longer product runs for a larger market, continuing the liberalized trade-driven restructuring process of the previous two decades. The market itself would grow because consumers would benefit from lower input costs. More intangibly, the competitive environment produced by the FTA would lead to "increased flexibility and dynamism," while reduced uncertainty with respect to the threat of U.S. protectionism would promote new industrial investment.

The department argued that "the economic benefits from the Agreement will begin to be realized shortly after its implementation ... investment spending for new plant and equipment will increase as Canadian firms move to take advantage of their enhanced and more secure access to the huge U.S. marketplace. Increased consumer and investment spending will result in stronger economic growth and enhanced job creation."[2]

It was estimated that the FTA would generate a long-run real output gain of 3.5 per cent, with the positive impacts highly concentrated in the manufacturing sector, which was forecast to enjoy a long-run real output gain of 10.6 per cent. These output gains would be shared by both highly protected and relatively unprotected industries, since the former would benefit most from lower U.S. tariffs and from the greater potential gains of specialization. In regional terms, Ontario, with its large manufacturing sector, was seen to be the major beneficiary of the FTA with a forecast real income (GNP) gain of 2.7 per cent compared to 2.5 per cent for the nation as a whole. No detailed sectoral forecasts were provided.

In terms of employment, the study estimated an economy-wide net gain of 120,000 jobs by 1993, plus the retention of 75,000 jobs at risk from U.S. protectionism. Again, no sectoral breakdown was provided. The extent of labour adjustment in response to FTA-driven restructuring was to be modest — an average 16,000 free trade-driven, inter-industry job shifts per year, or 25,000 job shifts counting intra-industry changes. This was placed firmly in the context of an average five million job changes in the economy per year.

While it was noted that industry would have to take advantage of the new opportunities provided by the FTA, there was barely a hint of concern that free trade could lead to a restructuring process with negative implications for at least a sizeable minority of manufacturing sector workers and businesses. The same is true of the more detailed sectoral estimates of job changes produced by the Economic Council of Canada, which found that over a ten-year period there would be a net gain of 19,000 manufacturing jobs as the result of 76,000 job losses and 95,000 job gains. A loss of 7,600 jobs per year would, as the Council noted, have a trivial impact in a sector employing more than two million workers.

Critics of the deal pointed to a number of flaws in the econometric studies, noting that the estimated gains from trade liberalization were relatively modest and dependent upon the largely unrealistic assumption of full employment. (In the world of econometricians, income and output gains from trade liberalization are axiomatic since resources idled in one sector move to more productive uses elsewhere.) The more fundamental criticism was that the abstract world of econometric models failed to correspond to the real world of the Canadian industrial structure.

The labour movement and the popular movements opposed to the FTA drew particular attention to high levels of U.S. ownership and the inherited branch-plant structure still prevalent in much of the manufacturing sector. Given that the FTA would lead to the phasing out of remaining tariff barriers as well as many non-tariff barriers (e.g., domestic processing requirements for resources, domestic procurement programmes) and given that it would assure U.S. multinationals access to the Canadian market if production were to be shifted from Canadian to U.S. plants, it was argued that many branch plants would simply be shut down or reduced to warehousing operations rather than restructured to serve the North American market as a whole in existing or more specialized product lines. In other manufacturing sectors with high levels of dependence upon the domestic market and enjoying still significant tariff protection — the "soft sectors," such as textiles, clothing, footwear, furniture, and food and beverages — it was argued that loss of tariff protection would also result in a loss of the domestic market to lower-cost U.S. imports.[3]

The rationale for such a shift of manufacturing production from Canada to the U.S. was seen to be a U.S. advantage in terms of cost competitiveness as the result of weaker unions, lower wages in many sectors, and the lower tax and regulatory burden on business in the U.S. For example, the pamphlet "What's the Big Deal" produced by the Pro Canada Network and massively distributed during the election argued that "a lot of Canadian companies will move down to the States ... to states that have no minimum wage, no health and safety laws, where unions are practically illegal ... or else they'll demand the same conditions as they can get in the States."

Another major argument advanced by critics of the deal involved the historical dependence of the Canadian manufacturing sector upon support through non-market mechanisms other than the tariff — regulated trade arrangements such as the Auto Pact; resource-processing requirements; regional and other industrial development subsidies; government procurement; crown corporations, and so forth. Put simply, space for the active exercise of industrial policy as opposed to the working of pure market forces was seen as essential to the maintenance of a healthy manufacturing sector. Take away many of the key instruments of national economic sovereignty, it was argued, and Canada's already weak manufacturing sector would suffer serious decline.

Somewhat astonishingly in retrospect, the proponents of free trade assumed the ability of Canadian manufacturing to compete in an integrated continental market. It was the left that drew attention to the competitive implications of Canada's stronger labour movement, larger public sector, and more advanced social programmes. To be sure, some business spokespersons were frank — or foolish — enough to acknowledge that the FTA would inevitably have repercussions for Canada's ability to maintain higher labour and social standards than those in the U.S., but the general line was that the free trade critics lacked faith in the competitive abilities of Canadians. Ironically, after four years of free trade, the need for massive social and economic changes to promote "competitiveness" vis-à-vis U.S. industry dominates the discourse of business and the right.

Before Free Trade

Contrary to the perception of "deindustrialization," the manufacturing sector did not significantly decline in the 1980s in terms of output. Indeed, our comparative position among the advanced industrial countries improved by some measures in the latter part of the decade before the free trade deal was signed.

Manufacturing contributed 19.3 per cent of GDP at factor cost in 1988, down only marginally from 19.7 per cent in 1980. The share of manufacturing in total employment fell from 20.8 per cent to 17.8 per cent over this same period, in large part because, as in all advanced industrial countries, labour productivity growth in the manufacturing sector rose at well above the average rate. In other words, it took a smaller share of the labour force to generate the same share of total output.

Total manufacturing employment (Labour Force Survey data) fell by 309,000 in the 1981–82 recession, from a peak of 2.13 million in January 1981 to a low of 1.82 million in November 1982. By mid-1988, the total number of manufacturing jobs had regained the pre-recession level, and the total peaked at 2.14 million in June 1989, six months after the FTA came into effect. Nineteen eighty-eight was a banner year for manufacturing job growth, with the total increasing by 4.3 per cent over 1987.

Over the 1979–88 period, real value added in manufacturing grew by an average 2.4 per cent per year, slightly less than the 2.8 per cent average recorded for the OECD countries and for the G-7, the seven largest industrial countries. This relatively poor performance was the result of the particular severity of the 1981–82 recession in Canada. In the 1983–88 period of recovery, manufacturing growth by this measure was significantly more rapid than for the OECD or the G-7, and Canada's relative status as an advanced industrial country thus improved.[4]

In the immediate pre–free trade period, Canada was enjoying a near industrial boom. Real manufacturing output grew by 4.0 per cent in 1987 and 4.8 per cent in 1988, with these increases fairly generalized but concentrated in the durable goods sector. Between 1986 and 1988, real output grew by 10.8 per cent in the motor vehicle sector, by 11.3 per cent in auto parts, by 22.6 per cent in aircraft, by 11.4 per cent in primary steel, and by 10.7 per cent in machinery. Expansion in the newer "high technology" sectors was particularly rapid — real output of electrical and electronic products rose by 22.2 per cent, and the sub-sector of office, store, and business machines recorded an output increase of 67.2 per cent.[5] Recent studies have documented the largely successful restructuring of the Canadian auto and steel industries, among others, in the 1980s.[6]

While the export orientation of the manufacturing sector — and levels of import penetration in the Canadian market — increased significantly in the 1970s and 1980s, a good part of the manufacturing expansion of the late 1980s was not external-trade driven. Exports as a share of Canadian (nominal) GDP did not, contrary to much of the rhetoric of "globalization," increase over the decade, and indeed fell from 28.3 per cent in 1980 to 26.3 per cent in 1988. (This drop is in large part attributable to the fact that the prices of many raw materials and semi-processed goods and, indeed, many manu-factured goods increased below the general rate of inflation.)

Between 1986 and 1988, when manufacturing expansion was at its most rapid, exports increased by 15.7 per cent in nominal terms compared to a 19.8 per cent increase in total nominal GDP. The growth of exports in real terms (the great majority of exports are manufactured goods) was lower than the growth of total manufac-turing production, and the major driving sources of expansion were domestic demand — consumer spending, investment in residential and non-residential construction, and investment in machinery and equipment by Canadian businesses. The overall dependence of the industrial expansion upon demand in the U.S. has thus been exag-gerated. This is also suggested by the fact that the expansion of the late 1980s was accompanied by a declining merchandise trade sur-plus with the U.S. (the surplus peaked at just over 12 per cent of total trade in 1984 and had fallen to 7 per cent by 1988) and by the fact that the U.S. share of Canadian exports fell from almost 80 per cent in 1985 to 75 per cent in 1988. That said, there is no denying the critical importance of the U.S. market to the major manufacturing industries — wood, pulp and paper, auto, aircraft, and so on.

Canadian manufacturers were cost competitive relative to U.S. manufacturers in much of the period of recovery from the 1981–82 recession. While there are many dimensions to competitiveness other than costs (technological and product quality advantages, quality of service, product uniqueness and design, etc.) and while wages are a modest and declining share of total manufacturing costs (which in-clude raw materials, energy, taxes, the cost of land, etc.), economists tend to pay great attention to unit labour costs — a measure that varies with wage rates and labour productivity (output per hour of labour). Cost competitiveness by this measure will decline if wage increases are not offset by greater labour productivity gains than those of competitors or by changes in the exchange rate.

In the recovery from the recession (1982–86), labour productivity in Canadian manufacturing rose at slightly below the rate in the U.S. (17.9 per cent compared to 20.0 per cent); wages rose slightly faster (21.4 per cent compared to 16.2 per cent), but the Canadian dollar depreciated 11.2 per cent against the U.S. dollar. As a result, the overall cost competitive position of Canadian manufacturers im-proved. From 1986, for reasons that have yet to be adequately ex-plained, labour productivity growth was much slower in Canada than in the U.S., and, likely as a result of a much stronger labour movement, wage growth was more rapid, though unexceptional relative to productivity growth and to wage growth in other industrial countries. Most importantly, the Canadian dollar appreciated sharply in value against the U.S. dollar from mid-1988 as a direct result of the restrictive monetary policies of the Bank of Canada.[7]

The key point is that the exchange rate the Canadian dollar — which averaged 74 cents U.S. between 1984 and 1988 — played an important part in promoting and then maintaining cost competitiveness in Canadian manufacturing relative to the U.S. in the pre-free trade period.

It should finally be noted that the latter part of 1980s saw substantial new investment in machinery and equipment in Canadian manufacturing and, to a lesser degree, in total manufacturing investment. From 1985 through 1989, machinery and equipment investment increased by an average 19.0 per cent per year (in nominal terms), significantly outstripping GDP growth. Total manufacturing investment increased by an average 13.6 per cent per year. Plant capacity was significantly expanded, new computerized technologies were installed, and the ground was laid for a substantial growth in productivity. This investment boom was a major source of growth for the Canadian economy as a whole, and from 1982 through 1988, investment growth was much more rapid than for the OECD countries as a whole.

None of these facts mean that the Canadian manufacturing sector did not face real and difficult problems in the immediate pre-free trade period. There were significant underlying structural weaknesses. But the evidence does show that the absence of an FTA was no impediment to significant industrial expansion in the aftermath of the 1981–82 recession and that in late 1988 Canada would not likely have been judged to be facing an imminent industrial crisis.

The Crisis of the Manufacturing Sector

Canada entered into an economy-wide downturn in the spring of 1990, a little more than one year after the FTA came into effect. Significantly, however, the downturn in the manufacturing sector, the sector most heavily exposed to direct U.S. competition and the most likely candidate for post-FTA "restructuring," began much earlier, in June 1989.

Since then total manufacturing employment (as measured by Statistics Canada's Labour Force Survey) has fallen almost continuously, from 2,144,000 to 1,783,000 in December 1992 — for a total loss of 361,000 jobs, or 17 per cent of all jobs in this sector. Over this same period, manufacturing output (adjusted for inflation) has fallen by a little more than 11 per cent. Output increased slightly during 1992, from a trough of 13 per cent below peak output, while employment continued to fall.

Table 5–1 breaks down these manufacturing job losses by major sector (on the basis of the Survey of Employment, Earnings and Hours, which provides such sectoral detail and indicates even larger net job losses than the Labour Force Survey). In literally scores of

Table 5–1

MANUFACTURING JOB LOSSES BY SECTOR

Jobs in Thousands

Sector	Jan. 1989	Jan. 1992	Loss/Gain	% Loss/Gain
Food and Beverage	224.10	191.50	-33	-14.5%
Rubber and Plastics	81.00	55.70	25	-31.2%
Clothing	94.70	61.60	-33	-35.0%
Textiles	66.70	46.90	-20	-29.7%
Wood Industries	109.20	75.10	-34	-31.2%
Furniture and Fixtures	63.10	41.40	-22	-34.4%
Pulp and Paper	125.50	108.70	-17	-13.4%
Printing and Publishing	142.00	114.00	-28	-19.7%
Primary Metals	99.40	80.80	-19	-18.7%
Metal Fabricating	160.40	120.00	-40	-25.2%
Machinery	100.40	77.20	-23	-23.1%
Aircraft/Aircraft Parts	43.70	42.00	-2	-3.9%
Motor Vehicles and Parts	128.50	104.20	-24	-18.9%
Electrical Products	129.00	100.40	-29	-22.2%
Non-Metallic Mineral	49.10	39.80	-9	-18.9%
Petroleum and Coal	19.40	22.30	3	14.9%
Chemicals	97.50	87.40	-10	-10.4%
Total	1900.9	1493.3	-408	-21.4%

(Includes Small Sectors)

Source: Statistics Canada, 72-002, *Employment, Earnings and Hours*

specific instances, manufacturing job losses can be directly tied to the complete closure of Canadian plants by U.S.-owned companies, which have, in most cases, transferred production for the Canadian market to their U.S. plants. In 1992 alone, seventeen U.S.-owned plants in Ontario employing 3,034 workers were closed, according to data compiled by the Ontario Ministry of Labour.

In other cases, closures of Canadian-owned plants are directly linked to free trade in so far as the market once served by those companies is now served by U.S.-based companies or, more rarely, because the Canadian-owned company has itself moved production to the U.S. In still other cases, the closures represent the spin-off effect of previous closures on a specific sector or upon the economy as a whole. For example, the closure of the profitable Caterpillar Canada plant in Brampton by U.S.-based Caterpillar Inc. resulted in an immediate loss of business for Canadian-based suppliers and, in a shrinking domestic market for manufactured goods, brought about the loss of hundreds of well-paid jobs in the community.

The pattern of recent job losses in manufacturing differs profoundly from that in previous downturns, reflecting the new circumstances of free trade with the U.S.

First, the impact of the recession has been disproportionately borne by the manufacturing sector. In the 1981–82 recession, total employment in manufacturing fell by 13.6 per cent from peak to trough, while total employment in the whole economy fell by 5.5 per cent. In this recession, total employment fell much less — 3.6 per cent from peak to trough — but the loss of manufacturing jobs has been greater — 17.9 per cent from peak to trough.

Second, manufacturing employment recovered relatively rapidly after the 1981–82 recession because most layoffs were temporary rather than the product of partial or permanent plant closures. Ontario Department of Labour data (unavailable for other provinces) show that just over one in five workers affected by major layoffs in 1982 was laid off because of a permanent plant shutdown. In 1991 and 1992, the comparable figure is three in five.

The difference shows up clearly in rehiring. After the 1981–82 recession, manufacturing employment began to grow as soon as the economy as a whole began to grow — and 130,000 of the jobs lost in 1981–82 were regained in 1983. By contrast, as shown in Table 5–2, manufacturing job losses have *continued* through 1992, even as a very modest recovery has begun.

At the end of 1992 there were no real signs of a broad-based recovery in manufacturing, after the worst crisis it had endured since the Great Depression. At best, output had recovered slightly while employment had bottomed out at a level almost 20 per cent below the 1988 level. It takes the perverse perspective of *Globe and Mail* editorialists to dress this crisis up as a healthy "productivity enhancing" free trade-driven shake-out that will leave Canada more productive and efficient.

The crisis of the manufacturing sector is the single major reason why the total number of people working full-time in 1992 had fallen by 500,000 since early 1990 and why the official unemployment rate

Table 5–2

CHANGES IN MANUFACTURING EMPLOYMENT
SEPTEMBER 1991 – SEPTEMBER 1992

	Change in Number of Jobs	Percentage Change
Food and Beverages	-400	-0.2%
Rubber and Plastics	-19,200	-25.8%
Clothing	15,100	-16.9%
Textiles	-7,100	-15.9%
Wood	-800	-0.8%
Furniture and Fixtures	-3,200	-6.5%
Pulp and Paper	-8,300	-7.5%
Printing and Publishing	-4,400	-3.3%
Primary Metals	-3,000	-3.5%
Fabricated Metal Products	-1,500	-1.2%
Machinery	-1,100	-1.7%
Aircraft/Aircraft Parts	-2,500	-5.8%
Motor Vehicles and Parts	-700	-0.5%
Electrical Products	-2,100	-1.6%
Non Metallic Minerals	-1,300	-2.8%
Petroleum and Coal	-2,700	-13.8%
Chemicals	-1,100	-1.3%
Total	**-67,200**	**-4.0%**

Source: Statistics Canada, 72-002. *Employment, Earnings and Hours*

rose steadily from 7.2 per cent to a high of 11.8 per cent in November 1992.

Job losses in manufacturing spread first to closely related service industries (rail, trucking, communications, and business services, such as advertising), which saw their customer base shrink. These sectors were also themselves often exposed to much more intensive competition from U.S.-based service providers, which resulted in a steady increase in Canada's deficit in the trade of services with the U.S.

Cumulative job losses in industry and closely related service sectors (the highest paid parts of the private sector economy) in turn had a huge depressing effect upon consumer spending and residential construction, ultimately depressing those sectors of the economy that were not so directly exposed to U.S. competition.

The steady erosion of Canada's private sector productive base has also led to an acute crisis in the public sector. On the expenditure side, soaring unemployment has translated into staggering increases in dependency upon unemployment insurance and, following the attack upon the UI programme, upon social assistance. In 1992, an average 9.97 per cent of the Canadian population were dependent upon social assistance, and more than one in four workers drew UI benefits at some time in the year. On the other side of the ledger, the decimation of well-paid, full-time jobs and the crisis of business sector after sector has resulted in a major squeeze on government revenues. Many governments have responded by cutting public sector jobs and services, further worsening the downward spiral.

At the end of 1992, there was no real end in sight to the unemployment crisis. The OECD noted in its December 1992 *Economic Outlook* that the gap between actual and potential output in Canada was — at almost 10 per cent — greater than in any major industrial country and greater than at any time since the Great Depression. Tellingly, the 3.8 per cent differential between Canadian and U.S. unemployment rates in 1992 (11.3 per cent vs. 7.5 per cent) was the highest ever recorded.

Is the FTA to Blame?

It is often argued — not without good reason — that the current industrial and economic crisis cannot be blamed on the Free Trade deal alone, and it is quite true that other factors have played a role. Most notably, the high interest rate/high dollar policy perversely implemented by the Bank of Canada just as the FTA came into effect dramatically worsened the cost competitiveness position of Canadian businesses in both the domestic and the U.S. markets from 1989 through to mid-1992. (There is, however, reason to believe that this policy and the FTA were not entirely unrelated, given the strongly expressed desire of the U.S. in the 1987 negotiations that the Canadian dollar be maintained at a high level. See Appendix II, this volume.)

The U.S. recession and the economy-wide Canadian recession brought about in part by high interest rates, the introduction of the GST, and continued cuts to government spending have also played major roles.

In practice, it is impossible to separate out the impact of the FTA from the impact of other policies and economic forces. But it is still the case that the *changing economic relationship between Canada and the U.S. has played a significant independent role in the crisis.* And it is surely undeniable that the FTA has had some influence upon trade and investment flows between Canada and the U.S.

The FTA has had two immediate, direct impacts and one more general impact. First, and least importantly, it has lowered Canadian tariffs and some previous non-tariff barriers (e.g., government procurement preferences), thus improving the competitive position of U.S.-based businesses in the Canadian market. Second, it has totally removed any concern on the part of business that relocation to the U.S. would be followed by any "discrimination" on the part of Canadian governments. The core of the FTA is the promise of "national treatment" for U.S.-based enterprises and the systematic removal of Canadian public policies favouring Canadian-based companies. Third, the FTA has prevented the Canadian government from implementing policies that might otherwise have been pursued to address the almost unprecedented scale and severity of the crisis.

Many of the economic impacts of the FTA are not directly measurable as job losses or as losses of market share. In many cases, companies have not closed down, but the increased bargaining leverage of business has been used to roll back the past gains of labour in terms of wages and working conditions.

All that said, there is clear evidence linking the current economic crisis to the direct impacts of the FTA.

As shown in Table 5–3, the U.S. share of the Canadian domestic market for manufactured goods in 1991 was significantly greater than in the period 1985–87. The U.S. share increased, often very significantly, in all major sectors except transportation equipment.

(The exception is explained by the fact that the non-North American import share of the Canadian market has risen faster than in the U.S. and by the fact that the Canadian share of auto pact production has risen slightly, for reasons that have nothing to do with the FTA.)

As shown in Table 5–4, since the FTA, U.S. merchandise exports to Canada have increased faster than Canadian exports to the U.S., resulting in a deterioration of the merchandise trade balance. This balance, which has historically been heavily tilted in Canada's favour, is needed to pay for the historically much greater Canadian

Table 5–3

U.S. SHARE OF THE CANADIAN MARKET

Industries	% U.S. Share 1985–1987	% U.S. Share 1991	% gain
Food Industries	5.1	8.0	+ 2.9
Beverage Industries	1.0	1.7	+ 0.7
Rubber Products	21.8	37.9	+ 16.1
Plastic Products	19.4	25.5	+ 6.1
Leather Products	4.3	7.5	+ 3.2
Primary Textiles	15.1	22.7	+ 7.6
Textile Products	9.1	19.5	+10.4
Clothing	1.3	3.2	+ 1.9
Furniture	5.9	26.4	+20.5
Paper	10.2	20.3	+ 10.1
Printing and Publishing	11.1	13.4	+ 2.3
Primary Metals	18.7	25.7	+ 7.0
Fabricated Metal Products	13.7	19.4	+ 5.7
Machinery	49.1	51.2	+ 2.1
Transportation Equipment	71.6	55.3	- 16.3
Electrical and Electronic Equipment	39.6	44.1	+ 4.5
Chemicals	21.9	26.9	+ 5.0
Non Metallic Mineral Products	11.5	19.1	+ 7.6
Refined Petroleum and Coal	4.9	5.9	+ 1.0

Source: Special Statistics Canada Data Package Compiled for the Office of the Minister for International Trade

deficit in trade in services with the U.S. and the large flow of interest and dividend payments from Canada to the U.S.

As shown in this table, both exports and imports have risen since the FTA, and both are now running at record levels (not adjusted for inflation). All the talk of Canada's "record" exports by the minister for international trade ignores the equally relevant fact that U.S. exports to Canada are also at record levels — and have risen even faster.

Overall, in the first four years of the FTA, 1989–92, the Canadian merchandise trade surplus with the U.S. was $59.9 billion, $8.8 billion *less* than the total balance in the four years immediately preceding the FTA. The balance for 1992 is lower than in 1985, 1986, and 1987, adjusted for inflation. The ratio of exports to imports has fallen. The conclusion is clear and inescapable — Canada's recent merchandise trade performance has been and still is weaker than immediately before the FTA.

This is a somewhat surprising fact because there are very strong reasons, quite unrelated to the FTA, to have expected that the Canada–U.S. trade balance would have improved in our favour over this

Table 5–4

MERCHANDISE BILATERAL TRADE ACCOUNT WITH THE U.S. ($ BILLIONS)

	Pre-FTA					Post-FTA		
	1985	1986	1987	1988	1989	1990	1991	1992
				Merchandise				
Exports	93.8	93.3	96.6	102.6	105.7	110.5	107.6	122.3
Imports	73.4	76.4	79.0	88.8	94.0	93.7	93.7	104.6
Balance	20.4	16.9	17.6	13.8	11.6	16.7	13.9	17.7
EX/IM	1.28	1.22	1.22	1.16	1.12	1.18	1.15	1.17

Source: Statistics Canada, 67-001, *Canada's Balance of International Payments*

The total Merchandise Trade Balance in the three years before the FTA (1986 – 88) was $48.3 billion. It fell 12.6 per cent (before adjustment for inflation) to $42.2 billion in the three years after the FTA, 1989–91.

Both exports and imports have risen to record levels (not adjusted for inflation) in 1992. The trade balance for the year was $17.7 billion — lower than in 1985, 1986, 1987, and 1990, when adjusted for inflation to $42.2 billion in the three years after the FTA, 1989–91.

The ratio of exports to imports has fallen significantly since 1985–1987.

period. In the period 1989 through 1992, the U.S. economy grew at almost three times the rate of the Canadian economy (annual average 1.1 per cent vs. 0.4 per cent in real terms). Under normal conditions, this growth would have resulted in significantly faster growth in exports than in imports since the U.S. market grew faster than the Canadian market. Put another way, U.S. exports have increased rapidly even though the Canadian market has been depressed, while Canadian exports have grown somewhat less rapidly despite the much faster growth of the U.S. market.

The deterioration in the merchandise trade balance is also surprising because the balance has historically tended to improve when the economy has been slack and to deteriorate in periods of expansion. Consider the last period of recession and expansion. Canada's trade balance with the U.S. rose to $3.3 billion in 1981 when the recession began, the highest level of the previous ten years. It then soared to $11 billion in 1982 and $13.7 billion in 1983. The trade balance with the U.S. then generally fell from 1985 through 1989, the years of economic expansion.

The major underlying reason our trade balance falls in periods of expansion and rises in periods of recession is the balance of trade in machinery and equipment. We produce only about half of our machinery and equipment needs, so an increase in business investment leads to a surge of imports. Conversely, when the economy is slack, business investment slows, and imports fall. The failure of this basic pattern to repeat itself — despite the fall-off of investment in the current downturn — shows that there has been a change in the underlying structure of Canada–U.S. trade, to the advantage of the U.S.

As shown in Table 5–5, Canada's manufacturing sector performed much more poorly than the U.S. manufacturing sector from 1989 through 1991. Declines in production, employment, and capacity utilization have been much more severe.

It has recently been noted by such advocates of free trade as the C.D. Howe Institute that Canadian exports of sophisticated "high-value-added" products have increased under the FTA and that this is proof that the deal is working for us. While the C.D. Howe study and the speeches of the minister for international trade misleadingly look only at Canadian exports rather than at the overall trade picture, it is true that Canadian exports of some such products have increased, and increased significantly, in recent years. However, this fact does not dramatically alter the basic picture.

Table 5–6 shows the balance of Canada–U.S. trade for some selected commodity groupings, comparing the first nine months of 1988 to the first nine months of 1992. The commodity groupings represent the main categories of consumer goods and investment goods (leaving out the resources category in which Canada runs and has always run a large trade surplus). The table shows that the ratio of exports to imports and the trade balance have improved significantly only in rubber, auto, aerospace, and electrical machinery and equipment, though we continue to run a huge trade deficit in the latter.

Looking to other sectors, the trade balance has fallen (and the export/import ratio has generally fallen) in chemicals, plastics and products, books and newspapers, glass and glassware, iron and steel, furniture, textiles, clothing, and footwear.

The best that can be said about post-free trade restructuring is that our traditionally huge trade deficit has fallen slightly in some "high

Table 5–5

U.S. VS. CANADIAN MANUFACTURING SECTOR PERFORMANCE IN THE RECESSION

	1989	1990	1991
% Change in Production			
U.S.	2.9	1.0	-2.3
Canada	0.3	-5.3	-6.7
% Change in Employment			
U.S.	0.4	-2.2	-4.0
Canada	0.5	-8.8	-13.7
Capacity Utilization Rate			
U.S.	83.9	82.3	78.2
Canada	83.8	78.0	72.7
% Change in Exports			
U.S.	14.0	8.1	9.0
Canada	4.8	10.3	0.3
% Change in Imports			
U.S.	4.8	2.4	1.1
Canada	5.5	0.2	2.9

Source: O.E.C.D. *Industrial Policy in O.E.C.D. Countries, Annual Review 1992*. Tables 12, 15, 19, 46

value added" areas, while our trade deficit in consumer goods (auto excepted) has increased. Part of the improvement in the former is the result of the fact that Canadian imports of machinery and equipment have fallen, or grown less rapidly, because of the underlying industrial crisis.

In any case, there has been no net job growth even in these "winning sectors," as Table 5–2 shows. What this means is that job losses have been vastly greater than expected by free trade advocates

Table 5–6

SELECTED CANADA–U.S. COMMODITY TRADE BALANCES
$ Millions

	Trade Balance Jan-Sept 1988	Trade Balance Jan-Sept 1992	Exports/ Imports Jan-Sept 1988	Exports/ Imports Jan-Sept 1992
Chemicals (HS 28, 29)	529	259	1.4	1.2 (-)
Plastics & Products (HS 39)	-834	-981	0.6	0.6 (=)
Rubber & (HS 40) Products	-154	13	0.8	1.0 (+)
Books, Newspapers (HS 49)	-606	-1,070	0.4	0.2 (-)
Glass & Glassware (HS 70)	-283	-406	0.5	0.4 (-)
Iron, Steel & Products (HS 72, 73)	650	288	1.3	1.1 (-)
Machinery & Equipment Mechanical (HS 84)	-7,211	-6,877	0.5	0.5 (=)
Electrical Machinery & Equipment (HS 85)	-3,695	-3,074	0.4	0.6 (+)
Vehicles & Parts (HS 87)	5,379	9,672	1.3	1.6 (+)
Aerospace Products (HS 98)	-828	124	0.5	1.1 (+)
Precision Equipment (HS 90)	-1,310	-1,589	0.3	0.3 (=)
Furniture (HS 94)	240	49	1.5	1.0 (-)
Textiles (HS 50-60)	-642	-651	0.3	0.5 (+)
Clothing (HS 61-63)	12	6	1.0	1.0 (=)
Footwear (HS 64)	6	-13	1.1	0.8 (-)

Source: Statistics Canada, 65-003, *Exports by Country* and 65-006, *Imports by Country*
Note: HS refers to Harmonized System commodity groupings

in labour-intensive sectors, while there has been little net job crea-
tion in the "high technology/high value added" sectors which were
supposed to provide enough jobs to compensate all of the workers
displaced from "losing" industries.

Turning to trade in services, Table 5–7 clearly shows that the large
U.S. surplus has increased steadily in the aftermath of the FTA, more
than doubling from $4.6 billion in 1988 to $10.6 billion in 1991 and
$13 billion in 1992 (based on the first half of the year). This increase
partly results from the increase in cross-border shopping (the travel
account), but it also reflects a significantly increased deficit in the
trade of business services. Increasingly, Canadian-based companies
have been purchasing services like advertising and consulting from
head offices in the U.S. or from other U.S.-based companies. There
has also been a smaller deterioration in the transportation balance,
mainly reflecting the increased U.S. share of the cross-border trucking industry.

The balance of merchandise trade can be added to the balance of
trade in services to yield an overall trade balance. The combined
balance thus calculated has almost evaporated — down from more
than $18 billion in 1985 to $9.2 billion in 1988 to just $2.6 billion
(annualized) in the first half of 1992.

In the recent tabloid released by the minister for international
trade, it was stated that "each $1 billion in exports generates 15,000

Table 5–7

BILATERAL SERVICES TRADE ACCOUNT WITH THE U.S.
($ BILLIONS)

	Pre-FTA				Post-FTA				
	1985	1986	1987	1988	1989	1990	1991	1992-Q1	1992-Q2
Exports	9.9	11.2	11.4	12.9	12.8	13.2	13.6	2.9	3.7
Imports	13.3	14.7	16.0	17.5	19.6	22.6	24.2	6.5	6.61
Balance	-3.4	-3.5	-4.5	-4.6	-6.8	-9.4	-10.6	-3.6	-2.9
(Business Services)	-2.4	-3.3	-3.2	-3.2	-3.8	-3.8	-3.8	-0.9	-1.2

Source: Statistics Canada, 67-001, *Canada's Balance of International Payments*
The services trade balance fell sharply in 1989 and has continued to fall.
The services trade deficit is mainly accounted for by travel and by business
services.

jobs." *By this measure, the change in Canada's net exports in goods and services to the U.S. between 1988 and the first half of 1992 cost us 99,000 jobs.*

In terms of merchandise trade alone, the export/import ratio fell from an average 1.22 in 1985 through 1988 to 1.17 in 1992. If the 1992 ratio had been the same as the 1985–88 average, 1992 exports would have been $5.3 billion higher. This decrease translates into a loss of 79,500 jobs.

The four years since the FTA came into force have seen not only a shift in trade flows in favour of the U.S., but also a major outflow of private capital from Canada to the U.S. Table 8 shows that there was a net outflow of business investment of $10.5 billion from 1989 through the first half of 1992. This is the total of net Canadian direct and indirect investment in the U.S., less the total of net U.S. direct and indirect investment in Canada.

Table 5–8

BILATERAL CAPITAL ACCOUNT WITH THE U.S. — BUSINESS INVESTMENT ($BILLIONS)

	1989	1990	1991	1992 Q1	1992 Q2
Net Canadian Direct Investment in U.S	-4.1	-2.8	-1.7	-0.4	0.0
Net Canadian Investment in U.S. Stocks	-2.1	-1.3	-3.9	-1.6	-0.5
Net Flow	-6.2	4.1	-5.6	-2.0	-0.5
Net U.S. Direct Investment in Canada	0.0	2.0	3.2	+0.2	0.0
Net U.S. Investment in Canadian Stocks	4.0	-1.5	-1.5	+1.0	0.0
Net Flow	4.0	0.5	1.7	1.2	0.0
Net Business Investment Flows	-2.2	-3.6	-3.9	-0.8	0.0

Source: Statistics Canada, 67-001, *Canada's Balance of International Payments*
   In the first three and a half years after the FTA, Canadian residents invested $18.4 billion in U.S. businesses, while U.S. residents invested $7.4 billion in Canadian businesses.

On the conservative assumption that $100,000 in investment is needed to create one job, this net outflow of private capital translates into a loss to the Canadian economy of 105,000 jobs.

The FTA and Industrial Policy

It must be stressed that analysis of changed patterns of employment, output, trade, and investment gives only a very partial picture of the costs of free trade in terms of its impacts upon the manufacturing sector.

The more profoundly important issue involves barriers to the pursuit of active industrial policies and managed trade policies created by the FTA. Beyond its direct negative impacts upon manufacturing, the FTA stands in the way of moving in a new and necessary direction.

There is an emerging analytical consensus that the Canadian manufacturing sector is not well equipped to meet the challenges of the emerging global economy; that traditional comparative advantage is eroding, and that we cannot and should not compete in international markets on the basis of low labour costs and low social standards. Rather, we must shift to the production of sophisticated services, to high-value-added goods production, which offsets labour costs through high productivity, and to the production of innovative, "knowledge-intensive" products that compete in international markets on the basis of uniqueness and customization rather than on the basis of cost.

Unfortunately, our natural resource advantage has not been optimally translated by business into the production of non-commodity-resource-based products or into the development of a strong indigenous machinery and equipment sector; our productivity and innovation record in secondary manufacturing is unimpressive, to say the least; and business investment in key areas, such as research and development and worker training, is grossly inadequate. As a result, we run huge deficits in the trade of sophisticated industrial goods and related services, and our internationally competitive industrial base remains dominated by the resource-based industries and by the auto sector, which grew up under the special conditions of managed trade. (The obvious partial exceptions, such as the telecommunications and aerospace sectors, modestly change the basic picture of technological and innovative backwardness, but they are themselves the product of past government intervention — telecom regulation, defence procurement, and public ownership — rather than proof of indigenous Canadian entrepreneurial capacity.)

The basic nature of our structural weaknesses — identified some two decades ago by the nationalist left — is now thoroughly familiar to readers of the Porter Report, the reports of the Ontario Premier's Council and the Science Council, and reports from other branches of the burgeoning competitiveness industry. Unfortunately, the original insight that many of our structural problems flow from a fundamental difference between the interests of international capital and the interests of Canadians has been all but forgotten.

There are essentially two choices available to us. First, accept the constraints of the FTA — with all that implies in terms of foreclosed policy options — and foster the international competitiveness of Canadian-based businesses through selective supply side interventions — principally in the area of skills training, public infrastructure, and support for innovation. This can be described as the "Field of Dreams" approach to economic development — "build it (tangible and intangible infrastructure), and they (the transnationals) will come." The second choice is to move in the direction of more interventionist industrial policy and managed trade.

The case for interventionism rests upon analysis of the weaknesses of our inherited industrial structure and of Canadian business and upon recognition that relative industrial success elsewhere — from Japan to the NICs to the EEC — has flowed from a much more socially organized and directed form of capitalism.

An alternative approach to industrial restructuring would begin from the immediate and pressing need to create jobs and rebuild productive capacity. Such an approach would involve several elements that directly conflict with the provisions of the FTA and NAFTA — hence the need to abrogate the agreement. It should be stressed that the point of terminating the FTA and staying out of NAFTA is not to return to the past, or to move to some illusory state of self-reliance, but to move forward in a different direction and relate to the new global economy in a different way.

Subsidies would play a role in such an industrial strategy. That is one reason to prefer the Dunkel draft of the GATT — with its explicit acceptance of "green light" subsidies for training, technological innovation, research and development, and regional economic development — to the FTA and NAFTA, which leave U.S. countervail laws intact. Another mechanism of support would be to co-ordinate public sector purchases of goods like computers, medical equipment, and construction equipment to provide an assured domestic market to Canadian-based companies. Such a procurement strategy — a central element in past Japanese industrial planning — is precluded by the FTA and NAFTA.

As part of an industrial strategy, there is a need for more stringent scrutiny of foreign investment and takeovers to make sure that Canadian development interests are served. Such action again involves direct conflict with the FTA/NAFTA. (NAFTA will even stop Investment Canada from insisting upon technology transfer or global product mandates as a condition for approval of a takeover.) There is also a role for some direct intervention to force resource-based companies to add more value to raw resources, for example, through an export tax on unprocessed fish or raw logs (in violation of FTA, though not GATT, rules.)

Even a rather mildly interventionist, market-oriented industrial policy would quickly encounter the tight constraints of the FTA, and that is precisely why the deal should be abrogated. Abrogation would also set the stage for conclusion of sectoral managed trade agreements.

It is clear that the FTA has by no means guaranteed free access to the U.S. market, and there is at least a reasonable possibility that managed trade arrangements could be negotiated and could work much better for sectors that have faced continued harassment under the FTA (e.g., steel, forest products, auto). There is also a strong case for managed trade in some service industries, for example, in cross-border trucking. As under the Auto Pact (where abrogation would restore the safeguards on Canadian content), managed trade deals can combine industrial restructuring to serve international markets with guarantees of continued Canadian market share and jobs.

Abrogation need not mean abandonment of the agreed upon path of tariff elimination, though tariffs not bound under GATT could be raised to limit U.S. access to the domestic market, if only as a negotiating tool to strike managed trade agreements. In some mainly domestic-oriented, labour-intensive sectors where existing capacity and jobs are being decimated by a flood of imports from the U.S. (e.g., furniture), tariffs might be at least temporarily restored to allowable GATT levels to slow down the pace of restructuring.

The fostering of a closer relationship between government and business to build up our manufacturing sector is effectively undercut by the hyper free market rules embodied in the agreement. This is a disaster for Canada precisely because our manufacturing sector is relatively weak in terms of its technology and needs to produce more high-value-added products. Leaving things to the market has clearly not been the solution to our underlying problems.

There is a wide range of views on the appropriate industrial policy, but it is clear that even practices that are commonplace in the European Community, Japan, and the NICs (subsidies, procurement policies, regulation of foreign investment, selective trade management) are precluded under the terms of the FTA. In the final analysis, that is the most compelling reason why we need to leave the FTA if we are to build a thriving manufacturing sector and to maintain the productive jobs that this sector sustains.

Chapter 6

Sector Profiles

Statistics Canada

The situation of Canada's manufacturing industry is profiled in the following tables prepared for the Ministry of International Trade by Statistics Canada and obtained through access to information legislation.

The manufacturing sector is the basis of an industrial economy. As measured by its contribution to Gross Domestic Product (GDP) at factor cost in constant $1986, Canadian manufacturing declined from its peak reached in 1989 of $95.8 billion to $84.9 billion in 1991. This decline occurred in the period corresponding to the implementation of the free trade agreement. Canada's manufacturing industries are profiled in the following tables prepared for the Ministry of International Trade by Statistics Canada and obtained under access to information legislation.

Manufacturing is divided into twenty sectors. In each table a profile is presented for 1991 that shows the GDP value of the sector, the value of product shipments, the number of people employed, the value of exports, and the exports to the U.S. In order to assess each sector under free trade, it is important to look at how Canadian exports are doing in the U.S. and how U.S. exports are affecting Canada. The tables look at the Canadian performance in the U.S. under the heading Southbound and at the impact of American exports on Canada under Northbound.

Taking the Southbound figures, for the first column (1991), the entry Export Dependence shows the percentage share of Canadian production that is exported. U.S. Concentration measures the percentage amount of those exports that go to the U.S. market. U.S. Penetration shows the percentage share of U.S. imports that are accounted for by exports from Canada. Generally speaking, if free trade was working well, one would expect to see increased U.S. penetration by Canadian exports. Where Canadian exports to the U.S. increased, but Canada's penetration of the U.S. market declined, this would be evidence that other countries were more successful than Canada in the U.S. market. In order to assess the export performance for each sector over time, three additional columns measure the changes between given time periods. The second column takes the average annual growth rate for 1982–84 and measures it against the average annual growth for 1989–91 (the first three years of free trade). The third column measures the period 1985–87 against the first three years of free trade. The fourth column measures 1985–87 against the data for 1991. In this last period, which measures the three years before free trade against the year 1991, only four industries showed a decline in their exports (Export Dependence). Nevertheless, for ten industries the Canadian share of the U.S. import market declined (U.S. Penetration), despite preferential access under free trade. Clearly, Canadian exporters are not winning a greater share of the U.S. market though exporters from other countries are.

Under the heading Annual Employment Growth, the percentage change is shown in the first column for the period 1990–91, and the average annual employment changes are then given for the mentioned periods. Only plastics and chemicals showed employment gains from 1985–87 to 1991, which shows the extent of job loss in manufacturing under free trade.

For the Northbound heading, the entry CDN Concentration shows the percentage share of exports to Canada of total U.S. exports.

The picture for the U.S. over the same period reveals a startling trend. While Canada is becoming a less important market for fifteen U.S. export sectors (CDN Penetration 2), fully fifteen U.S. export industries were able to increase their share of the Canadian market.

Manufacturing Industries Definitions and General Notes

Southbound

1. For the entry Annual Employment Growth in the following tables, the first period for employment is 1983–84. The first column shows the percentage variation in employment for 1990

to 1991. The other three columns present the compound annual growth rates between the mentioned periods.

2. Export Dependence is the industry dependence on exports, i.e., its total exports as a proportion of its total shipments.

3. U.S. Concentration indicates the importance of the U.S. in Canadian exports. It is Canadian exports to the U.S. divided by total Canadian exports.

4. U.S. Penetration shows the importance of Canadian exports in terms of total U.S. imports. Canadian exports to the U.S. are divided by total U.S. imports from the world.

5. Change in tariffs represents the change in duty collected by the U.S. on Canadian exports as a proportion of total Canadian exports to the U.S.

Northbound

6. CDN Concentration shows the importance of Canada to U.S. exporters. It is defined as the share of U.S. exports to Canada in total U.S. exports to the world.

7. CDN Penetration 1 measures the degree of penetration of U.S. exports in terms of Canadian imports. It is the share of U.S. exports in total Canadian imports from the world.

8. CDN Penetration 2 shows the degree of penetration of U.S. exports in terms of Canadian domestic demand. It is the proportion of the Canadian domestic demand that is met by imports from the U.S. (Imports from U.S./(Canadian shipments + Canadian imports - Canadian exports)).

9. Change in tariffs represents the change in duty collected by Canada in U.S. exports to Canada as a proportion of total U.S. exports to Canada.

Table 6–1
TOTAL MANUFACTURING

Profile Data

GDP in 1991:	84,927 (1986$ million)
Gross Value of Shipments in 1991:	277,672 ($ million)
Employment in 1991:	1,674,488
Value of Exports in 1991:	113,152 ($ million)
Exports to the United States in 1991:	89,744 ($ million)

		Share Trend		
	1991	*1982-84 to 1989-91*	*1985-87 to 1989-91*	*1985-87 to 1991*
Southbound				
Export Dependence	40.9	5.29	2.62	4.69
U.S. Concentration	79.3	-0.65	-4.44	-4.10
U.S. Penetration	17.9	-1.68	-0.58	0.57
Annual Employment Growth	-10.5	1.25	0.22	-1.74
Northbound				
CDN Concentration	21.9	-5.83	-12.38	-14.50
CDN Penetration 1	65.9	-6.12	-2.74	-3.36
CDN Penetration 2	28.0	2.58	0.69	1.94

Table 6–2
FOOD INDUSTRIES

Profile Data

GDP in 1991:	9,458 (1986$ million)
Gross Value of Shipments in 1991:	38,388 ($ million)
Employment in 1991:	184,796
Value of Exports in 1991:	4,995 ($ million)
Exports to the United States in 1991:	3,083 ($ million)

		Share Trend		
	1991	*1982-84 to 1989-91*	*1985-87 to 1989-91*	*1985-87 to 1991*
Southbound				
Export Dependence	13.1	1.33	-0.12	-0.32
U.S. Concentration	61.7	7.32	-1.32	3.86
U.S. Penetration	14.0	3.72	2.40	2.98
Annual Employment Growth	-4.9	1.25	0.43	-0.58
Northbound				
CDN Concentration 1	5.8	4.16	-0.08	0.03
CDN Penetration 1	58.4	9.63	11.38	14.62
CDN Penetration 2	8.0	2.13	2.05	2.87

Table 6–3
BEVERAGES INDUSTRIES

Profile Data

GDP in 1991:	2,263 (1986$ million)
Gross Value of Shipments in 1991:	6,008 ($ million)
Employment in 1991:	26,683
Value of Exports in 1991:	714 ($ million)
Exports to the United States in 1991:	633 ($ million)

Share Trend

	1991	1982-84 to 1989-91	1985-87 to 1989-91	1985-87 to 1991
Southbound				
Export Dependence	11.9	0.67	4.06	4.45
U.S. Concentration	92.8	-4.05	-0.36	-0.38
U.S. Penetration	14.6	-1.02	1.72	2.34
Annual Employment Growth	-14.6	-1.73	-2.56	-4.21
Northbound				
CDN Concentration	12.0	-10.73	-9.35	-11.10
CDN Penetration 1	16.4	4.22	4.72	6.03
CDN Penetration 2	1.7	0.66	0.65	0.70

Table 6–4
TOBACCO INDUSTRIES

Profile Data

GDP in 1991:	569 (1986$ million)
Gross Value of Shipments in 1991:	1,891 ($ million)
Employment in 1991:	4,812
Value of Exports in 1991:	259 ($ million)
Exports to the United States in 1991:	187 ($ million)

Share Trend

	1991	1982-84 to 1989-91	1985-87 to 1989-91	1985-87 to 1991
Southbound				
Export Dependence	13.4	1.19	1.84	6.99
U.S. Concentration	72.2	40.29	26.48	36.40
U.S. Penetration	13.1	7.65	5.25	6.28
Annual Employment Growth	0.0	-5.91	-5.62	-4.89
Northbound				
CDN Concentration	0.3	-2.77	-0.37	-0.34
CDN Penetration 1	58.7	-20.47	-4.66	-3.78
CDN Penetration 2	1.1	-1.71	-0.27	-0.09

Table 6–5
RUBBER PRODUCTS INDUSTRIES

Profile Data

GDP in 1991:	1,041 (1986$ million)
Gross Value of Shipments in 1991:	2,515 ($ million)
Employment in 1991:	17,260
Value of Exports in 1991:	1,125 ($ million)
Exports to the United States in 1991:	1,079 ($ million)

		Share Trend		
	1991	*1982-84 to 1989-91*	*1985-87 to 1989-91*	*1985-87 to 1991*
Southbound				
Export Dependence	45.0	10.98	7.28	11.05
U.S. Concentration	96.0	1.62	2.45	2.84
U.S. Penetration	24.6	-2.12	1.13	4.41
Annual Employment Growth	-14.3	-0.18	-2.15	-3.97
Northbound				
CDN Concentration	45.6	5.42	3.42	-2.13
CDN Penetration 1	70.1	1.52	6.25	5.70
CDN Penetration 2	37.9	14.96	14.31	16.09

Table 6–6
PLASTIC PRODUCTS

Profile Data

GDP in 1991:	1,654 (1986$ million)
Gross Value of Shipments in 1991:	5,439 ($ million)
Employment in 1991:	57,405
Value of Exports in 1991:	1,116 ($ million)
Exports to the United States in 1991:	1,023 ($ million)

		Share Trend		
	1991	*1982-84 to 1989-91*	*1985-87 to 1989-91*	*1985-87 to 1991*
Southbound				
Export Dependence	20.7	6.99	3.15	5.64
U.S. Concentration	91.6	8.34	1.67	1.52
U.S. Penetration	19.4	1.83	1.02	2.71
Annual Employment Growth	-2.8	6.71	8.20	5.99
Northbound				
CDN Concentration	39.4	0.97	-4.56	9.56
CDN Penetration 1	79.9	-5.90	-0.69	-0.13
CDN Penetration 2	25.5	4.43	3.82	6.11

Table 6–7
LEATHER AND ALLIED PRODUCTS

Profile Data

GDP in 1991:	341 (1986$ million)
Gross Value of Shipments in 1991:	1,006 ($ million)
Employment in 1991:	14,447
Value of Exports in 1991:	148 ($ million)
Exports to the United States in 1991:	119 ($ million)

		Share Trend		
	1991	*1982-84 to 1989-91*	*1985-87 to 1989-91*	*1985-87 to 1991*
Southbound				
Export Dependence	15.5	5.78	5.13	6.13
U.S. Concentration	80.2	-5.94	-6.54	-5.86
U.S. Penetration	0.6	-0.36	-0.12	-0.22
Annual Employment Growth	-23.2	-7.77	-9.78	-11.86
Northbound				
CDN Concentration	10.0	-3.48	-3.45	-5.24
CDN Penetration 1	11.9	0.36	2.30	2.62
CDN Penetration 2	7.5	2.47	2.57	3.20

Table 6–8
PRIMARY TEXTILES

Profile Data

GDP in 1991:	943 (1986$ million)
Gross Value of Shipments in 1991:	2,625 ($ million)
Employment in 1991:	18,157
Value of Exports in 1991:	706 ($ million)
Exports to the United States in 1991:	432 ($ million)

		Share Trend		
	1991	*1982-84 to 1989-91*	*1985-87 to 1989-91*	*1985-87 to 1991*
Southbound				
Export Dependence	27.1	12.19	10.22	14.63
U.S. Concentration	61.2	19.48	5.18	11.28
U.S. Penetration	8.1	4.51	3.57	4.65
Annual Employment Growth	-10.8	-5.18	-4.71	-6.06
Northbound				
CDN Concentration	22.1	-4.44	-8.12	-8.27
CDN Penetration 1	48.4	-2.11	7.65	10.02
CDN Penetration 2	22.7	4.56	5.38	7.62

Table 6–9
TEXTILE PRODUCTS

Profile Data

GDP in 1991:	851 (1986$ million)
Gross Value of Shipments in 1991:	2,872 ($ million)
Employment in 1991:	26,355
Value of Exports in 1991:	295 ($ million)
Exports to the United States in 1991:	206 ($ million)

Share Trend

	1991	1982-84 to 1989-91	1985-87 to 1989-91	1985-87 to 1991
Southbound				
Export Dependence	10.4	3.41	2.71	3.58
U.S. Concentration	70.0	9.57	-1.45	-1.04
U.S. Penetration	5.3	0.49	0.22	0.37
Annual Employment Growth	-5.2	-0.15	-2.40	-3.55
Northbound				
CDN Concentration	27.4	4.70	3.71	3.42
CDN Penetration 1	61.9	8.06	14.60	19.42
CDN Penetration 2	19.5	5.00	6.27	10.40

Table 6–10
CLOTHING

Profile Data

GDP in 1991:	2,123 (1986$ million)
Gross Value of Shipments in 1991:	5,945 ($ million)
Employment in 1991:	90,557
Value of Exports in 1991:	441 ($ million)
Exports to the United States in 1991:	369 ($ million)

Share Trend

	1991	1982-84 to 1989-91	1985-87 to 1989-91	1985-87 to 1991
Southbound				
Export Dependence	7.4	0.97	-0.59	0.80
U.S. Concentration	83.7	12.80	0.04	-0.10
U.S. Penetration	1.1	-0.06	-0.27	-0.16
Annual Employment Growth	-17.8	0.46	-2.76	-5.18
Northbound				
CDN Concentration	7.9	-2.23	-2.03	-2.64
CDN Penetration 1	10.4	0.99	3.82	5.49
CDN Penetration 2	3.2	0.94	1.31	1.93

Table 6–11
WOOD

Profile Data

GDP in 1991:	4,328 (1986$ million)
Gross Value of Shipments in 1991:	13,120 ($ million)
Employment in 1991:	98,078
Value of Exports in 1991:	6,545 ($ million)
Exports to the United States in 1991:	4,133 ($ million)

Share Trend

	1991	1982-84 to 1989-91	1985-87 to 1989-91	1985-87 to 1991
Southbound				
Export Dependence	50.4	-4.76	-2.84	0.24
U.S. Concentration	63.1	-10.68	-15.15	-15.48
U.S. Penetration	54.4	-8.61	-6.30	-13.87
Annual Employment Growth	-14.5	1.53	1.44	-1.44
Northbound				
CDN Concentration	18.0	-6.54	-14.99	-18.65
CDN Penetration 1	85.4	2.95	1.80	2.45
CDN Penetration 2	10.6	1.04	1.09	1.99

Table 6–12
FURNITURE AND FIXTURES

Profile Data

GDP in 1991: 1,285 (1986$ million)	
Gross Value of Shipments in 1991:	3,797 ($ million)
Employment in 1991:	51,520
Value of Exports in 1991:	1,315 ($ million)
Exports to the United States in 1991:	1,247 ($ million)

Share Trend

	1991	1982-84 to 1989-91	1985-87 to 1989-91	1985-87 to 1991
Southbound				
Export Dependence	34.7	17.83	12.99	14.53
U.S. Concentration	94.9	4.80	1.05	-0.14
U.S. Penetration	18.9	-4.39	-0.93	-3.13
Annual Employment Growth	-10.8	2.05	0.08	-2.45
Northbound				
CDN Concentration	30.0	10.36	8.94	1.55
CDN Penetration 1	70.6	11.96	25.08	28.97
CDN Penetration 2	26.4	14.30	14.95	20.54

Table 6–13
PAPER AND ALLIED PRODUCTS

Profile Data

GDP in 1991:	7,859 (1986$ million)
Gross Value of Shipments in 1991:	20,934 ($ million)
Employment in 1991:	112,886
Value of Exports in 1991:	14,111 ($ million)
Exports to the United States in 1991:	9,581 ($ million)

Share Trend

	1991	*1982-84 to 1989-91*	*1985-87 to 1989-91*	*1985-87 to 1991*
Southbound				
Export Dependence	67.2	6.96	5.88	9.31
U.S. Concentration	67.9	-2.45	-3.43	-3.28
U.S. Penetration	78.5	-5.50	2.27	4.11
Annual Employment Growth	-7.3	0.76	0.48	-0.90
Northbound				
CDN Concentration	20.9	0.88	-2.11	-1.40
CDN Penetration 1	84.4	-3.96	4.35	6.97
CDN Penetration 2	20.3	6.12	5.98	10.13

Table 6–14
PRINTING AND PUBLISHING

Profile Data

GDP in 1991:	4,720 (1986$ million)
Gross Value of Shipments in 1991:	12,469 ($ million)
Employment in 1991:	131,008
Value of Exports in 1991:	492 ($ million)
Exports to the United States in 1991:	423 ($ million)

Share Trend

	1991	*1982-84 to 1989-91*	*1985-87 to 1989-91*	*1985-87 to 1991*
Southbound				
Export Dependence	4.0	-0.45	-1.76	-1.76
U.S. Concentration	85.9	-4.38	-5.79	-6.82
U.S. Penetration	17.3	-6.53	-6.50	-8.35
Annual Employment Growth	-8.3	2.67	1.19	-0.57
Northbound				
CDN Concentration	48.4	-28.39	-35.74	-36.81
CDN Penetration 1	86.0	-2.48	-0.11	1.37
CDN Penetration 2	13.4	-0.87	0.85	2.27

Table 6–15
PRIMARY METALS

Profile Data

GDP in 1991: 6,764 (1986$ million)
Gross Value of Shipments in 1991: 17,713 ($ million)
Employment in 1991: 85,010
Value of Exports in 1991: 11,380 ($ million)
Exports to the United States in 1991: 7,130 ($ million)

	1991	1982-84 to 1989-91	1985-87 to 1989-91	1985-87 to 1991
		Share Trend		
Southbound				
Export Dependence	64.1	14.00	23.65	28.78
U.S. Concentration	62.7	-14.68	-22.00	-21.34
U.S. Penetration	32.9	8.12	5.19	8.22
Annual Employment Growth	-6.9	-1.83	-2.17	-3.46
Northbound				
CDN Concentration	21.2	-16.32	-28.80	-32.76
CDN Penetration 1	66.4	-1.48	-0.89	1.21
CDN Penetration 2	25.7	3.67	4.35	7.02

Table 6–16
FABRICATED METAL PRODUCTS

Profile Data

GDP in 1991: 5,568 (1986$ million)
Gross Value of Shipments in 1991: 15,831 ($ million)
Employment in 1991: 134,051
Value of Exports in 1991: 2,740 ($ million)
Exports to the United States in 1991: 2,280 ($ million)

	1991	1982-84 to 1989-91	1985-87 to 1989-91	1985-87 to 1991
		Share Trend		
Southbound				
Export Dependence	17.3	2.83	1.56	3.41
U.S. Concentration	83.2	1.39	-5.81	-2.90
U.S. Penetration	18.6	-2.58	-1.75	-0.47
Annual Employment Growth	-14.4	2.04	0.45	-2.16
Northbound				
CDN Concentration	38.3	12.46	1.90	9.09
CDN Penetration 1	69.7	-0.59	1.56	2.03
CDN Penetration 2	19.4	3.77	3.55	5.71

Table 6–17
MACHINERY INDUSTRIES

Profile Data

GDP in 1991:	2,957 (1986$ million)
Gross Value of Shipments in 1991:	8,926 ($ million)
Employment in 1991:	66,054
Value of Exports in 1991:	4,659 ($ million)
Exports to the United States in 1991:	3,385 ($ million)

		Share Trend		
	1991	*1982-84 to 1989-91*	*1985-87 to 1989-91*	*1985-87 to 1991*
Southbound				
Export Dependence	52.5	-3.35	-1.75	2.09
U.S. Concentration	72.7	2.85	0.83	-2.29
U.S. Penetration	10.1	-4.45	-0.10	-0.65
Annual Employment Growth	-17.5	1.83	0.40	-3.52
Northbound				
CDN Concentration	21.3	-2.53	-13.38	-19.36
CDN Penetration 1	69.6	-7.83	2.11	2.58
CDN Penetration 2	19.4	3.77	3.55	5.71

Table 6–18
TRANSPORTATION EQUIPMENT

Profile Data

GDP in 1991:	11,392 (1986$ million)
Gross Value of Shipments in 1991:	49,561 ($ million)
Employment in 1991:	196,481
Value of Exports in 1991:	38,045 ($ million)
Exports to the United States in 1991:	35,534 ($ million)

		Share Trend		
	1991	*1982-84 to 1989-91*	*1985-87 to 1989-91*	*1985-87 to 1991*
Southbound				
Export Dependence	76.5	-9.80	-10.40	-8.79
U.S. Concentration	93.4	0.73	-1.50	-2.19
U.S. Penetration	32.1	-4.35	2.94	2.38
Annual Employment Growth	-10.3	3.22	1.80	-0.40
Northbound				
CDN Concentration	33.2	-18.76	-31.22	-35.13
CDN Penetration 1	73.4	-9.83	-7.55	-10.79
CDN Penetration 2	55.3	-15.82	-15.39	-16.29

Table 6–19
ELECTRICAL AND ELECTRONIC PRODUCTS

Profile Data

GDP in 1991:	7,685 (1986$ million)
Gross Value of Shipments in 1991:	17,589 ($ million)
Employment in 1991:	133,991
Value of Exports in 1991:	11,057 ($ million)
Exports to the United States in 1991:	8,904 ($ million)

	1991	*Share Trend*		
		1982-84 to 1989-91	1985-87 to 1989-91	1985-87 to 1991
Southbound				
Export Dependence	63.1	14.13	12.62	21.67
U.S. Concentration	80.5	6.66	1.33	3.34
U.S. Penetration	8.1	0.98	1.73	2.53
Annual Employment Growth	-14.3	2.10	0.34	-2.40
Northbound				
CDN Concentration	15.8	-5.16	-5.25	-6.08
CDN Penetration 1	57.9	-10.19	-5.44	-8.12
CDN Penetration 2	44.1	0.18	2.65	4.55

Table 6–20
NON-METALLIC MINERAL PRODUCTS

Profile Data

GDP in 1991:	2,513 (1986$ million)
Gross Value of Shipments in 1991:	5,945 ($ million)
Employment in 1991:	44,033
Value of Exports in 1991:	1,033 ($ million)
Exports to the United States in 1991:	901 ($ million)

	1991	*Share Trend*		
		1982-84 to 1989-91	1985-87 to 1989-91	1985-87 to 1991
Southbound				
Export Dependence	17.4	3.28	2.90	4.55
U.S. Concentration	87.3	0.85	-4.67	-5.71
U.S. Penetration	12.6	-2.23	-0.09	-1.10
Annual Employment Growth	-15.6	1.43	-0.06	-2.69
Northbound				
CDN Concentration	17.7	-0.18	-7.83	-15.59
CDN Penetration 1	63.9	-1.88	2.15	2.86
CDN Penetration 2	19.1	4.60	5.08	7.55

Table 6–21
REFINED PETROLEUM AND COAL

Profile Data

GDP in 1991:	1,891 (1986$ million)
Gross Value of Shipments in 1991:	16,882 ($ million)
Employment in 1991:	17,713
Value of Exports in 1991:	3,505 ($ million)
Exports to the United States in 1991:	3,120 ($ million)

		Share Trend		
	1991	*1982-84 to 1989-91*	*1985-87 to 1989-91*	*1985-87 to 1991*
Southbound				
Export Dependence	21.5	11.62	9.97	12.07
U.S. Concentration	89.0	-2.53	-1.36	-4.47
U.S. Penetration	18.4	6.62	5.03	9.09
Annual Employment Growth	-8.7	-4.04	-3.58	-4.68
Northbound				
CDN Concentration	11.7	0.93	-7.18	-10.57
CDN Penetration 1	55.1	-8.11	-3.44	-1.38
CDN Penetration 2	5.9	3.25	1.48	0.97

Table 6–22
CHEMICAL AND CHEMICAL PRODUCTS

Profile Data

GDP in 1991:	6,619 (1986$ million)
Gross Value of Shipments in 1991:	22,269 ($ million)
Employment in 1991:	89,067
Value of Exports in 1991:	6,107 ($ million)
Exports to the United States in 1991:	4,213 ($ million)

		Share Trend		
	1991	*1982-84 to 1989-91*	*1985-87 to 1989-91*	*1985-87 to 1991*
Southbound				
Export Dependence	27.5	-3.29	-3.11	-1.97
U.S. Concentration	69.0	5.83	5.82	6.04
U.S. Penetration	15.4	-7.45	-1.35	-3.83
Annual Employment Growth	-4.9	1.97	2.08	1.02
Northbound				
CDN Concentration	17.7	0.46	-2.19	-2.80
CDN Penetration 1	74.1	-2.14	1.06	2.88
CDN Penetration 2	26.9	2.78	2.75	4.95

Table 6–23
OTHER MANUFACTURING

Profile Data

GDP in 1991:	2,105 (1986$ million)
Gross Value of Shipments in 1991:	5,950 ($ million)
Employment in 1991:	74,124
Value of Exports in 1991:	2,365 ($ million)
Exports to the United States in 1991:	1,731 ($ million)

Share Trend

	1991	1982-84 to 1989-91	1985-87 to 1989-91	1985-87 to 1991
Southbound				
Export Dependence	40.3	1.10	-1.80	0.17
U.S. Concentration	73.2	0.72	-2.99	-0.23
U.S. Penetration	3.4	-0.74	-0.54	-0.30
Annual Employment Growth	-4.6	0.88	0.40	-0.64
Northbound				
CDN Concentration	14.7	-4.71	-6.13	-7.92
CDN Penetration 1	59.4	-3.26	3.11	3.62
CDN Penetration 2	41.3	0.58	3.40	4.93

Chapter 7

Auto Sector

Sam Gindin

The auto sector is Canada's most important export industry. One incentive for production in Canada was the right for producers that could meet the Auto Pact standards to import duty-free from the U.S. With the removal of tariffs under the FTA, this incentive disappeared.

In this chapter, Sam Gindin outlines the effect of the threat to move jobs to Mexico and the impact of the Japanese multinationals on Canadian auto production.

The government is fond of citing the auto industry as an example of the benefits of free trade. Under the Auto Pact, companies had to assemble one vehicle for every one they sold here. And they had to produce sixty cents overall in Canadian content for every one dollar in sales they had in Canada. The Auto Pact, in other words, was not a free trade agreement. Its success was directly linked to safeguards put in place, such as penalties and duties and the protection of Canadian jobs. The FTA eroded these safeguards and imposed a ban on Canada extending this principle to new companies (like the Japanese multinationals).

Since the FTA, some seventy-five Canadian Auto Worker (CAW)-represented auto parts plants have been lost along with many others not represented by CAW. About 15,000 independent parts jobs have also been lost. Labour-intensive parts operations, such as the production of safety harnesses and steering wheel covers, have been the most vulnerable in auto parts. These are usually the lower-paid jobs, and they have the greatest proportion of women workers. Under the FTA, these jobs were the most vulnerable to lower-cost southern U.S. operations and, especially, to Mexican plants. (In Mexico, workers make in a day less than Canadians earn in an hour). But Canada is also losing higher-paid parts and assembly jobs. GM has announced some 8,500 jobs losses in Canada. Over the last decade (1985 – 1995) GM's employment in Canada has gone from about 48,000 to 30,000. Meanwhile, GM's employment in Mexico has gone from 8,000 to about 64,000. The reality is that any new international agreement in the auto industry must deal with the threat to move jobs to Mexico and the impact of the Japanese multinationals. Imports from Japan along with sales from Japanese multinationals account for 37 per cent of our market. This percentage is higher than in any other major auto-producing country in the world. The Big Three North American-produced cars are now down to 54 per cent of the Canadian market (62 per cent in the U.S.).

If we compare the number of jobs provided by the North American-based companies relative to their sales, with that provided by the

Table 7–1

CANADA/U.S. MARKET SHARE – 9 months, 1992
(1989 Data in Brackets)

	Canada		U.S.	
Big 3, North American-assembled	53.8%	(62.6%)	61.9%	(64.3%)
Imports *	37.4%	(33.1%)	23.8%	(27.8%)
Transplants	8.8%	(3.9%)	14.3%	(8.1%)

* 7.4 per cent of Canadian imports are captives, i.e., Big 3-produced outside N.A.

JAPANESE SHARE

	Canada		U.S.	
Imports, Japanese Multinationals	23.3%	(19.7%)	15.9%	(17.2%)
Imports, Captives from Big 3	5.4%	(5.1%)	2.0%	(2.7%)
Transplants	8.0%	(3.8%)	14.1%	(8.0%)
TOTAL	**36.7%**	**(28.6)**	**32.0%**	**(27.9)**

Note: Of total Japanese share, in U.S. 44 per cent are transplants (more content); in Canada only 22 per cent are transplants.

major Japanese-based companies (Toyota, Honda, Nissan, and Mazda), we find that the former provide ten times as many jobs. In other words, if GM, Ford, and Chrysler only had the same commitment to Canada as the Japanese multinationals, we would have 60,000 fewer jobs (even fewer if we include the parts manufacturing jobs).

A key weakness of NAFTA is that it deals with none of these issues. The Japanese-based multinationals can continue to capture our market without any commitment to jobs in Canada. Incredibly, NAFTA would prevent us from ever extending or expanding the principle of the Auto Pact to new companies. Plants will continue to be free to move to Mexico to escape Canadian wages and workplace and environmental standards. The Big Three can continue to move jobs to the U.S. south or Mexico. NAFTA also erodes the Auto Pact because the auto pact penalties will no longer apply on imports from the U.S. and Mexico. Under NAFTA, the North American content rule would be increased from 50 per cent to 62.5 per cent, but there are no domestic safeguards. Though the 62.5 per cent North American content could take place in Mexico or the U.S., the final product would gain duty-free access to Canada.

Canada needs to require corporations that want access to our market to make a commitment to a proportional number of jobs in our country. Specifically, within NAFTA, the CAW argued for an overall North American (Canada, U.S., Mexico) content requirement of 80 per cent (by company and relative to dollar sales). Further, it is essential that each country have its own content requirement to get its fair share of jobs. The CAW proposes a 65 per cent content rule for each country. Clearly, the struggle against NAFTA is not against Mexican or U.S. workers but for sectoral trading agreements to give workers in each country their fair share of jobs.

Those who argue that they support NAFTA out of concern for the citizens of Mexico could instead express that concern by supporting the cancellation of the Mexican foreign debt, which is squeezing the lifeblood out of the Mexican economy. Further, they could insist that union, political, and human rights be ensured as a precondition for any international agreement. Instead of the FTA and NAFTA, we need an international "trade and development pact" that respects sovereignty, the need for democratic control over the economy, and the right to regulate foreign investment and trade.

Chapter 8

The Garment Industry

Jan Borowy

The clothing industry is a major Canadian employer. Until free trade it was a growing industry. In this chapter, Jan Borowy explains how working conditions are affected by the push to free trade and presents a case study that shows how the shift of employment outside Canada does not necessarily benefit Canadian consumers.

Garment manufacturing plays a critical role in providing jobs to women and immigrant workers. It is often the first and only source of employment for women, particularly immigrant women. While women make up approximately 29 per cent of the goods-producing sector, 80 per cent of workers in the garment industry are women. In Metro Toronto in 1986, 94 per cent of sewing-machine operators were born outside of Canada (compared to 43 per cent of the overall workforce). And the garment industry is the largest manufacturing industry in the City of Toronto.

Since the signing of Free Trade Agreement, the garment industry has been under direct attack. As a labour-intensive industry, it is at the forefront of the effects of trade liberalization and economic restructuring, which seek to reduce direct labour costs as much as possible. The garment industry is following a low-wage strategy in two ways. First, factories are closing. They have moved to the low-wage parts of the United States, like Dade County, or to Mexico. Forty-two unionized factories have closed since 1988. Many may have thought that garment production was a sunset industry before free trade; however, between 1971 and 1988 employment actually increased. But from 1988, the number of garment workers in Canada dropped from 95,800 to an estimated 62,800. In Ontario alone, employment has fallen off drastically from a high in 1988 of 27,700 to 16,800.[1] Second, production that stays in Canada is shifting out of unionized factories. Garments that are sewn here are produced through a complex chain of contractors, subcontractors, and homeworkers.

Take a concrete example: Vogue Bra, a prominent Canadian manufacturer of a wide range of women's intimate apparel. This company operated a manufacturing plant in Cambridge, Ontario, prior to August 1992, which produced a large proportion of its products. The remainder of their products were made in a plant in Quebec and in another plant near Ottawa. In January 1992, Vogue opened a factory in Mexico and assured all workers that this move would not affect their factory in Cambridge. In August 1992, Vogue Bra announced that it was closing its Cambridge operation. This factory had employed up to 80 workers. It downsized over a year and half period, and by August 1992, 40 workers remained when the plant closed completely. Vogue Bra said production for the Canadian market would be done at the remaining Canadian production facilities.

Here is what has happened. First, Vogue Bra workers — who are mainly immigrant women — are left without decent unionized jobs; their only option is to turn to the unemployment lines. Second, Vogue moved production to a maquiladora — a free trade zone. Interviews with women garment workers from the September 19th Union in Mexico show that the entire garment industry in Mexico is under attack. Free trade zones force Mexican workers to make goods for export only to benefit northern countries. It is a myth that free trade is benefiting all Mexican workers. The problem is that Mexican domestic factories are closing, leaving many Mexican garment workers out of jobs. Unemployment in Mexico is at an all time high. It has been estimated in a study by the *Banco de Mexico* that 340,000 jobs will be lost as a result of NAFTA. We know that wages in the maquiladora zones are about fifty cents per hour. Legitimate unions in Mexico are threatened with production moving further south to Guatemala if they demand too much money to make the garments.

Supporters of free trade claim that Canadian consumers will benefit. Take a look at these bras made by Vogue Bra. Zellers, a store owned by the Hudson's Bay Company with 1991 profits of $158.2 million, tells a very different story. The store is flooded with Vogue bras from Mexico. A bra made in Mexico is sold for $19.50. These bras are retailing for the same price as Canadian-made bras. Canadian-made bras are sold for $20.50, yet the Canadian-made bra required many more operations and is a much more complicated item. It would take a worker approximately a half hour to produce this full garment. That means the worker in Mexico received about 25 cents to make it.

Who's pocketing the difference? Clearly, Canadian workers are not benefiting, Mexican workers are not benefiting, and consumers are not seeing any savings. We need to ask Zellers and the Hudson's Bay Company — Canada's oldest department store — some very tough questions. How is it that a major retailer is able to sell a garment made in Mexico, where a worker is paid only a quarter for it, at the same price as a Canadian-produced garment?

Low Wage Economies

Homework is exploding within the Canadian scene. Homework refers to garments made mainly by immigrant women in their homes. Here are the results from interviews done with Chinese-speaking sewers in Toronto in 1991.

- Twenty-one of thirty homeworkers were not being paid minimum wage. One was earning as little as $1.00 per hour; the average was was $4.64 per hour. The minimum wage was $6.00. Only two highly skilled workers earned an average of $7.00.
- Only one homeworker was being paid the vacation pay she was entitled to. None of their employers were making unemployment insurance or pension contributions. Only one employer had a permit to employ homeworkers as required under the Employment Standards Act.
- Homeworkers have to pay for their own equipment and cover the costs of their operating expenses out of their meagre wages. The industrial sewing machines often cost more than $3,500.
- Homeworkers are not entitled to premium pay for overtime hours under Ontario law. The average work week was forty-six hours. In the busy times, homeworkers worked an average of seventy hours a week.
- Almost half of the homeworkers reported that other family members, especially children, assisted them, providing unpaid labour to the contractor.

- Twenty-seven of the thirty homeworkers interviewed experienced health problems related to their work — often allergies to the dust from the fabric, stress resulting from the time pressures, and ergonomic problems with the work.
- The homeworkers have no control over the scheduling of their work or the rate of pay. Twelve reported problems in getting paid for the work they had done. Twenty-one worked for sub-contractors, nine for factories; all but four worked for more than one employer.
- All but one woman reported that they had turned to homework as the only option because they could not afford child care. More than two-thirds said they would rather work outside the home. With few exceptions, their last job had been in a garment factory, and they had begun their homework while on maternity leave.
- Only one of the women interviewed reported that she could converse in English. All but two had less than high school education, completed in their country of origin.

There are other changes as part of the restructuring brought by free trade:

- More low-paying, often part-time warehouse jobs. If production isn't in Canada, then Canadian workers can only shuffle goods around.
- Greater concentration by U.S. retailers. With the U.S.–Canada free trade deal, U.S. retailers, like Talbots and the GAP, have taken over more of the Canadian market. They bring U.S.-made goods, and they keep intact their entire network of American-based suppliers, rather than engage in the painful process of re-establishing new Canadian-based suppliers.

NAFTA will further these trends in drastic ways. NAFTA not only extends all of the negative features of the FTA by linking with Mexico, but it also moves even further to weaken Canada's apparel industry. And NAFTA is only the tip of the iceberg. At this moment other mini free trade agreements have been signed within Central and South America. The Enterprise of the Americas and the Caribbean Initiative are pitting worker against worker from Canada to Peru, all in search of a low-wage strategy. We are looking at a race to the bottom — to the lowest wages, working conditions, and quality of life possible. It is a race that directly attacks women.

Alternative Policies

There are a number of policy alternatives to the Free Trade Agreement.

- Garment Sector Managed Trade: As with the Auto Pact, if a corporation wants to trade with Canada in the garment industry, it must ensure that it is meeting Canadian needs and creating Canadian jobs with decent wages and working conditions.
- Canadian Retail Content Legislation to ensure that consumers will have the choice of buying Canadian-made garments. Retailers must be regulated so that a proportion of the goods available in stores are Canadian-made.
- The provinces should introduce and enforce tough procurement policies. They should use the buying power of the provincial governments to buy unionized and Canadian-made goods.
- Introduce new labour legislation to protect homeworkers.
- Invest directly in the textile industry so that textile production can be regenerated.
- Create a universal, affordable child care system in the provinces.

Section III
NAFTA: Renegotiating the FTA

Chapter 9

Investment

Jim Stanford

The free trade agreements are about investment. For Canada, the main concern is that liberalized investment flows lead to disinvestment and capital outflows not just to new investment. In this chapter, Jim Stanford outlines the different faces of foreign investment and shows the effects of continental economic integration on Canada. He points to the importance of flows of financial capital within the free trade area, flows that generally do not enhance domestic output and employment. His examination of the workings of the FTA and the investment provisions of NAFTA suggests that a "laissez-faire" approach to foreign capital leads to the same approach being adopted towards the economy as a whole, including domestic capital.

Free Trade and Foreign Investment

Ask someone to define "free trade," and they will typically think of the free flow of commodities across a national boundary. Indeed, it is this idea that has sparked most of the economic theory and political debates dealing with free trade dating back to the early 1800s, when economist and politician David Ricardo first argued for the free import of corn into England. And it is the free flow of commodities that Conservative politicians must have had in mind during the 1988 election campaign, when they defended the Canada–U.S. FTA as a "simple commerical agreement."

To judge from the amount of text devoted to foreign investment issues, however, the agreement has more to do with the free movement of capital than with the free flow of goods. The elimination of tariffs on commodity trade is fully described in only two chapters (Chapters 3 and 4) of the NAFTA, while at least seven others are devoted to the elimination of various barriers to foreign investment and the international operations of private firms.

Far from being "simple commercial agreements," the capital mobility provisions of the FTA and the NAFTA are unprecedented in their scope and their potential effect. Of course, major shifts in the pattern of foreign investment in North America are occurring and will continue to occur with or without continental free trade agreements, but the new investors' rights enshrined in these agreements have reinforced and accelerated this process. What effects will these new continental freedoms for investors have on the Canadian economy?

The Tory government has claimed that the liberalization of foreign investment will benefit Canada by encouraging more capital flows into the country, which will result in job creation, increased output, and, perhaps, greater export capability. The usual response of critics has been to argue that Canada's reliance on foreign capital has been a negative, not a positive, feature of our economic development and that encouraging more foreign investment in Canada is a counterproductive strategy. Criticisms of foreign investment have focused on the loss of economic control that accompanies a reliance on foreign investment, the skewed nature of economic development that tends to result (with a focus on export-oriented and raw materials industries), and the long-term drain on the balance of payments that occurs when interest and dividends are repaid to foreign owners.

In the 1990s, however, this traditional critique of foreign investment may need to be modified somewhat. First, the consequences of the *flight* of foreign capital from Canada (especially in manufacturing industries and especially since the FTA was implemented) seem to be rather more severe than the consequences of allowing that foreign capital into Canada in the first place. In other words, it would be understandable if residents of economically hard-hit communities were to conclude that foreign investment is better than no investment at all. Canadian concerns about foreign control of the domestic economy have tended to exhibit a procyclical relationship with the business cycle, becoming less intense when the national economy is weak, and the current era is no exception. Moreover, the globalization of Canadian firms has allowed them to be as responsive and mobile with respect to foreign opportunities as any other multinationals.

Questions about the long-term net costs and benefits of foreign investment in Canada must continue to be raised. But a more urgent concern can be raised with the prior assumption of the Tory strategy — that is, the belief that liberalizing international capital flows in North America will lead to more foreign investment in Canada in the first place. In other words, even if the benefits of incoming foreign investment outweigh its longer-run costs, it is highly questionable whether the capital mobility provisions of the FTA and the NAFTA will indeed increase real investment expenditure in Canada. To the contrary, the enhanced mobility of capital within North America may more likely result in an outflow of capital from Canada, both foreign- and Canadian-owned.

The Different Faces of Foreign Ownership

Foreign investment flows affect Canada in many different, contradictory ways, and deciphering the impact of the FTA and the NAFTA requires that these various effects be considered. In the first place, Canada is both a "home" country and a "host" country in the foreign investment relationship. Canadian firms have extensive foreign investments in the U.S. and Mexico, and thus Canada is the "home" country for some foreign investment abroad. To the extent that the FTA and the NAFTA make it easier for Canadian firms to invest abroad, their provisions will likely accelerate the transfer of capital by Canadian firms (like those of other nationalities) to regions like the U.S. South and the Mexican *maquiladora,* where lower wages and weaker social and environmental standards allow for higher profits. In general, this will hurt Canadian employment and GDP. However, some Canadian companies and investors will benefit from cheaper production costs, greater competitiveness, and higher profits; this may result in certain positive spin-off effects that partly offset the damage to the Canadian economy.[1]

But Canadian foreign investments abroad are more than outweighed by the investments of other nations (especially the U.S.) in Canada — investments for which Canada is the "host." To the extent that the FTA and the NAFTA make it easier for foreign firms to invest here, free trade advocates will argue that Canada will benefit from resulting job creation, production, and exports. To assess these claims, the motives underlying the various types of foreign investment in Canada must be examined.

Most foreign investment in manufacturing in Canada has been dedicated to the construction of facilities that serve Canadian consumers. The foreign firms must possess some edge (such as brand-name recognition or a unique technology) that gives them an advantage over competing Canadian firms. But these foreign firms face a fundamental choice regarding how to supply the Canadian market: whether to service Canadian consumers through foreign investment and made-in-Canada production or through imports from the firms' home plants in the U.S. or elsewhere.

In the case of service industries (such as financial or retail services), foreign firms are forced to invest in Canadian facilities because the commodity cannot generally be imported (that is, the service is "non-tradeable").[2] But for manufactured products, firms can evaluate the relative costs of producing a commodity abroad and importing it to Canada versus the costs of producing it within Canada. Several factors enter this calculation. For example, in addition to relative production costs, firms must consider transportation costs and import tariffs. The lower these costs are, the more likely the firm is to import its product rather than to establish Canadian factories. This is why Canada's early high tariffs (part of John A. Macdonald's National Policy) indirectly promoted foreign control of the Canadian economy: if foreign firms wanted to sell to Canadian consumers, they found that it was cheaper for them to invest in Canadian factories than to pay high tariffs on imports.[3] Foreign investment aimed at the domestic market, therefore, requires that the cost of production in Canada be competitive relative to the total landed cost of imports.

On the other hand, a certain share of foreign investment in Canada has been intended for the service of *export markets*. In this case, the cost of production in Canada must be especially competitive, because the product must be affordably priced in foreign markets even *after* transport costs and tariffs have been added. This type of foreign investment has been especially common in natural resource industries, in which Canada's cost advantage derives from its ready abundance of resource supplies. These resource-oriented foreign investments, of course, have been important in the development of certain regionally concentrated industries in Canada (most notably the petroleum industry). The long-run net benefit of this type of foreign investment for Canada, however, is even more questionable than in other industries. Natural resource prices are notoriously volatile and tend to decline relative to manufactured goods;[4] this circumstance makes it unlikely that a nation dependent on natural resource exports can maintain its standard of living in a global economy increasingly dominated by exporters of innovative high-technology products. Critics have thus tended to be especially opposed to the tendency for foreign investors to concentrate in Canadian resource industries, making Canada a "hewer of wood and a drawer of water."

Not all foreign investment in resource industries is intended for export markets, but usually this has been the case. In some instances (such as the early development of Canadian oil and gas production), foreign capital was dedicated to facilities that served Canadian markets. Similarly, not all foreign investment in manufacturing has been intended for the domestic market — but most has. Under the Auto Pact, for example, for a certain period of time (ending in the 1980s), Canada was a preferred production location for the Big Three producers, primarily because of lower labour costs. The absence of tariffs on auto trade in this case reinforced Canada's desirability as a production site, since our labour-cost advantage was not offset by U.S. tariffs on sales south of the border.

In this manner, free trade in goods and freedom of foreign investment are closely related and, indeed, can be *cumulative* in their effects. If trade in commodities is free, then capital will move (if it is legally able) to wherever production costs are minimized.[5] A high-cost region needs to regulate *either* commodity trade *or* capital mobility in order to protect local investment — in the former case, it regulates through tariffs (as in the National Policy) or managed trade arrangements (such as the Auto Pact); in the latter case, through direct limits on capital outflows[6] or incentives for domestic investment.

It is worth drawing attention to one final distinction between categories of foreign investment. So far, we have considered different reasons why foreign firms will invest in the construction of real facilities — factories, mines, stores, or offices — that result in real employment and production in the host country. This can be thought of as "real" foreign investment.[7] On the other hand, many international flows of financial capital do not result in the creation of new production facilities but rather are used for other purposes: speculating in asset, currency, or real estate markets, purchasing government bonds, or financing consumer credit (for example, using foreign loans to pay off a foreign trade deficit). This type of *financial* capital flow is more unambiguously negative in its long-run net impact on Canada than the real investment flows discussed earlier. No new jobs or output are created, but a long-run obligation to remit interest or dividends to the foreign investor is nevertheless incurred. Some foreign direct investment even falls into this category, in those cases when foreign investors merely purchase existing facilities from Canadian investors instead of constructing new ones.[8]

Continental Free Trade and Canada's Foreign Investment Position

Given the existing structure of foreign investment, what will be the effects of continental economic integration on investment in Canada? These effects are complex and contradictory — and will vary according to the particular industry being considered — because, as we have seen, the motives that lead foreign firms to locate in Canada vary greatly from one sector to another. At least five different effects can be identified:

1. *An Investor Confidence Effect (all sectors)*: Continental free trade agreements commit member countries to pursuing economic policies that are broadly in line with the current status quo. This is certainly true of trade and investment policies, but it is even true of those other elements of economic policy (such as interest rates and government taxes and spending programmes) that are not explicitly constrained by the terms of the international agreement. Signing an FTA or a NAFTA is thus a signal to foreign investors — both real and financial and in all sectors of the economy — that their investments will not be threatened by sudden or radical changes in government policies, such as the nationalization of private companies or the implementation of capital or foreign exchange controls.[9]

In this context, when investors evaluate the risks and opportunities of a foreign investment and compare different potential locations for that investment, they will look more favourably on a country that has made such a commitment. This is the dominant reason why the Mexican government has been so anxiously committed to a NAFTA, in hopes that the consequent ability to attract private real and financial capital would help to ease that country's debt crisis. The investor confidence effect is much less important in the case of Canada, where (despite official, exaggerated U.S. complaints about the old Foreign Investment Review Agency and other mildly interventionist policies) an essentially stable and known investment climate already existed. Nevertheless, it is possible that membership in a continental trade bloc will make Canadian assets somewhat more appealing to foreign investors.[10]

The investor confidence effect can have a damaging side-effect; an increase in the relative appeal of investment assets in the country can lead to a rise in the value of the country's currency. Indeed, to some extent, the nation's money is itself a potential investment asset, subject to financial market speculation, and hence a free trade deal could result directly in a rising exchange rate, if foreign speculators decide to hold more Canadian dollars. Alternatively, an inflow of other foreign investments could indirectly push up the currency by increasing net capital inflows and strengthening the overall balance of payments. Both effects help to explain the recent rise in the Mexican exchange rate, with capital flowing into Mexico in antici-pation of the NAFTA. To some extent, this effect may also explain the big increase in the Canadian exchange rate that followed the FTA although by far the more important reason for the appreciation of the Canadian dollar was the unnaturally high interest rate policy pursued by the Bank of Canada. In Canada's case, the rising exchange rate has greatly exacerbated the loss of cost competitiveness, which also accompanied the FTA.

2. *A Strategic Positioning Effect (all sectors)*: In addition to the investor confidence effect, the new and apparently permanent market environment created by continental free trade may spark another type of real foreign investment flow. North American integration forces firms to "think continentally" in their planning and investment strate-gies. Some smaller firms, particularly in specialized manufacturing industries, may simply not have targeted foreign markets in the past. Alternatively, the onset of new competition from elsewhere in the continent may force firms to attempt to break into new foreign markets as a defensive measure. Either way, the result is likely to be a one-time wave of restructuring, mergers and acquisitions, and con-solidations as firms position themselves for the newly integrated market environment.

This restructuring will involve two-way flows of capital as both Canadian and American firms attempt to position themselves better in each other's markets. Examples of this pattern of buy-outs and strategic positioning include the takeover of Consolidated Bathurst by Stone Containers of Chicago.[11] The net effect on investment in Canada, however, is most likely negative: U.S. firms play a much larger role in Canadian industry than do Canadian firms in the U.S., and hence any consolidations of production facilities (where firms reduce costs by centralizing production and capturing economies of scale) will tend to occur at larger U.S. plants. At any rate, these mergers and acquisitions do not necessarily result in any new real investment expenditure — that is, the relationship between two-way buy-outs and the actual construction of new production facilities is fuzzy. A more important long-term effect of free trade on foreign investment will be felt via more fundamental decisions regarding the location of *new* investment, which we discuss in more detail below.

3. *A Canadian Market Access Effect (especially manufacturing)*: Continental free trade ensures that goods produced in any part of North America are permitted essentially free access to Canadian consumers. This alters the key industrial location decision that has historically faced multinational firms: Should Canadian markets be served with made-in-Canada production or with imports from abroad? Relative to the cost of made-in-Canada production, it becomes more appealing under free trade for firms to concentrate production at cost-minimizing production sites anywhere in North America and then service consumers across the continent through exports. Unfortunately for Canadians, these cost-minimizing production sites are not usually found inside Canada.

The line in Figure 9–1 shows the level of unit labour costs[12] in Canada relative to those in the U.S.; the U.S. labour cost includes the average Canadian tariff on imports from the U.S. (since this cost must also be considered by a firm deciding whether to produce in Canada or import from the U.S.). The bars in Figure 9–1 also show the rate of investment in the Canadian manufacturing industry. When tariff-protected Canadian relative labour costs have been low (as in the late 1960s and 1970s), investment in Canadian manufacturing has been very strong. But when relative labour costs are high, manufacturing investment has slowed. The FTA's gradual elimination of tariffs (together with the rise in the Canadian dollar that followed the signing of the FTA) significantly reduced relative U.S. labour costs "landed" in Canada and hence greatly reduced the incentive to locate manufacturing facilities in Canada.

At one time, as Figure 9–1 indicates, Canada had a labour-cost advantage in North American commodity trade and hence would have attracted extra manufacturing investment under a free trade regime. Canadian wages were low relative to the U.S.; initially, this was offset by much lower productivity, but as Canada's industries developed in the 1960s and 1970s, Canadian productivity increased rapidly (and thus unit labour costs fell). The different directions of social development in Canada and the U.S. have changed that comparison, however. Real wages in Canada have continued to increase, albeit slowly, and trade unions and other socioeconomic institutions have helped Canadian workers to capture a more-or-less steady share of the gains in national output. In the U.S., however, unions have

Figure 9–1
LABOUR COSTS AND MANUFACTURING INVESTMENT

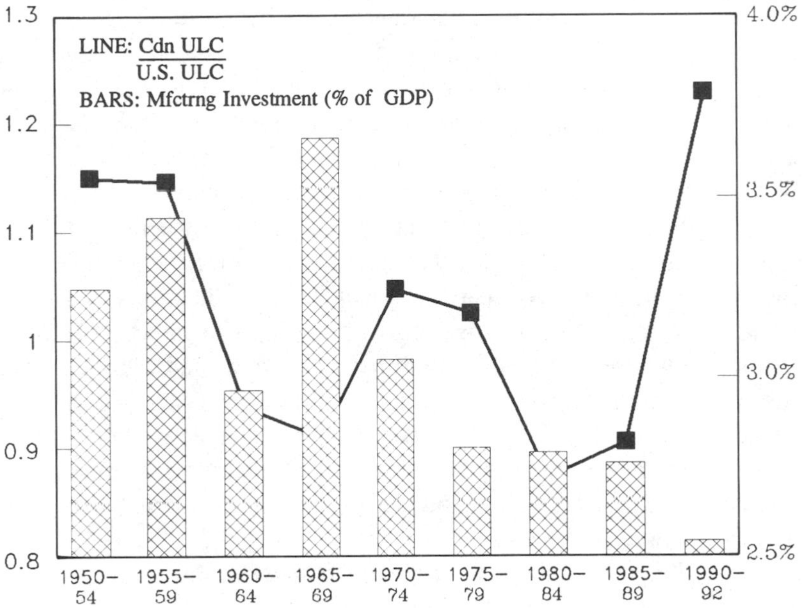

Source: US Bureau of Labor Statistics. Statistics Canada, and author's calculations. U.S. unit labour costs are in $ Cdn. with tariff added. 1992 data is first three quarters at annual rate.

withered in the face of a hostile political and industrial relations climate,[13] and real wages have fallen steadily for twenty years (making the U.S., ironically, a "low-wage" economy by the standards of the industrialized world). The recent sharp decline in Canadian manufacturing investment, employment, and output is a direct result of this divergence in socioeconomic standards. As suggested above, without measures to restore unit labour-cost competitiveness[14] or else to regulate *either* trade flows *or* the location of investment, the long-run deindustrialization of Canada will certainly be accelerated by continental free trade.

Note that other industrialized countries (notably Japan and Germany) also have much higher unit labour costs than the U.S.; yet they are able to continue successfully producing manufactured goods. However, these countries possess certain advantages that Canada does not — in particular, their domestic firms have internal attributes (technology or product quality advantages) that largely offset their production cost disadvantage, and their markets are a long distance from the U.S. (and hence the transport costs facing U.S. competitors are high). Note also that many of these firms (such as Japanese and German car manufacturers) have been locating more of their facilities in the U.S. in order to take advantage of restrictive industrial relations practices and lower labour costs. Without the long-run development of unique products or technologies in Canada[15] or else a fundamental and repressive shift in Canadian socioeconomic relations to reduce relative labour costs, it seems inevitable that the process of disinvestment in Canadian manufacturing will continue.

4. *A U.S. Market Access Effect (especially resources)*: In certain industries, foreign investment in Canada has been motivated by a desire to service the U.S. market — especially in natural resource industries, where the advantage of production in Canada derives from the simple fact that the resources are located here. By improving the security of access to the U.S. market, continental free trade may thus increase export-oriented real investments (including foreign investments) in Canadian primary industries, such as forestry, petroleum, and electricity.

Ironically, with respect to resource industries, the FTA provides assurance of market access to the U.S. more through restrictions on the *exporting* country than on the importing country — that is, unlike other types of commodity trade, with natural resources the FTA was more concerned with eliminating existing and potential restrictions on exports rather than with tariffs and non-tariff barriers on imports. This is especially true, of course, with respect to the energy trade provisions of the FTA: essentially, free trade in energy products already existed prior to the FTA, but the treaty assured investors that no future Canadian government could implement interventionist measures (similar to those of the National Energy Policy of the 1980s) that might undercut the value of their export-oriented investments. All other things being equal, this would make export-oriented foreign investment in Canadian resource industries more attractive.

Free trade proponents have placed much emphasis on the benefits of incoming resource investments for Canadians. However, even if large amounts of new foreign investment are attracted, it is doubtful that resource exporting constitutes a beneficial strategy for Canada's long-term economic development. More immediately, however, the effect so far of continental free trade on investment in the resource sector has been rather small anyway, making the argument over its net benefits somewhat beside the point. New foreign investment in resource industries has been limited by a couple of factors. First, the much vaunted access to the U.S. market granted by the FTA has not proven to be very reliable; U.S. tariffs on wood and agricultural products show that the contingent protectionist policies of the U.S. (especially its use of anti-dumping and countervailing duties) will continue to be applied to Canadian exports, despite Canada's "preferential" status. More importantly in the long run, the tremendous weakness in natural resource prices (especially oil, agricultural goods, and wood products) means that these industries are likely to be unattractive investment prospects for the forseeable future, regardless of access to U.S. markets.

In addition to resource industries, free trade boosters have argued that continental integration will also attract export-oriented foreign investment in the manufacturing sector, particularly from non-North American firms who could now service the entire North American market from factories located in Canada. The Canadian government has been particularly eager to attract Japanese auto investments. But the outlook for this type of foreign investment is not bright for the same reasons that underlie the current crisis in Canada's manufacturing industry in general. Even if Japanese auto firms and others decide to construct new facilities in North America, why should they choose Canada — where labour costs are significantly higher and the distance to major markets tends to be greater? While Canada initially attracted a large share of Japanese direct investment, more recent transplant facilities have been located — like those of the Big Three North American auto producers — in the U.S. south, where wages are lower and unions virtually impossible to organize.[16]

5. *Effects on Financial Capital Flows*: In addition to these various effects on the pattern of real investment, it is worth reviewing the likely impact of continental free trade on international flows of financial capital into and out of Canada. Canada continues to be a large importer of financial capital from the rest of the world, a pattern that has not changed in the aftermath of the FTA. These financial flows are potentially more damaging than real foreign investment because they do not necessarily result in the construction of new productive facilities, which would increase future Canadian income and hence make it easier eventually to reimburse the foreign investors.[17]

The two dominant factors that drive Canada's reliance on inflows of foreign financial capital are domestic interest rates and Canada's habitual deficit in its balance of payments. Indeed, the two tend to be closely related. High interest rates attract financial flows from abroad as investors move their capital from country to country in search of the highest return. This investment may drive up the value of the Canadian dollar, making Canadian products uncompetitive at home and abroad and producing a balance of payments deficit. But the causation can also run in the other direction: If Canadian products are initially uncompetitive (as is likely to be true within North America, at least for manufactured goods), then a balance of payments deficit arises.[18] In order to finance this external imbalance, Canada must attract financial capital from abroad by increasing the interest rate. Either way, output declines in Canada, and Canada's indebtedness to international financial investors increases — which only makes the problem worse in the long run, since this debt must be repaid with interest in the future, but the economy's real ability to make these repayments has not improved.

Without measures that result in lower interest rates and an improved balance of payments, Canada's net financial indebtedness will continue to grow, with severe long-run consequences. To some extent, it can be argued that both high interest rates and a poor current account balance have been exacerbated by continental economic integration, which has worsened Canada's reliance on foreign capital. Canadian interest rates (relative to the U.S.) increased sharply following the FTA, pushing up the exchange rate.[19] At the same time, Canada's balance of payments with the U.S. (and with the world at large) has worsened dramatically since the FTA, as indicated in Figure 9–2. As expected, this is partly the result of a deterioration in Canada's trade balance (particularly in manufactures) following the elimination of tariff protection against low-cost imports from elsewhere in North America: Canada's inflation-adjusted bilateral merchandise trade surplus with the U.S. was about $6 billion (or over 25 per cent) lower, on average, in the four years following the FTA compared to the four years before. However, an equally important contributor to Canada's deteriorating balance of payments situation has been a tripling of Canada's deficit in services trade — especially on the travel account, with FTA-induced cross-border shopping by Canadians now making tourism a large net drain on Canada's balance of payments.

For all of these reasons, it could be suggested that continental integration has enhanced Canada's reliance on foreign capital but not necessarily in the manner that both proponents and opponents of the FTA might have initially suspected. Imports of *financial* capital are therefore perhaps the dominant foreign investment issue facing Can-

Figure 9–2

CANADA-U.S. BILATERAL BALANCE OF PAYMENTS

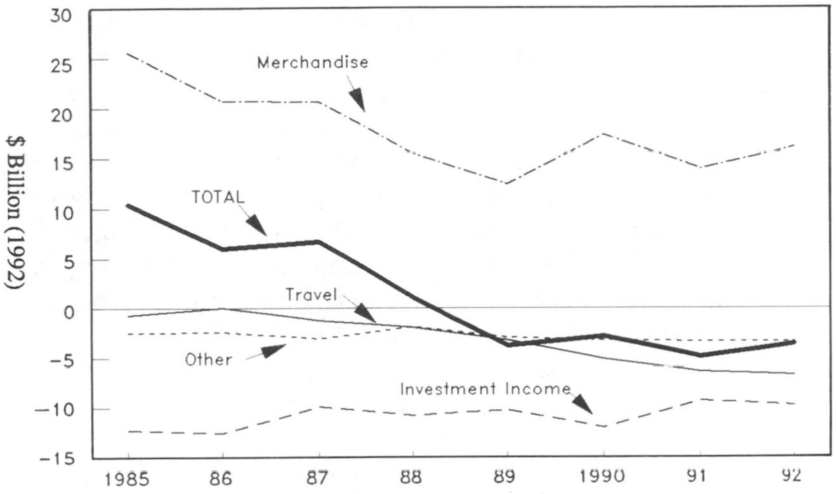

Source: Statistics Canada Catalogue 67-001. 1992 figures are first three quarters at annual rate.

ada at the present time. Indeed, these financial flows generally dwarf the real foreign investments that have been the focus of so much debate. Moreover, most of the foreign debt that results is incurred not to the U.S. but to financial investors in other industrialized countries. As Figure 9–3 indicates, Canada's net foreign investment position[20] with the U.S. has deteriorated by somewhat more than $20 billion since the FTA was implemented.[21] But this figure accounts for barely one-third of the total decline in Canada's net investment position with the entire world. In other words, it is inflows of financial capital from Japan, Europe, and elsewhere — motivated by Canada's high interest rates, trade deficit, and sales of government bonds — that have been the dominant foreign investment development since the FTA. It is important to remember that the U.S. is largely in the same boat: it is also accumulating foreign financial debt (especially to Japan) at a rapid pace. However, the current account balance of the U.S. has *improved* since the FTA by an amount equivalent to about 1.5 per cent of GDP, while Canada's has declined by a roughly equivalent relative proportion.

Canada's Foreign Investment Experience Since the FTA

The preceding discussion casts grave doubt on the claims of free
trade supporters that continental integration will lead to an inflow of
new foreign investment to Canada. Of course, it is still controversial
whether or not that foreign investment would be beneficial for Canada in the long run (especially in export-oriented natural resource
industries). But this may be a moot point because for various reasons
it appears unlikely that foreign investors will flock to Canada despite
the free trade treaties. In manufacturing industries, Canada's higher
unit labour costs make it generally unattractive as a site for new
investment in the context of an integrated continental market. In
resource industries, Canada's cost advantage is outweighed by the
generally gloomy profit outlook facing these industries. The main
inflow of foreign capital to Canada seems to be in the form of
financial flows, which do not generally enhance domestic output and
employment.

This perception is verified by a review of Canada–U.S. capital
flows since the implementation of the FTA (see Figure 9–4). As
suspected, net new direct investment by U.S. firms in Canada has
been insignificant since 1989 (although the net outflow of direct
investment from Canada prior to 1989 has ceased, primarily thanks
to terrible conditions in the U.S. real estate market where most
Canadian investments were concentrated). Financial capital flows
from the U.S. have been substantial, particularly in 1992,[22] but these
flows are much smaller than similar inflows from other countries. As
for real investment expenditure, especially in the key manufacturing
sector, it seems that the liberalization of foreign investment in North
America will much more likely lead to flows of capital *out* of Canada, rather than in.

The Further Impact of the NAFTA on Foreign Investment

NAFTA supporters insist that the enhanced freedom of mobility for
foreign investment will benefit host countries by creating jobs and
expanding local output. As discussed above, this expansion is unlikely to occur in Canada (other than in some resource industries)
because of Canada's current lack of cost competitiveness as an investment site. But even on its own grounds, the pro-investment
argument of free trade advocates is weakened by the presence of
several provisions in the NAFTA that will restrict the ability of host
countries to increase the positive spin-offs from foreign investment.

Figure 9–3

CANADA'S NET FOREIGN INDEBTEDNESS

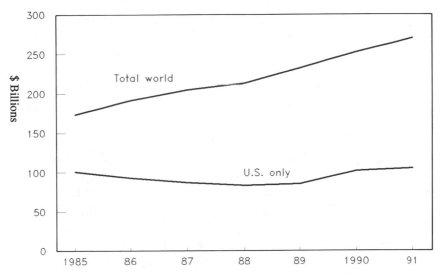

Source: Statistics Canada Catalogue 67-202.

Figure 9–4

NET CANADA-U.S. CAPITAL FLOWS

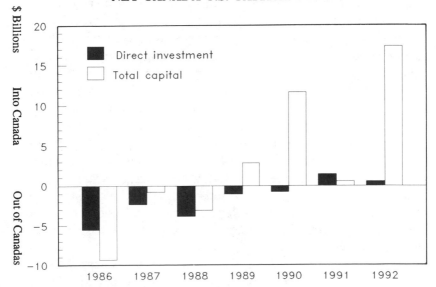

Source: Statistics Canada Catalogue 13-533. 1992 figure is first three quarters at annual rate.

In other words, even if it is *agreed* that foreign investment in the domestic economy is beneficial (or at least not as harmful as was once thought), various provisions of the NAFTA will prevent host countries from taking measures that would increase their net benefits from that investment. These provisions restrict or outlaw a variety of measures that host governments have traditionally taken to tailor the pattern of foreign investment in the interests of the host country's long-run economic development. These measures may prove to be among the most insidious elements of the FTA and NAFTA agreements because they create a regime in which future governments will be restricted in their ability to regulate investors of *any* nationality. They generally fall within the broad category of "performance requirements"; in fact, the NAFTA goes considerably further than the FTA (and much further than Canada's other international trade obligations, such as the GATT) in restricting government interference with private investment.

Performance requirements and other measures to regulate the nature of foreign investment have been widely used in both Canada and Mexico in the pursuit of a variety of policy objectives. Foreign capital may be encouraged or channelled into particular sectors of the economy in the interests of balanced long-run development (e.g., in order to encourage the manufacturing sector), thus serving as a form of industrial policy. Similarly, if foreign investment is channelled (via direct regulation or indirect subsidy) into particular regions of the host country, it can serve as a type of regional development policy.[23] Foreign investors have often been required to utilize a certain amount of domestic content in their operations in order to maximize the host country spin-offs resulting from the investment. In Canada, these measures have been applied in the oil and gas industry (where foreign investors in Canadian frontier regions were required to purchase Canadian inputs and hire a certain share of Canadians for the best-paying jobs) among others. Foreign investors have also been required to transfer a certain share of their proprietary technology to the host country, either directly, through the importation and shared knowledge of their production processes and patents, or indirectly, through requirements for the in-house training of domestic employees.

By prohibiting or restricting these and other measures, NAFTA will make it difficult for host countries (Canada and Mexico in particular) to influence the nature of investment and thus promote long-run industrial and regional development goals. Without this ability to regulate, foreign investment in both countries will tend to become focused in the host countries' areas of "natural" specialization: natural resource extraction in Canada and low-skill labour processes (and to a lesser extent natural resources) in Mexico. The host countries will be less able to ensure that investment is balanced across industries and regions and less able to increase the local spin-offs that could otherwise benefit the host economy.[24] The more specialized, skilled, and higher-paying stages of industrial processes (e.g., design, planning, and co-ordination tasks) will tend to be concentrated in a few "headquarters" cities, primarily in the U.S. Investors will then have the run of the rest of North America (including the rest of the U.S. itself) to obtain other needed inputs (namely, raw materials and labour) wherever they are available at the lowest price. Lacking the power to encourage (through the regulation of investment) a more balanced pattern of indigenous growth, the outlying regions will have no choice but to compete with one another for the attention of investors in the peripheral stages (raw materials production and final assembly) of the production process.

Ironically, this deregulated approach runs counter to the lessons that have been learned from the most successful experiments in economic development and industrialization that have been conducted in recent decades: namely, the rapid growth and international success of the newly industrializing countries of East Asia. South Korea and the other Asian countries, following Japan's example to a large extent, did not develop so quickly by relying on free markets and *laissez-faire* investment decisions. Rather, governments were heavily involved in influencing the pattern of investment expenditure through subsidies, performance requirements, and, occasionally, direct regulation in order to promote development in key leading sectors that would maximize domestic spin-offs and lead to a more all-round development.[25] Government intervention of exactly the type prohibited by NAFTA was a crucial element in the success of these countries in moving past low-wage, labour-intensive manufacturing sub-processes to a more wide-ranging and beneficial type of economic development.[26] This is one reason why NAFTA may hamstring Mexico's development process, even though it is likely to lead to new investment and new job creation in Mexico. The *laissez-faire* orientation of the treaty will prevent Mexico from taking the measures that will be needed if it is to move beyond the labour-intensive, low-wage processes that are the current preoccupation of unregulated multinational businesses.

Finally, it is also important to note that NAFTA — both directly and indirectly — even prevents governments from imposing these performance requirements on *domestic investors*. For example, domestic content requirements for investment projects (such as those that are regularly imposed by provincial electric utilities in Canada) are outlawed by the national treatment provisions of the NAFTA. And even where a government would be nominally free to impose certain restrictions on a domestic investor (e.g., by requiring certain in-house employee-training programmes or other measures to promote the employment of domestic workers), doing so would place the domestic firm at a competitive disadvantage relative to its North American competitors. It is in this sense that NAFTA does more than simply promote foreign investment (which carries both costs and benefits); it enshrines a *deregulated* regime in which investors of any nationality will be unconstrained by various measures that might force them to enhance the net benefits of their undertakings for the residents of the host region.

It is worth noting that these provisions of NAFTA are unique relative to other international trade agreements. They go much farther than GATT or even the EC agreements in limiting the ability of governments to regulate the pattern, location, and effects of investment.[27] In this regard, NAFTA sets a bad precedent in international trade law, enshrining the hands-off approach that the U.S. has traditionally promoted in global trade negotiations.[28]

The following specific provisions of NAFTA, listed in no particular order, are examples of the treaty's restrictions on investor performance requirements.

Chapter 3, Appendix B, Annex 300-A: This appendix phases out Mexico's version of the Auto Pact. It consisted of a set of performance requirements on foreign investors in the auto industry that required a certain domestic content in all Mexican auto production and required foreign auto producers essentially to balance their own imports and exports (so that overall auto trade in and out of Mexico was roughly balanced). This concession may not be so significant right now for Mexico, since its attractiveness as a low-cost production site is likely to allow it to run a large and growing trade surplus in autos for the foreseeable future (since Mexican auto output will probably grow much faster than consumer purchases of autos, especially if the tough wage restraint programme of the current government is maintained). However, this provision of NAFTA is a warning that all types of performance requirements (ultimately including the

Canada–U.S. Auto Pact, even though it is exempted from the terms of NAFTA for now) are fundamentally incompatible with the de-regulation bias of this method of continental integration.

National Treatment Provisions (Articles 301, 1102, 1202, 1703): These provisions prevent governments from discriminating between domestic or regional firms or products and the firms or products of any other NAFTA-member country. Directly, then, it prevents the implementation of performance requirements and other measures aimed specifically at foreign investors. It also prevents domestic-content provisions from being applied even to domestic or publicly owned firms (such as the buy local policies of many local and provincial governments, electric utilities, and crown corporations). Indeed, by opening up international competition in public procurement programmes, NAFTA indirectly constrains demand-boosting fiscal policy measures by local, provincial, or even national governments: since governments are less assured that a large share of the demand injection provided by public spending will stay in the local area, the incentive for increasing regional public works spending during economic downturns is reduced.

One area of current interest where national treatment provisions may be important is in native economic development: native groups in many provinces are pushing for (and have sometimes won) guarantees that a certain share of the employment and supply purchases associated with large energy and other developments on their traditional lands be allocated to natives and native firms. It is likely that, if challenged, such measures would be found to be incompatible with national treatment provisions. One concrete demand that could be made for the revision of NAFTA would be to include native development programmes in the exceptions to national treatment provisions listed in Section A of Annex 301.3 and elsewhere.

Performance Requirements (Articles 1106, 1107): This section is the most damaging with respect to the preceding comments. It prevents host countries from imposing restrictions regarding the trade balance, domestic content, and technology transfer activities of foreign investors — and hence those of *any* investors, foreign or domestic (for the reasons discussed above). This measure would prevent any auto pact-type measure designed to ensure local production in important industries.

Article 1107 deals particularly with requirements (which have in the past been imposed in Canada's petroleum industry, among others) that a certain share of a subsidiary's directors be domestic citizens. One issue that this might touch on in future years might be any effort to implement German- or Swedish-style laws providing a certain number of director seats to the local *workers* of a firm.

Note that Article 1108 allows for existing performance requirement measures (including, presumably, many of the buy local rules currently in place in some local and provincial governments and some crown corporations) to be grandparented under NAFTA. This suggests another potential area for concrete political action in the period leading up to the implementation of NAFTA. First, local communities will want to identify important existing measures in Canada and ensure that they are included in this list. Second, for those provisions that fall under provincial or local jurisdiction, critics can fight (wherever possible) to have new performance measures passed during the two years that the NAFTA allows before the corresponding list of non-conforming measures for these levels of government needs to be finalized.

Intellectual Property (Articles 1709, 1710, 1713): Similar to Article 1106, these measures may prevent attempts to require investors to ensure that their undertakings raise the overall level of skill and technical development of their employees and the host economies (through the training of local employees in high-tech skills and so on).

Subsidies: Like the FTA, NAFTA is silent on the subject of how subsidies will be defined for purposes of countervail and anti-dumping law. This controversy is closely related to the performance requirement issues discussed above because subsidies are another key measure used in many countries for industrial and regional development planning: they are, so to speak, the "carrot," where a direct performance requirement is the "stick," in an effort to channel investment into desired industries or regions. The U.S. will continue to be able to apply its very broad definition of export subsidy (which, precedent has shown, includes industrial and regional policy measures) in its own countervail law; the mere size of its market means, therefore, that this definition will set the dominant tone for policy planning throughout North America.

This is another area, therefore, in which political demands for the reform of North American trade laws might be fruitful. Opponents of free trade need to build support for the notion (accepted in the EC and most of the rest of the world) that government measures to influence the level and location of investment are entirely legitimate instruments of economic policy and should not be subject to the discipline of international trade law. The failure of the *laissez-faire* U.S. approach to industrial development and investment policy, under which U.S. technological leadership in key industries has been lost, should make this a somewhat easier but all the more urgent task.

Conclusion

In framing opposition to the treatment of foreign investment in the FTA and NAFTA, it is worth drawing an analogy between free commodity trade and free capital mobility in North America. Many free trade critics have stressed that they are not necessarily opposed to "free trade" in the sense defined at the beginning of this chapter: the international movement of commodities free from tariffs or other taxes. Rather, it is argued that free trade need not be *laissez-faire* trade; allowing for some type of public policy role in planning and tailoring trade flows will more likely ensure that the benefits of trade will be mutually enjoyed. The Auto Pact is the greatest example of how this can happen. Popular opposition to the FTA and NAFTA can be defined not primarily in terms of opposition to the abolition of tariffs on North American trade (which are quite low to begin with) but rather with respect to the FTA's enshrinement of a generally deregulated approach to economic policy.

The same distinction applies to a critical analysis of foreign investment in an integrated North American economy. One need not necessarily oppose foreign investment *per se,* especially in these tough times when any type of investment is badly needed and will be greatly appreciated by depressed communities. Rather, what needs to be targeted is NAFTA's enshrinement of a hands-off approach to investment policy, one that will effectively apply to both domestic and foreign investors. This tendency towards the deregulation of investment will prevent the potential benefits of foreign investment from being fully shared by host communities, and it will weaken governments' ability to tailor economic development — just when more and more North Americans are recognizing that a free-market industrial strategy is not serving this continent well in the current global economy.

In other words, the point needs to be made that an *integrated* continental economy — marked by international flows of commodities, capital, and labour[29] — need not be equivalent to a *deregulated* continental economy, in which crucial decisions about investment, income distribution, workplace and environmental standards, and economic development policy are left primarily up to free markets.

In investment policy, as in many other areas, the FTA and NAFTA reflect the latter orientation, tearing down as "trade barriers" measures that have rather been intended to exert a certain degree of collective social control over economic processes.

Chapter 10

Trade Law

Scott Sinclair

Reducing the impact of U.S. trade law on Canada's ability to introduce regional development programmes was a major objective in the FTA negotiations. This issue was set aside for further negotiations, and under NAFTA it has been postponed indefinitely. Instead, a dispute-settlement system was introduced in the FTA and extended by NAFTA.

In this chapter, Scott Sinclair shows that the dispute-settlement mechanism provides no real advantages to Canada. Indeed, trade harassment has increased under the FTA. Instead of legitimizing a process that Canada opposes — the unilateral application of American trade law — Canadian interests could be better served through multilateral efforts to change U.S. trade legislation under GATT.

The treatment of trade remedy laws has been a major issue in both the Canada–U.S. Free Trade Agreement (FTA) and the North American Free Trade Agreement (NAFTA). The Mulroney government's main objective in the FTA negotiations was to gain secure U.S. market access by curbing the use of U.S. trade remedy laws against Canadian exports. Secure U.S. market access is also central to the Salinas government's efforts to attract foreign investors to Mexico.

As tariffs have been reduced through multilateral negotiations, domestic trade remedy laws have become more important as "non-tariff" barriers to trade. The GATT has singled out the United States as "one of the most frequent users of anti-dumping and countervailing duties actions," actions that challenge the allegedly unfair trade practices of its trading partners. In addition, the U.S. pioneered potent "unfair trade" provisions, such as Sections 301 and 337 of U.S. Trade Law, which threaten to restrict access to the large U.S. market, largely as a lever to obtain concessions for U.S. companies operating abroad.

The unilateral application of U.S. trade laws not only undermines market access, but also it creates pressure to adjust or abandon domestic policies judged contrary to U.S. interests. Canadian and Mexican energy, cultural, regional development, agricultural, environmental, and even social programmes have been targeted under U.S. trade remedy laws. During the free trade debate, the Mulroney government assured Canadians that it could negotiate U.S. market access without compromising vital national programmes.

For Canadian and, to some extent, Mexican negotiators the most important test of a free trade agreement is the degree to which it assures secure U.S. market access by curbing U.S. trade remedy laws, while at the same time protecting key domestic programmes from attack as trade distortions or unfair subsidies. U.S. negotiators, on the other hand, wished to maintain and strengthen trade remedies. Congressional leaders had made it clear from the outset that they would not approve a trade agreement that undermined U.S. trade legislation. U.S. negotiators also sought to restrict specific Canadian and Mexican government programmes alleged to be trade-distorting subsidies. But the key U.S. objectives lay in other areas: for example, investment, services, intellectual property rights, and energy. Their goal with respect to trade remedies was to deflect Canadian and Mexican demands for a common set of rules and create an agreement that would be acceptable to Congress and serve as a model for future trade negotiations.

The FTA Experience

In the FTA negotiations, the Canadian *objective* was to get exempted from U.S. trade laws or, at least, to negotiate new binding rules to curb them. Prime Minister Mulroney said: "Our biggest priority is to have an agreement that ends the threat to Canadian industry from U.S. protectionists who harass and restrict exports through the misuse of trade laws."[1] The *results*, however, fell short.

In the end, despite an eleventh-hour walkout of the Canadian negotiating team and the temporary breakdown of the talks, U.S. trade remedy laws were largely unchanged. Of the five laws of most concern to Canada, only safeguard rules have been modified marginally in Canada's favour.[2] Under the FTA, each country continues to apply its domestic trade laws against the other's exports (Article 1902). Either country is free to change its trade remedy laws without the other's agreement. If a new trade law specifies the other country, then it will apply (Article 1930). The most contentious issues were initially postponed. The FTA simply set up a working party to nego- tiate a substitute system of rules for countervailing duties and subsi- dies. Under NAFTA, the provisions for further negotiation were dropped.

At the request of either government, a binational panel may be set up to consider any dispute arising from "any actual or proposed measure or any other matter that it considers affects the operation of this Agreement" (Articles 1804–1807). In addition, binational review panels now replace domestic judicial review when a countervailing duty or anti-dumping ruling is appealed (Article 1904). However, Chapter 18 panels are not binding, and Chapter 19 panels can merely rule on whether the domestic laws of the investigating country have been applied properly, not on the merits of the case or the fairness of the laws themselves.

Canadians also learned to their peril the importance of American implementing legislation. Section 409 of the U.S. FTA implementing legislation (the Baucus-Danforth amendment) has the perverse result of making it easier to harass successful Canadian exporters. A U.S. company, trade association, or union that believes a successful Ca- nadian exporter may be subsidized can get the U.S. trade repre- sentative to investigate without first proving that the so-called subsidies injured U.S. industry.[3] The section also permits higher penalties on Canadian exports than were possible before and, per- versely, makes it easier for a U.S. industry to initiate a trade action against Canada than against other GATT signatories. At first Section 409 singled out Canada by name, but after protests by the Canadian government, the U.S. changed this provision to apply to "any other country ... benefiting from a reduction of tariffs or other trade barriers under a trade agreement that enters into force after January 1, 1989." Hence (thanks to Canada), these discriminatory provisions will presumably apply to Mexico under free trade with the U.S.

These shortcomings of the FTA are serious. Through the FTA, Canada has accepted the continued application of U.S. trade remedy laws.[4] Baucus-Danforth actually creates a new, easier method to harass Canadian exports. The U.S. is by far and away the global leader in the use of trade remedy laws. Between 1980 and 1988, for example, the U.S. filed 264 countervailing duty cases against its trading partners (14 of these were against Canada). Over the same period, Canada filed only one.[5]

This imbalance has not been corrected by the FTA. During the first year of the deal alone some of the U.S. actions against Canadian trade included:

● anti-dumping tariffs against raspberry producers, paving equipment manufacturers, and steelmakers;
● countervailing duty actions against steelmakers, pork producers, and limousine manufacturers;
● extension of a 20 per cent tariff against shakes and shingles;
● refusal to agree to end a 15 per cent softwood export tax;
● action against West Coast fish conservation regulations;
● GATT action against supply management for dairy and poultry producers;
● action against regional development and anti-pollution measures using the Baucus-Danforth amendment;
● import quotas against sugar products;
● legislation to prohibit import of Canadian lobsters; and
● massive border delays of Canadian clothing, auto parts, and red meat.[6]

Even Deputy Prime Minister Don Mazankowski was forced to admit, "We expected fewer hassles, but we appear to be getting more ... U.S. countervail actions are tantamount to harassment."[7]

During the first eighteen months of the FTA twelve cases were referred to dispute settlement. Not surprisingly, all but one of these were initiated by the Canadian side.

Canada lost the first two Chapter 18 cases, regarding the Pacific fishing industry and the East Coast lobster fishery. In some Chapter 19 cases, the decisions of U.S. agencies have been remanded because they were based on inaccurate technical information. A remand for technical reasons is no assurance, however, that the trade harassment will cease or that the penalty will be lifted. More importantly, the body of rulings against Canadian exports built up over time by the binational panels will be based on the application of U.S. trade law. By participating in these panels, Canada legitimizes the very trade practices that free trade was supposed to end.

The failure to gain secure market access was predictable. From the very beginning the instructions to U.S. negotiators were clear.

The Senate Finance Committee, which authorized negotiations by the narrowest possible margin, directed that the FTA must "ensure that United States persons retain full access to United States trade remedy laws affecting imports from Canada."[8] The U.S. has never taken the Canadian demand for a new trade remedy regime seriously. Deputy U.S. negotiator William Merkin stated after the deal had been concluded that "basically, the subsidy negotiations in the FTA went nowhere." President Reagan made it clear that U.S. trade remedy laws must remain intact in letters and speeches before, during, and after the talks. After the chief Canadian negotiator, Simon Reisman, walked out of the talks, it required political intervention at the highest levels to hammer out a face-saving gesture: the dispute panels.

Regional Development Policies

Despite the lack of progress in securing access to the U.S. market, the FTA puts numerous restrictions on government measures to redress regional disparities. Because it surrenders many important policy instruments — including the right to review most foreign investment, the right to impose local content and local employment requirements on American investors, the right to restrict the repatriation of the profits of U.S.-based transnational corporations, and the right to independent resource and energy pricing — the FTA greatly reduces the ability of Canadian governments and communities to challenge terms dictated by transnational resource corporations and to ensure fairer returns to regional economies.

During the oil price shocks of the 1970s, Canada put an export tax on western oil sold in the U.S. market. The proceeds from this levy cushioned the impact of higher prices for oil imported to Quebec and Atlantic Canada. Article 408 of the FTA specifically prohibits such an export tax, a measure that is allowable under the GATT.

By phasing out U.S. tariffs on processed goods, the free trade deal was expected to provide incentives for higher value-added processing of Canadian resources prior to export. But early experience under the dispute-settlement process is not encouraging. Through a two-pronged GATT–FTA action, the U.S. has successfully challenged Canadian regulations that require the processing of Canadian salmon and herring prior to export. The GATT struck down the processing requirements, and in the first decision of a Chapter 18 panel, an alternative Canadian landing requirement was struck down.[9] If the FTA were not in effect, Canada would also have the alternative of using an export tax to replace the fish-processing regulations challenged under the GATT. In this important industry, Canadian policy is now unable to prevent North American resource companies from shipping unprocessed fish south for further processing closer to American markets, exactly the opposite effect predicted.

Chapter 4 of the FTA, Border Measures, and parallel provisions in Chapter 8, on energy, severely constrain the ability of Canadian governments to conserve natural resources or relieve domestic shortages of essential goods and resources. Even in an emergency, Canadian policy will be unable to favour domestic consumers over U.S. customers. If export restrictions are put in place, the U.S. must be guaranteed the same proportion of total Canadian supply as it used in the most recent thirty-six-month period. Furthermore, the FTA prohibits Canadian policies that charge U.S. customers more for Canadian resources and other goods than those paid by Canadians.

Most governments of the world — federal, state, or provincial — bargain with potential investors over the terms of major investments. Such bargaining is especially crucial in generating local benefits from investments in underdeveloped or resource-dependent regional economies. The investment provisions of the FTA greatly diminish the ability of Canadian governments to get regional benefits from U.S. investment. In a confidential memo to former Treasury Secretary Baker and Trade Representative Yeutter, the U.S. State Department assessed the investment provisions of the deal this way: "Henceforth Canada will impose no export, local content, local sourcing, or import substitution requirements on U.S. investors ... The real achievement of the Agreement is that henceforth, the vast majority of new U.S. investments in Canada will occur with no interference by the Canadian government."[10]

In a series of legal actions beginning in the early 1970s, the U.S. has clearly demonstrated that it rejects the legitimacy of Canadian regional development programmes. In a single countervailing duty case against fresh Atlantic groundfish, over fifty federal and provincial government programmes to assist the Atlantic fishery were subject to trade penalties. Monies spent under virtually every major Canadian regional development programme have been judged illegal subsidies under U.S. trade law.[11]

At least one case against Mexico was later used as a legal precedent for the actions against Canadian regional development practices. In *Carbon Black from Mexico,* the U.S. Department of Commerce ruled that where the availability of natural resources at a discounted price was "partially dependent on regional location" the preferential prices conferred a bounty or grant and were countervailable. Another Mexican "government program (FONEI) which granted long-term credit at below market rates to enterprises that located in specific regions was a countervailable subsidy."[12]

Prior to the signing of the FTA, Donald Macdonald and other prominent supporters of free trade argued that Canadian regional development programmes might be protected through a trade-off recognizing the U.S. right to subsidize military production and Canada's right to promote regional development. After all, Canada spends only a small fraction on regional development of what the U.S. pours into its military-industrial strategy. This trade-off never materialized. Although Article 2000 of the FTA exempts national security expenditures, there is no exemption for regional development spending. The only practical option for protecting regional development programmes is through the GATT, where other countries, including the European Community, share Canadian concerns. The Dunkel Uruguay Round draft text makes regional development programmes a protected category, within certain limitations. The U.S. will find it difficult to accept the Dunkel formula.[13] That Canada's hopes for insulating regional development programmes from challenge have reverted to the GATT calls into question the major concessions made in the FTA, and now cemented in NAFTA.

NAFTA Provisions

During the FTA negotiations, the U.S. and Canada were, not surprisingly, unable to agree on a set of bilateral rules to govern countervailing duties and subsidies or anti-dumping and trans-border pricing practices. Instead, the FTA committed the two countries to continue negotiating in order to develop "a substitute system of rules in both countries for anti-dumping and countervailing duties as applied to their bilateral trade" (Article 1906). If agreement on a new regime was not reached within five to seven years, either party could abrogate the FTA on six months' notice (Article 1906).

NAFTA eliminates the deadlines for negotiating bilateral rules on countervail, anti-dumping, and subsidies and replaces them with a looser pledge to "consult on the potential to develop more effective rules and disciplines concerning the use of government subsidies and the potential for reliance on a substitute system of rules for dealing with unfair transborder pricing practices and government subsidization" (NAFTA Article 1907.2) The FTA Working Group (Article 1907) created to develop a substitute system has been abolished (cf.,

NAFTA Annex 2001.2). The recourse to abrogation (Article 1906) if agreement cannot be reached has also been deleted from NAFTA.

NAFTA, like the FTA, provides for advance notification of amendments to trade remedy laws (FTA/NAFTA Article 1902(2)(b)) and consultation, upon request (FTA/NAFTA Article 1902(2)(c)). NAFTA Article 1903, like the virtually identical FTA Article 1903, allows a party to request a dispute panel to review whether an amendment to the other party's anti-dumping or countervailing duty laws is consistent with the GATT's anti-dumping and subsidy codes, or the "object and purpose" of the NAFTA. The panel may issue a declaratory opinion only; that is, it has no binding force or effect (Article 1903(1)). NAFTA, like the FTA, reserves the right of each country to apply its anti-dumping and countervailing duty laws. If an amendment specifies the other party, then it will apply (FTA/NAFTA Article 1902.2(a)). Moreover, Section 102 of the U.S. FTA implementing act states that the laws of the U.S. are to prevail in a conflict with the FTA.

The FTA provided for binational panel review to replace domestic judicial review of anti-dumping and countervailing duty decisions (FTA Article 1904(1)). NAFTA reproduces these provisions, extending them to all three parties (NAFTA Article 1904(1)). An "involved party" will be able to request binational panel review of an anti-dumping or countervailing duty decision against its exports.

NAFTA strengthens the "extraordinary challenge" procedures established by the FTA. Under the FTA, an extraordinary challenge committee could be established to investigate allegations of "gross misconduct" or "serious conflict of interest" by panel members; a serious departure from a fundamental rule of procedure; or a case where the panel "manifestly exceeded its powers, authority or jurisdiction." NAFTA broadens these grounds to include the example of "failing to apply the appropriate standard of review." According to Gordon Ritchie, Canada's deputy chief negotiator for the FTA, this opens the door for further "extraordinary challenges," such as the USTR's unsuccessful appeal in the processed pork case.

NAFTA Article 1905 "Safeguarding the Panel Review System" creates recourse to a "special committee" if a party considers that "the application of another Party's domestic law" has denied it the opportunity for binational panel review of an anti-dumping or countervailing duty decision or has prevented the implementation of the decision of a panel. The special committee will be selected from the "extraordinary challenge" roster of judges or former judges. These provisions seem to be designed to address the differences in Mexico's trade law administration. If the special committee rules in favour of the complainant, the complaining party may "suspend the operation of Article 1904 with respect to the Party complained against; or suspend the application to the Party complained against of such benefits under this agreement as may be appropriate under the circumstances" (NAFTA Article 1905.8).

NAFTA Article 1908 designates a section of the new North American Free Trade Commission to "facilitate the operation of" Chapter 19 panels or committees. The commission absorbs the binational secretariat established by the FTA to service Chapter 19 panels and committees (FTA Article 1909).

Evaluation

Chapter 19 of NAFTA marks the final retreat from the Tory rationale for pursuing bilateral free trade with the U.S. in the first place: the desire for a common set of rules to govern trade between the two countries. As its representatives made clear from the outset, the U.S. was never interested in negotiating common rules to discipline the use of trade remedies. NAFTA's Article 1902, "Retention of Domestic Anti-dumping and Countervailing Duty Law," concedes that the demand was a non-starter.

The Conservatives now claim that the GATT was always their preferred route to a common set of rules. But in 1987, the supposed obstacles to negotiating thorough the GATT were presented as the motive for negotiating one on one with the U.S. From Canada's point of view, continental free trade is a policy without a justification. Privatization, deregulation, and corporate rights, locked in by one-sided Canadian concessions and secured by U.S. power, are the ends in themselves.

The recourse to binational panels was conceived as a temporary, stopgap measure. NAFTA makes it permanent (see Chapter 16, this volume). The mandate of the panels is confined to applying the importing party's domestic laws and practices (Article 1902). For the purposes of panel review under Chapter 19, "the anti-dumping and countervailing duty statutes of the Parties, as those statutes may be amended from time to time, are incorporated into this Agreement" (NAFTA Article 1904 (3)). As the U.S. Department of Commerce observed in the 1992 softwood lumber ruling, "nothing in the FTA precludes the Department from applying the U.S. countervailing duty law against a countervailable [Canadian] program."[14]

With respect to Canadian exports and public programmes, the body of rulings and precedents being built up by the panels is based on U.S. trade law. The U.S. can change these laws unilaterally to negate the effect of an unfavourable panel ruling. Prior to participating in these binational panels, Canada had never agreed that its agricultural marketing, regional development, or transportation programmes were trade-distorting or illegitimate subsidies. In these instances and others, *binational* panels have now upheld U.S. rulings against such programmes. This marks an important shift in Canada's trade diplomacy. Canadian participation in the panel process sanctions adverse decisions, weakening Canada's position in subsequent international subsidy negotiations and national support for important domestic programmes.

The successful U.S. demand for stronger extraordinary challenge procedures indicates dissatisfaction with even minimal checks on unilateralism and, as former trade negotiator Gordon Ritchie told the *Globe and Mail*, "adds time, expense and uncertainty to the [dispute-settlement] process." Under NAFTA, Canada and Mexico remain subject to the most potent U.S. unfair trade law of all. Section 301 has been used twice against Canada in 1992, to "self-initiate" the countervailing duty case against Canada softwood lumber and to attack Ontario's GATT-consistent environmental levy to promote reuse of alcohol containers.

Relation to Uruguay Round

Neither Canada nor Mexico has sufficient leverage to secure changes in U.S. domestic trade legislation on its own. Any disciplines depend on the outcome of the Uruguay Round, where the U.S. position may be shifted through combined pressure from the EC, Japan, and the LDCs. A GATT settlement will in all likelihood subsequently be incorporated into the NAFTA.

A GATT agreement that significantly modifies U.S. trade legislation will meet with stiff opposition from U.S. administrative agencies (like the Department of Commerce) and the Congress. Large U.S. industries have complained to the USTR that the current Dunkel text would require changes in U.S. trade law covering research and development and regional development programmes. Recently, multilateral steel talks foundered as a result of European insistence on, and U.S. opposition to, a "green light" for regional subsidies. The Bush administration's objections also resulted in environmental subsidies, which were protected in the 1990 Brussels GATT draft, being dropped from the Dunkel text.

If the Uruguay Round fails, NAFTA, the hub-and-spoke option represented by Enterprise for the Americas, and bilateral initiatives with eastern Europe and the smaller Pacific Rim countries will be important fallback positions for the U.S. Anticipating that the Uruguay Round could end without a comprehensive agreement, U.S. NAFTA negotiators strengthened enforcement in services, investment, and intellectual property rights without relinquishing trade remedy powers.

However, globally competitive U.S. corporations may support limited curbs on U.S. trade remedy powers in exchange for strengthened enforcement and more binding dispute settlement in U.S.-based TNCs' priority areas, such as national treatment, right of establishment, intellectual property rights, and traded services. The intent of new unfair trade laws like Section 301, Special 301, and Super 301 is mainly expansionist, that is, to gain concessions for globally competitive U.S. corporations rather than to cushion U.S. businesses or workers hurt by import competition. A GATT agreement that largely preserves U.S. trade remedies, while strengthening supranational enforcement and dispute settlement, will further shift power to the largest U.S.-based TNCs and doubly prejudice the agenda of social movements in Canada and Mexico.

In the Canadian case, the impact of U.S. trade laws, although significant, has been greatly exaggerated by the federal government and the corporate community for ideological purposes. The transfer of democratic regulatory authority to a secretive, unaccountable, corporate-dominated, supranational enforcement and dispute-settlement process could set back the agenda of the social, labour, and environmental movements more than adjustment to U.S. trade remedies. This is a clear case of a cure that is worse than the disease.

Efforts to regulate corporate behaviour democratically and to increase corporate accountability are a sound basis for co-operation among social movements in the three countries. Overemphasizing trade remedy and market access issues, like countervailing duty laws, can obscure this possibility. There are sovereign options open to Canadian and Mexican governments to respond to unilateral U.S. trade actions on a case-by-case basis. The present Canadian and Mexican governments have simply been unwilling to explore independent action. Instead, they have preferred to use the bogey of U.S. "protectionism" as a cover for entering into overarching trade and investment agreements that greatly diminish national sovereignty and decisively shift democratic power away from citizens and social movements in all three countries to the largest TNCs on the continent.

Chapter 11

Public Services

Matthew Sanger

The important differences between Canada and the U.S. in the provision of public services have narrowed in recent years. In this chapter, Matthew Sanger examines the constraints imposed on governments at all levels by the FTA and now NAFTA. If an active public sector is part of Canadian democracy, then many will be surprised at the extent to which the trade deals affect the powers of governments to deliver social and public services and promote economic development. In particular, the ability of the provinces to carry forward their constitutional responsibilities is subject to new, important limitations. This chapter is adapted from briefing materials prepared for the Canadian Union of Public Employees.

The most important trade provisions of both the FTA and NAFTA deal with "non-tariff barriers," a term that refers to a broad range of legislation, regulations, programmes, and standards that are seen as obstacles to imports. What constitutes a non-tariff barrier depends very much on the political and commercial interests involved. NAFTA considers a very broad range of government measures to be non-tariff barriers. Eliminating these measures will significantly limit the powers of provincial and federal governments. Free trade restrictions limit the ability of governments to respond to the most significant problem raised by globalization: how to maintain and improve living standards for individuals, families, and communities in a world of extraordinary capital mobility.

People, unlike capital, have limited mobility. Even those with the legal right to live and work in other countries have commitments to their families, to their communities, and to Canada. Public services are essential to maintaining a relatively high standard of living in Canada. As a result of our more extensive public services, income disparities are smaller than in the U.S., and Canadians have better access to education and health care.

The differences between the Canadian and U.S. public sectors reflect the differences between our two countries. Canadians support an active public sector because of our relatively small population, our large land mass, our reliance on resource industries, and our proximity to a large, powerful neighbour.

Global economic integration reduces the effectiveness of many of the mechanisms that support our public services. Corporations can relocate to jurisdictions with lower corporate taxes, eroding the Canadian tax base. International financial markets can put pressure on interest rates and disrupt monetary policy.

These changes increase the need for governments to manage the economy actively and to support public services. An active public sector response to globalization would include:

• performance requirements and other forms of regulation to ensure that foreign investments benefit Canada;
• strategic public investments to support Canadian companies;
• expanded training and adjustment programmes;
• regulation of resource exports;
• tax reforms to increase corporate tax revenue and make the personal income tax system more progressive; and,
• mobilization of domestic pools of capital to finance public infrastructure

Table 11–1

CANADA'S PUBLIC SECTOR COMPARED

	Canada	United States	European Community
Government Revenue/GDP	40.1%	31.8%	43.6%
Public Spending/GDP	44.6%	36.1%	47.4%

Note: All data is for 1989
Source: OECD, *Economic Outlook,* December 1992

A government with the political will to pursue these policies would face difficult, but surmountable, obstacles. However, the alternative provided by the Conservative government surrenders the tools we need to respond to changes in the global economy. Canadians pay a high price for abdication of government responsibility.

With the most optimistic forecasts predicting a "jobless recovery," Canadians' need for social assistance, health care, and other public services continues to grow. Instead of supporting these services, the federal government has dismantled them. In the "laissez-faire" climate of free trade, and despite assurances to the contrary, the federal government has eroded Unemployment Insurance, first by eliminating federal contributions and then by restricting eligibility and shortening benefit periods. These changes force more out-of-work Canadians on to social assistance, offloading the costs of unemployment on to provincial and local governments. It also undertook further changes that punish workers who decide to leave their jobs and further offload costs to the provinces and local governments.

Unilateral changes to federal-provincial funding arrangements have forced provinces and municipalities to fund more of the costs of medicare, post-secondary education, and social services. The federal government is reducing its share of funding at a time of burgeoning demand on these programmes. In Metro Toronto, for instance, the number of welfare cases has increased at an annual rate of 20 per cent since 1990. Beginning the same year, the federal government imposed a 5 per cent cap on increases in its annual Canada Assistance Plan transfers to Ontario, Alberta, and British Columbia. Over three years this cap has cost the Ontario government $3.7 billion in lost revenue for social assistance programmes.

Established Programs Financing (EPF), which funds a portion of provincial costs for medicare and post-secondary education, was first cut in 1986 and has been frozen since 1990. Cuts to EPF transfers have been deepest for some of the poorest provinces. According to the *Canadian Tax Journal,* 1992 revenues from EPF transfers were down by over 13 per cent in Nova Scotia and New Brunswick. Under the current funding formula, EPF cash payments to provinces will be eliminated by the middle of the next decade. Unlike tax transfers, these cash payments enable the federal government to enforce national health insurance standards under the Canada Health Act. When they are eliminated, it will have no way of ensuring that provincial health-care systems uphold the principles of universality, accessibility, comprehensiveness, portability, and public administration. These principles have already been compromised in almost every province as a result of bed closures, privatization, contracting out of services, and the removal of some previously insured services. Access to post-secondary education has also been severely reduced by EPF cuts. Reduced funding for colleges and universities has resulted in enrolment quotas, larger class sizes, and substantial increases in tuition and user fees.

These federal policies have compounded the damage done by free trade and the recession. The NAFTA deal will restrict the ability of any other government — federal, provincial, or local — to reverse these measures and pursue more active economic and social policies.

Provincial and Local Powers Restricted

Important areas within provincial jurisdiction, including most services, are affected by NAFTA. Yet the federal government did not seek active provincial participation in the NAFTA negotiations. Furthermore, provincial governments cannot directly respond to challenges to provincial measures through the dispute-resolution mechanism. They must rely on the federal government to resolve disputes regarding areas of provincial jurisdiction. NAFTA requires the federal government to "ensure that all necessary measures" are taken to enforce the rules of the agreement on provincial and local governments.[1] This general obligation is qualified in two ways. First, provincial and local government measures are exempted from some parts of the agreement. However, provincial measures are subject to the most significant rules regarding investment, trade in services, energy, natural resources, procurement policies, financial services, and certain restrictions on crown corporations. Local governments, including municipalities, libraries, school boards, and municipal hospitals, are exempted from these specific rules. However, the general provisions regarding NAFTA's scope include local government. Given that NAFTA sets out a process for continually expanding its coverage, it is highly likely that these local government bodies will soon be subject to the same rules as the provinces.

Second, it is not clear that the federal government has the constitutional power to force provincial governments to observe NAFTA rules affecting areas of provincial jurisdiction.[2] This discrepancy between the federal governments's NAFTA obligations and its constitutional authority will create new federal-provincial conflicts and exacerbate existing ones. A province could violate the agreement by introducing a measure in an area of exclusive provincial jurisdiction:

for instance, by creating a public waste management corporation, or by setting performance requirements on investments by foreign-owned resource companies or by requiring provincial crown corporations to favour domestic suppliers of goods and services.

If such a measure were successfully challenged under NAFTA, the federal government would be obliged to ensure that the province repealed or changed it to conform to the finding of the NAFTA dispute panel. If it could not effect changes in an area of provincial jurisdiction, the federal government would be required to pay compensation costs in order to avoid trade retaliation. Such conflicts are likely to result in effective changes in the federal-provincial division of powers. During the debate over the Charlottetown Accord, Canadians rejected the federal government's proposal to take over certain economic powers within provincial jurisdiction. NAFTA may enable it to assume such powers as a result of trade actions instead of democratic decision-making.

A Hostile Framework

The framework established by NAFTA is fundamentally hostile to public services and to an active public sector role in the economy. Like the Canada–U.S. FTA before it, NAFTA treats many public services as commodities that must be opened up to the competitive pressures of the marketplace. This private market approach constitutes a fundamental break with the long-established Canadian tradition that certain social and economic decisions should be determined by democratically accountable representatives and on the basis of community values as opposed to market principles. NAFTA treats public services as anomalies that conflict with the underlying principles of the deal. Where existing services are exempted from the deal, they are termed "non-conforming measures" and their future expansion is prevented.

Private Sector Rights

The key provision affecting public services is the principle of national treatment. In the chapter on services, the national treatment rule requires Canadian governments to give U.S. (and Mexican) service firms the same rights and privileges as Canadian service providers.[3] In other words, governments are prevented from exercising policies that favour Canadian public or private service providers. NAFTA also prevents governments from requiring an American service provider to establish a "local presence." Services can be provided entirely from outside the country. For instance, this "right of establishment" would allow an American company to bid on a public contract for data-processing work without having an office in Canada.[4] The work could then be transmitted electronically to lower-paid clerical workers in the United States.

Supporters of NAFTA argue that existing social programmes are not subject to its rules on trade in services. The following provision, which appears in the chapter on investment as well as the chapter on services, does appear to prevent a wholesale privatization of our basic public services:

> Nothing in this Chapter shall be construed to prevent a Party [i.e., NAFTA government] from providing a service or performing a function such as law enforcement, correctional services, income security or insurance, social security or insurance, social welfare, public education, public training, health, and child care, in a manner that is not inconsistent with this Chapter.[5]

However, this protection is limited in significant ways that will allow a gradual deterioration of public services and the transfer of many important functions to the private sector. First, the provision is qualified by the requirement that publicly provided services be consistent with the rules set out in the rest of the services chapter. But the commercial rules set out in the chapter, particularly those concerning national treatment, will certainly conflict with the social and cultural purpose of providing certain services through the public sector. This kind of conflict could arise in public services that are currently contracted out to Canadian providers. For instance, the B.C. government currently contracts a locally based firm to prepare grade twelve examinations. There are good reasons for requiring that this service be provided locally. As well as a knowledge of the subject matter, the contractor would have to know about cultural aspects of the curriculum and be familiar with practices of the B.C. school system. Yet, because NAFTA recognizes services only as an economic commodity, the B.C. government would be obliged to let American contractors bid on an equal basis with B.C. contractors.[6]

A second limitation to the protection of public services appears in the annex to the agreement. This annex specifically excludes existing public services from coverage by certain rules, including national treatment and right of establishment.[7] However, this protection applies to social programmes only "to the extent that they are social services established or maintained for a public purpose." This qualification is important because it opens the door to interpretations regarding which aspects of public social programmes are social services in this sense. Various support functions — such as food and janitorial services in hospitals and universities or data processing in social assistance programmes — could be open to challenge on this basis. Public sector bodies increasingly contract out or privatize such support services in an effort to cut costs. Similar challenges could affect certain health-care services that are largely deinstitutionalized. These include home care and long-term health care, which are funded by government but delivered by profit and non-profit agencies outside of government. A successful challenge under the agreement's dispute-resolution mechanism could force a government to open these services to competition from U.S. companies. It could accelerate the pace of contracting out and privatization, resulting in the deterioration of important public services.

The third limitation on the protection of public services is found in rules that restrict the ability of governments to improve existing services or introduce new services. These rules create a "ratchet" effect, which permits a government to change its social programmes only by further opening them to market forces and prevents it from expanding the public provision of services. The procedure for grandparenting existing services that do not conform to the national treatment rule is more restrictive than under the Canada–U.S. FTA, which automatically exempted these services. Under NAFTA, the federal government must submit a list of all provincial and federal non-conforming services within two years of the agreement taking effect. Federal and provincial governments can continue to provide exempted services only so long as any change to these services "does not decrease the conformity of the measure" with certain NAFTA rules, including national treatment.[8] This rule will prevent federal and provincial governments from deciding to expand the public provision of existing services by, for instance, shifting work back from private contractors to public sector workers. Furthermore, the agreement puts in place a process for continually reducing the scope of non-conforming public services. The lists of existing non-conforming public services must spell out how governments intend to bring these services into line with the NAFTA rules.[9]

Governments are obliged regularly to review any quantitative measure — such as a quota or monopoly — that restricts the number of service providers or the operations of service providers. NAFTA specifies that these reviews must be conducted at least every two years, and they must "endeavour to negotiate the liberalization or removal" of quantitative restrictions.[10] These limitations significantly compromise NAFTA's formal protection of existing public services. The corporate rights contained in NAFTA, and the powerful mechanism it provides for enforcing them, will ensure that government powers are restricted and that public sector activities are attacked by firms that claim these activities infringe their ability to make an expected level of profit.

The NAFTA agreement limits the use of important tools of public economic policy. These restrictions will prevent governments from effectively managing a rapidly changing economy.

Procurement

Chapter 10 of NAFTA limits the use of government procurement as an industrial policy measure. As in the FTA, this chapter requires governments to open tendering for purchases above a specified amount to companies from other NAFTA countries. It outlines tendering procedures that prevent governments from giving preference to domestic suppliers. The NAFTA chapter on procurement goes further than the FTA in several important respects. First, it covers government purchases of services in addition to goods.[11] While the chapter lists the goods and purchases covered, it also applies to all purchases of services unless specifically exempted.[12] Secondly, the NAFTA chapter covers a much longer list of federal government bodies, including crown corporations.[13] It applies also to provincial government bodies, which are to be listed pending negotiations with the federal government.[14]

Third, the NAFTA agreement contains more elaborate enforcement procedures, which empower a domestic reviewing authority to delay the awarding of a disputed contract.[15] Also, the governments commit themselves to further negotiations "towards the substantial liberalization of their respective procurement markets."[16] This process would be facilitated by exacting requirements to provide other NAFTA governments with detailed information on government procurement.[17]

Because of Canada's larger public sector, including crown corporations, restrictions on government procurement have a greater proportionate impact in Canada than they do in the U.S. A study by the former Ontario government estimated that purchases of goods and services by all levels of government were worth $74 billion in 1984. Of this amount, $24 billion was purchased federally, $32 billion provincially, and $18 billion by local governments, health-care organizations, universities, and schools.[18] Without the restrictions imposed by NAFTA, this level of collective spending power could be a powerful tool to support Canadian priorities for Canadian economic development. Since provincial governments provide the largest procurement market, U.S. negotiators will certainly ensure that a broad range of provincial bodies are covered by this chapter. Given that major federal crown corporations, such as Canada Post and Via Rail, are covered, the federal government will likely insist on including provincial crown corporations in this chapter. One example gives an indication of the potential impact on jobs and provincial economic policies. In 1991, Ontario Hydro alone spent $2.234 billion on procurement of goods and services. It applies a "Buy Canadian Policy" to all purchases, regardless of value.[19] If federal-provincial negotiations under Article 1024 include Ontario Hydro in the agreement, as is highly likely, all contracts over a threshold of $250,000 ($8 million for construction contracts) would be subject to bidding by American and Mexican firms. (Thresholds are $50,000 for government departments and agencies.)

Performance Requirements

The NAFTA also increases constraints on governments' ability to impose performance requirements on foreign investors. Performance requirements are important tools of industrial policy that ensure that foreign investments benefit the Canadian economy. Like the FTA, NAFTA prohibits national content laws requiring transnational companies to produce a portion of the goods they sell within the country or to purchase inputs and services domestically. To these provisions, NAFTA adds new constraints against requiring corporations to balance their exports and imports, to transfer technology, or to assign world or regional product mandates to their local subsidiaries.[20] This provision applies immediately to federal government measures that are not specifically exempted under the agreement. After a two-year phase-in period, provincial government measures are also covered. Local government measures are exempted.[21]

Crown Corporations

NAFTA contains significant new restrictions on federal and provincial crown corporations. These restrictions will further subject them to private market principles, compromising their ability to carry out public policy objectives. Chapter 15 of NAFTA requires any federal crown corporation to act "solely in accordance with commercial considerations in its purchase or sale of the monopoly good or service."[22] "Commercial considerations" is defined as "consistent with the normal business practices of privately-held enterprises in the relevant business or industry."[23] The most significant specific restriction concerns cross-subsidization. This restriction could prevent a federal crown corporation, such as Canada Post, from introducing a new service at lower prices than are charged by private couriers. Provincial crown corporations are not required to operate solely on commercial principles. However, in their sale of goods and services, provincial crown corporations are required to treat U.S. and Mexican firms identically to Canadian firms. This means, for instance, that Ontario Hydro would be prevented from providing electricity at preferential rates to a Canadian company.[24]

Public Investment Funds

International capital mobility has greatly increased in recent years. This change in the international economy makes it essential for Canadian governments to mobilize domestic sources of capital for strategic investment in the Canadian economy.

Public sector pension plans are an important source of such capital. Equity in these plans should be used, at a fair rate of return, to finance the badly needed expansion of public infrastructure. As well as repairing our deteriorating stock of roads, railways, and sewers, a large infrastructure investment programme could enhance our telecommunications network to provide public access to a wide range of new technologies. It could also expand environmental protection facilities. Such a programme for investing in public infrastructure would create jobs throughout the Canadian economy. It would also contribute to economic growth.

Recent American studies show that investment in public infrastructure contributes significantly to economic growth and has a particularly positive impact on regional economic performance.[25] NAFTA will prevent a Canadian government from making this kind of strategic use of public investment funds. Chapter 15 prevents state enterprises, which include publicly guaranteed investment funds, from employing policies that discriminate against U.S. investors.[26] The obligation to allow American companies to bid on public contracts to rebuild Canada's public infrastructure would defeat the strategic purpose of creating such a fund: mobilization of domestic pools of capital to finance public infrastructure.

Conclusion

It is ironic that the Canadian government is proposing an agreement that would restrict its ability to manage the economy at a time when the new U.S. government shows signs of adopting a more active economic role. NAFTA establishes a framework in which public services are seen as economic commodities to be exchanged for profit. This position conflicts with fundamental Canadian values, which hold that there is a public benefit to providing certain services through the public sector. NAFTA will allow a gradual deterioration of public services and the transfer of many important functions to the private sector. Moreover, NAFTA undermines the democratic right of Canadians to determine the direction of our social and economic policies.

Chapter 12

Environment

Michelle Swenarchuk

The environment crisis concerns the way we produce goods and services and exploit resources. Yet the direct links between the economy and the environment are not fully appreciated. At the time of the FTA, the government denied it included environmental implications, though the deal clearly reduced the ability of the Canadian government to control the rate of resource exploitation through, for instance, eliminating the use of export taxes on resources.

In this chapter, Michelle Swenarchuk examines the workings of the FTA and assesses the implications of NAFTA for protecting the environment.

In the current era of public debate, Canadians are aware of the economic problems we face. But political leaders have not yet acknowledged that we live in an era of unprecedented ecological crises. It means, now, that we must approach most questions, including questions of trade, from that perspective.

The global ecological crisis has become clear. Global warming will have an enormous impact on our lifestyles, on agriculture, forests, fisheries, on sea levels, and on coastal regions around the world. Depletion of the ozone layer is already causing increased rates of eye diseases in Chile and skin cancer in Australia. We face catastrophic and increasing levels of poverty in the Third World, and we know that poverty is both a cause and result of environmental problems. Industrialized nations, including our own, exploit resources at accelerating rates, and international problems of ecosystem pollution —

of air, soil, and surface and groundwater — abound. As Lester Brown points out in *Ecodecision*: "Every major indicator shows a deterioration in natural systems; forests are shrinking, deserts are expanding, croplands are losing topsoil, the stratospheric ozone layer continues to thin, greenhouse gases are accumulating, the number of plant and animal species is diminishing, air pollution has reached health threatening levels in hundreds of cities, and damage from acid rain can be seen on every continent."

This is the context in which we examine the relationship between environment and trade and the international trade agreements that provide the structure for the international economy. The proposed North American Free Trade Agreement repeats the environmental problems of the Canada–U.S. Free Trade Agreement and worsens some of them. Briefly summarized, the FTA:

1. Committed us to supplying the American market in perpetuity with all of our natural resources, including water, through the "proportionality clause" and explicitly repeated that commitment with regard to energy (Chapter 9).[1] This requirement applies even in times of shortage and creates enormous barriers to initiatives for conservation of natural resources.

2. The FTA required harmonization of our pesticide standard with the American one[2] in accordance with the American approach of risk-benefit analysis, which requires the balancing of the health effects of a pesticide against the economic loss to producers of preventing its registration. This standard is lower than the Canadian standard in the *Pesticide Products Control Act,* Regulation Section 18(d), which is exclusively based on health considerations. Fortunately, this harmonization has not in fact occurred in its widest sense. At this time, those involved in designing the programme to implement the recommendations of the Pesticide Registration Review will have to consider the harmonization problem. However, the strictly health-based standard has been lost.

3. The FTA has been used to strike down a Canadian regulation under the Fisheries Act that required the landing of fish caught off the West Coast for biological sampling.[3] It was also used by the Canadian government as part of the successful challenge to the plan of the U.S. Environmental Protection Agency to phase out the use of asbestos in the U.S. (*Corrosion Proof Fittings et al. U.S. Court of Appeals for the Fifth Circuit, 1991*). These cases join the international jurisprudence in which numerous environmental standards

have fallen as a result of challenges based on international trade agreements.

4. The FTA committed us to a dispute-resolution process that entrenched the right of the U.S. to continue to use its countervail and anti-dumping laws, unfettered by any agreement on what constitutes unacceptable subsidies. This process has had a direct impact on the Canadian forest industry, in which we are now facing the third countervail action in nine years initiated by the U.S. Previous cases focused on the Canadian stumpage system, but the current one is aimed at eliminating Canadian laws that prohibit the export of raw logs. These provisions were explicitly protected in the FTA, but they were nevertheless and the FTA panel decision of May 6, 1993 found that despite the FTA provision, U.S. countervail law can still be used against Canadian prohibitions of raw log exports (*U.S.–Canada FTA Article 1904 Binational Review Panel: Softwood Lumber*). Restrictions on the rights of Canadians to require local processing of resources for the purpose of economic diversification and job creation stymie efforts to move to the conserver society, with an emphasis on conservation of resources, not on accelerated primary extraction. Further, the best-paying jobs in the forest sector are not in the woodlands, cutting raw timber, but in the mills, processing it. The lack of discipline on the aggressive American use of its countervail laws threatens these jobs and the whole range of public policy options (local processing requirements, subsidies for environmental protection programmes, government procurement policies, requirements of reusable beverage containers for waste reduction, etc.).

5. The trade agreements now constitute an overarching international legal regime that limits our government's powers and has invalidated laws passed according to our democratic processes. Nevertheless, the agreements are negotiated in secret, and trade dispute panel processes are also secret. Access to information and to accountable government standard-setters are crucial to the environmental movement in achieving further environmental protection. Since trade agreements have the effect of making new laws and striking down current ones, their secret processes undermine campaigns for better environment protection.

NAFTA

1. The NAFTA continues the requirement of perpetual supply of the American market with all of our resources, including energy while granting Mexico an exemption from that requirement regard-

ing energy, and other resources.[4] Canadian difficulties with conservation initiatives remain.

2. The NAFTA provides a limited protection for trade-related actions taken pursuant to three international environmental agreements: the Convention on the International Trade in Endangered Species; the Montreal Protocol on Substances That Deplete the Ozone Layer; and the Basel Convention on the Control of Transboundary Movements of Hazardous Wastes and Their Disposal. Also incorporated are the Canadian-American agreement on transboundary hazardous waste and the U.S.–Mexico one regarding the border area. The protections are limited in that, in applying those agreements, we must use the strategy that least contravenes the NAFTA. There are many other important initiatives at the international level regarding environmental protection, including those from the Rio Conference, which the U.S. would not sign. These have been excluded from the NAFTA.

3. The NAFTA includes a comprehensive programme of harmonization of standards in sections dealing with Sanitary and Phytosanitary Standards and Technical Barriers to Trade.[5]

Sanitary and Phytosanitary Standards (SPS)

This section is subject to the overall federal responsibility to ensure provincial compliance and so marks a new incursion into provincial SPS-related standards.[6] It also extends to non-governmental standard-setting bodies, such as the Canadian Standards Council, Canadian Standards Association, and so forth.[7] SPS measures are given a broad definition (Article 724) but they basically concern plant and animal health standards, including pesticides and, as they apply to humans, food additives. Although the word "harmonization" is not used, the chapter outlines a comprehensive approach to the harmonization of these standards by a group of international bodies.[8] Some of these bodies have not previously been engaged in setting standards. Codex Alimentarius is an experienced standard-setting body, but its members include large corporate producers. None of the organizations include consultation with the public and environmental groups in their processes.

While the chapter does allow parties to set SPS standards higher than those set internationally, those standards must be based on scientific principles as defined in the chapter and on risk assessment.[9] Parties have the right to determine their "appropriate level of protection" but only in accordance with Article 715, which establishes stringent conditions, that is, risk assessment, including consideration of international methodologies of risk assessment, and economic factors, such as loss of production or sales from presence of a pest or disease.

In setting SPS standards, parties remain subject to an overall obligation not to create "a disguised restriction to trade between the Parties."[10] This is the same standard applied by dispute panels in the past and ensures that any future SPS standards may be subject to the same treatment in trade dispute panels. Essentially, the power of the panels to determine whether a standard will be upheld still remains.

In setting new SPS federal standards, our government will need to give notice to the U.S. and Mexico and consider their comments on them.[11] It must also take "appropriate measures" to require provinces to do the same.[12] These requirements will require additional government resources and raise concerns that backroom deals with other governments are going to defeat SPS initiatives here.

Overall, despite the words that reserve our rights to set our own standards, the obstacles within the agreement are considerable. Higher, different standards will be in danger from trade challenges. Furthermore, many environmentalists consider that our government does not intend to set separate, higher standards. *The Foreign Policy Framework of External Affairs and International Trade* entitled "Managing Interdependence" stated:

> Strong environment standards are compatible with encouraging development of a more competitive Canadian economy. However, we shall have to pay attention to adjustment costs *and move in step with our major trading partners to avoid the risk of being undercut by environmentally irresponsible competitors. We must also be wary of "green protectionism,"* given our vulnerability in the resource sector.[13]

Plans to move "in step" with trading partners suggests using the same standards they use. With regard to "green protectionism," we would not need to be wary if we dealt with the environmental problems caused by our resource sectors.

Technical Barriers to Trade (Chapter Nine)
This chapter pertains to an even broader range of standards related measures (defined in Article 915) and to environmentally related issues, such as packaging. Specifically, it pertains to measures in-

cluding those relating to safety, protection of human, animal, and plant life and health, the environment, and consumers and measures to ensure their enforcement or implementation.[14] Like the SPS subchapter, it contains a comprehensive approach to harmonization of these measures, with some rights for separate standards reserved. Parties may establish such levels of protection as they consider appropriate,[15] but they must do so in a non-discriminatory manner and without creating a disguised restriction on trade.[16] The protection for national levels of protection does not extend to protection against challenges under the "nullification and impairments of benefits section"[17] even if those measures are otherwise consistent with the NAFTA. (The right to establish the level of protection is "Notwithstanding any other provision of this *Chapter*, not *this Agreement.*"[18]) Nor can such measures have the effect of creating an unnecessary obstacle to trade.[19]

The legitimate objectives for which measures may be adopted include safety, plant and animal health, the environment, and sustainable development.[20] Parties are to use international standards, but they can also use higher levels of protection as required to meet a legitimate objective.[21] The chapter contains further requirements for consideration of compatibility and equivalence of standards, risk assessment, conformity assessment, and notification of intended new measures.

Whether or not this chapter in fact allows Canada to use different and higher standards than those arrived at by the named international bodies will not be clear until trade panels rule on any possible challenges. What is clear is that there is room for challenges and that the rights to establish national standards are significantly qualified.

The standards in question are very important environmentally. Subcommittees will be examining standards concerning packaging, uniform chemical hazard classification, good laboratory practices, assessment of environmental hazards of goods, risk assessment, and testing of chemicals, including industrial and agricultural chemicals, pharmaceuticals, and biologicals.[22] The NAFTA contains the same entrenchment of U.S. trade remedy law[23] as the FTA.

NAFTA does contain provisions not in the FTA regarding trade disputes involving environmental issues. Parties challenged with regard to SPS or other standards-related measures, or in relation to actions related to the named international environmental agreements, may require that the NAFTA dispute mechanism be used, in preference to GATT, and the mechanism provides for scientific panels to advise on environmentally related matters.[24] In choosing the experts to sit on those panels, parties and international bodies will be contacted, not environmentalists.

It has been the experience of many in trying environmental cases that in any discipline there exists a range of opinions among experts. Frequently, the experts who testify on behalf of environmental groups bring a perspective to such proceedings that is very different than those provided by government and industry. Yet such individuals (and the public, including environmental groups) are excluded from these secret judicial processes.

Conclusion

The negotiations for NAFTA, like those for the FTA, were carried out in secrecy, with minimal consultation with a few environmentalists, and the trade panels will continue to operate in secrecy and make public decisions with no disclosure of which panel members are associated with minority or majority opinions.[25]

Although an attempt was made to prohibit actions that would encourage investment on a "pollution haven" basis, it was unsuccessful, and the NAFTA merely notes that such actions are "inappropriate." It provides for consultations if a party lowers standards to attract investment, but doesn't provide access to a dispute panel in such circumstances.[26]

The NAFTA falls short of containing provisions that would allow us to respond to the enormity of the ecological crisis that confronts us in Canada and in the world. By constraining our governmental powers to regulate exports and imports of resources, to use local and regional development strategies, local content requirements, subsidies, and strong, locally based environmental standards, it is an environmentally damaging agreement.

We need to change our economic practices significantly, not entrench them for all time. In signing an agreement with a less developed country, we need to offer technical and economic assistance (not in parallel accords, but in the agreement itself) rather than constrain the Mexican government's powers to act in the interest of the majority of its people.

Chapter 13

Culture

Graham Carr

Much controversy has been generated by the cultural provisions of the free trade agreement. The Canadian government argued that culture had been exempted by the agreement. But the very definition of culture established by the agreement had a distinctly American flavour.

In this chapter, Graham Carr shows that for American negotiators the bilateral agreement was part of a much larger economic agenda, including redefining culture as information, private property, or a service.

Since the day that FTA went into effect, Canadians have been treated to a steady barrage of American threats and imprecations about the need to liberalize trade in culture further. The American government has never entirely accepted Canada's claim that special protective measures that fully and permanently exempt culture from the rules of free trade are "enshrined" in Article 2005 of FTA.[1] Instead, the U.S. trade representative has consistently declared that the two countries "agree to disagree" about the meaning and application of the exemption for culture contained in the agreement. These declarations have been made with increasing vigour since June 1991, when trilateral talks began on the prospect of reaching a North American Free Trade Agreement (NAFTA) involving Canada, Mexico, and the United States. Complaining that it is unfair that Canada "should have substantial trading barriers on such a large segment of trade," the U.S. administration repeatedly stated that culture must be open to negotiation in the NAFTA round.[2]

Predictably, these statements infuriated many Canadians, including senior government officials, who insist that an exemption for culture is "a basic cornerstone of the Canada–U.S. deal," which must be respected in any follow-up negotiations.[3] Outraged by what they interpret as further evidence of "bullying U.S. insensitivity to deep-rooted Canadian concerns," most commentators are adamant that Canada should just say no to the Americans.[4] Unfortunately, while such hair-trigger condemnations of the U.S. position resonate powerfully in the chambers of Canadian nationalism, they are of limited utility as the inspiration for public policy because they are based on a fictional reading of FTA and a misunderstanding of American intentions in the cultural sphere.

It is not necessary to subscribe to the official American version of FTA to realize that any Canadian loyalty to the existing agreement is based on a misperception of what its cultural provisions contain. In particular, the blanket assertion that culture is exempt from FTA is simply untrue. Not only does the treaty explicitly mandate several changes to Canadian cultural policies and adjust tariffs on numerous cultural products, it is also ambiguous about the range of cultural activities it covers and fails to shield application of the exemption from retaliatory actions that are justified by other provisions of the agreement. Furthermore, by giving the appearance that its sole purpose is to enable Canadians to subsidize and regulate their cultural activities in ways that would otherwise be inconsistent with the goals of trade liberalization, the exemption perpetuates the common, but inaccurate, belief that the United States is a free trader in culture and manages to create an implementing framework that needlessly invites American scrutiny of Canadian policies.[5]

Apart from the dubious wisdom of standing firm by an agreement that is obviously porous in construction and contested at its foundations, a more fundamental problem with the cultural exemption approach is that it fails to comprehend the U.S. position fully. While some observers dismiss Washington's aggressive rhetoric on culture as cynical posturing that is designed to pry concessions in other areas of trade, many seem almost stunned by the administration's unyielding demands and professed to be "very surprised" when the U.S. tried to exploit the NAFTA talks in order to "do things through the back door ... that they couldn't get through the front door."[6] These views badly underestimate the firmness of American diplomatic resolve. But, more important, they fail to recognize, or else ignore, the degree to which the interpretation the U.S. is wont to put on FTA accurately reflects the administration's belief that is has already furthered its cultural agenda by implementing the agreement.

This failure of perception poses a series of problems. First, it indicates that there are many dimensions to U.S. thinking about free trade and culture of which Canadians are generally unaware. Second, it reveals that Canadians are not fully cognizant of the potential implications of the agreement. And third, it suggests that Canadians are relatively unprepared for the type of cultural initiatives that the U.S. undertakes. While the Canadian discourse on culture turns almost entirely on issues of national sovereignty and is predicated on the possibility of isolating culture from other policy areas by means of an exemption, much of the relevant American literature challenges the meaning of culture itself and dwells on the extent to which it can be subsumed by other political and economic realities. These divergent interpretations raise fundamental questions not only about the status of culture under FTA but also about the best way for Canada to respond to continued U.S. pressure for liberalization.

At the core of many Canadian misperceptions about U.S. strategy is the tendency to view American policy strictly through the narrow lense of bilateralism and from only one direction. This tendency magnifies the extent to which U.S. actions are driven by the desire to gain greater access to Canadian cultural markets while it glosses over the depth and scope of U.S. multilateral interests in the cultural sphere. Although Canadians have every right to be concerned about the further Americanization of their cultural resources, it is far from clear that this is the main goal of U.S. policy. Considering that Canada is already far and away the biggest export market for U.S. periodicals, books, films, and television programmes and that American capital holds controlling shares in a host of Canadian cultural enterprises, the potential for future investment growth and market expansion here seems comparatively limited. This impression is borne out by recent Department of Commerce forecasts, which clearly identify the EC countries and Eastern Europe as the most promising areas for future expansion by U.S. cultural industries.[7]

Instead, the principal and ongoing objective of U.S. strategy in negotiating cultural issues with Canada is to establish "improved rulemaking" and set precedents that can subsequently be applied in other bilateral or multilateral treaties. Various official statements made since the FTA was implemented could be cited to confirm this, but none are as blunt or revealing as the Bush administration's stern warning that it will retaliate against undue Canadian "reliance" on the exemption "in such a manner as to discourage the creation of similar non-tariff barriers in other countries."[8]

If the U.S. approach to culture under FTA is best understood in a multilateral, rather than a bilateral, context, it must also be examined in relation to other sectors of American foreign and trade policy. The common nationalist assumption that culture is more vital to Canada's interests than it is to the U.S., and the corollary belief that American meddling in this issue is motivated by mischief and arrogance, ignores the discernible pattern of U.S. foreign policy that has evolved during the past several years. Far from being a secondary or isolated item on the international policy agenda, the cultural dossier has long held an important place in American diplomatic strategy and is increasingly integral to the overall framework of U.S. commerce.

The most obvious reason for the growing importance of culture to U.S. policy is that it is extremely valuable to the domestic American economy. Not only does cultural production generate millions of jobs and billions of dollars in annual GNP, cultural exports are vitally significant as favourable items in the U.S. balance of payments. Historically, the U.S. has enjoyed a global competitive advantage in many areas of cultural production, such as theatrical films, recorded music, and broadcasting. But with the saturation of its domestic markets and the growth of English "as the world's second language," expanded access to foreign consumers has become even more imperative to the sustained development of many cultural industries. For example, since 1988, sales of American recorded music in EC countries alone has exceeded values garnered in the domestic U.S. market. In 1989–90, the value of exports of American periodicals increased by 20 per cent over the previous year. Meanwhile, the value of foreign book sales increased by 13 per cent, capturing a full 9.5 per cent of total industrial shipments, which is "the highest level ever achieved by the U.S. book industry." Similarly, income from the foreign distribution of American films accounts for approximately one-third of the total revenue in that industry and contributes in excess of US$4 billion per year to the overall U.S. balance of payments, making motion pictures one of the country's "most successful exports."[9]

Quite apart from their tangible economic worth, cultural exports are politically valuable to the larger interests of U.S. trade and foreign policy. The "geopolitical significance" of trade is a leading theme in contemporary American foreign policy, which bids to consolidate U.S. hegemony in a post–Cold War world.[10] Culture is a proven instrument of such diplomacy. The global distribution of American films, music, television, videos, books, and periodicals, as well as private and state-sponsored tours by leading artists and entertainers, are essential tools for inculcating values or reinforcing tastes that advance U.S. economic and security interests.

Considering the relative significance of culture to the larger framework of U.S. commercial and foreign policy, it is not surprising that, increasingly, the preferred diplomatic strategy for accomplishing the goal of cultural expansionism is free trade. Yet, in trying to promote liberalized trade in culture globally, the U.S. has run up against two major obstacles: the lack of an acceptable economic rationale for bringing culture under the rubric of relevant international trading agreements, such as the GATT, and international resistance to the potential use of culture as an instrument of political domination. Although culture has always been inseparable from economic factors in terms of its production, distribution, and reception, cultural products have traditionally been excluded from international agreements on trade liberalization on the grounds that they do not function according to the same set of use values or market relations as material goods and that they have an extraordinary potential to shape public opinion and behaviour.

Unlike most material goods, cultural products are not necessarily created with an "ascertainable market" in mind, and they may actually increase in value the more they are used or exchanged rather than in relation to their relative scarcity. Therefore, in such areas as copyright legislation, governments have historically tried to balance the public's right of access against the legitimate proprietary claims of creators or other owners.[11] Similarly, in the name of national sovereignty, all governments, including that of the U.S., have long insisted on the right to intercept, limit, or regulate the cross-border flow of cultural materials and the right to put parallel restrictions on foreign investment in cultural institutions. But governments introduce other non-tariff barriers on cross-border cultural exchange too. Because many forms of culture are inherently unprofitable, they have always been dependent on some measure of patronage in order to survive and flourish. In many countries, including the U.S., this patronage often takes the form of hidden or direct government subsidization or public ownership. Even in areas where cultural production is profitable, however, government intervention also occurs for the purpose of stimulating domestic production and nurturing infant industries that are deemed essential to national economic development.

Although it is misleading to assume the existence of a national consensus on cultural policy in the U.S., contemporary American commercial and diplomatic strategy seeks to overcome these obstacles to freer trade in this area by effectively redefining culture and eliminating qualitative distinctions between it and other forms of socioeconomic activity. There are two related thrusts to this endeavour, both of which are executed in a variety of bilateral and multilateral contexts. The first thrust, which began in the late 1970s, involves attempts by successive American administrations to connect culture to the concept of information through association with knowledge and communication and, in turn, to link the doctrine of free flow in information to free trade. The second strategy, which is more clearly a product of the 1980s, involves efforts to commodify the meaning of culture by emphasizing intellectual property rights and the role of culture as a service industry. By redefining culture as information, private property, or a service, the U.S. can more easily lobby for the liberalization of trade in cultural products. But there is a hidden advantage to this tactic, too. Blurring the distinctions between culture and other forms of intellectual and economic activity involving knowledge provides a potential for tremendous, if unforeseeable, spin-offs in other sectors of economic activity resulting from policy gains made through the liberalization of culture. This does not mean that there is something conspiratorial about the U.S. strategy with respect to free trade in culture. On the contrary: the strategy as a whole in still in process of formation, but its main components have been articulated individually in various international forums and have been a matter of public record for roughly a decade.

The assimilation of culture and information as concepts has been an axiom of U.S. policy since the mid-1970s. On one level it is justified by arguing that the substantive distinctions between paintings and advertisements, for example, are "largely arbitrary" because, in essence, both things contain and communicate knowledge. Moreover, in the case of paintings and advertisements, there is evident potential for symbiosis in the application of graphic techniques to commercials or in the appropriation of artistic images — the *Mona Lisa* or *American Gothic* — to sell chocolate bars or cornflakes. According to a 1990 congressional study on communications, culture and information are virtually indistinguishable from each other because "communications is the process by which culture is developed and maintained," and "information, the content of communication, is the basic source of all human intercourse." The reality of culture as information is embodied and communicated "in an ever-expanding variety of media, including spoken words, graphics, artifacts, music, dance, written text, film, recording, and computer hardware and software."[12]

Moving beyond the question of content, the rationale for effacing distinctions between culture and information is also justified on socioeconomic and technological grounds. Culture and information are often produced industrially, sold for profit, and subject to legal protection under copyright or patent law. There are genuine overlaps, too, in their means of production, delivery, and interpretation. These overlaps are illustrated by the reality that contemporary writers and musicians are just as likely to be dependent on computers, cables, or satellites as stock market analysts or data processors. These socioeconomic and technological convergences suggest that traditional ways of separating culture and information are anachronistic and serve to highlight the potential for confusion in the development of public policies in fields like telecommunications.

Intellectually, the net effect of a line of reasoning that conflates culture and information is to neutralize the meaning of culture by linking it, on the one hand, to empirical, and presumably beneficial, concepts, such as knowledge and, on the other, to ostensibly value-free, physical objects, such as technology. But the argument that culture and information are identical to each other is also functionally significant because it serves to incorporate culture into the international debate on the doctrine of free flow in which the U.S. is a leading participant.

The advocacy of free flow in information is a cardinal element of U.S. foreign policy. Couched mainly in ideological terms, the burden of the American argument is that national policies that interfere with the free expression of ideas, dissemination of information, and transfer of relevant communications technology or that give unfair privilege to host groups or institutions must be eliminated because they are discriminatory, anti-democratic, and economically counterproductive. However, American enthusiam for free flow is also inextricably bound up with its commercial interests, which are increasingly dependent on the fortunes of its information industries and information-based economy. U.S.-dominated foreign trade in information is increasingly a factor in this equation. As early as 1983, the licensing and assignment of patents and copyrights generated US$4.7 billion worth of benefit to the American balance of payments. More recently, in 1990, foreign sales of U.S. information, data-processing, and network services contributed 20 to 30 per cent of revenues in those industries.[13] Apart from these tangible advantages, the unrestricted ability to move information across borders is also commercially vital because of the advantages of privileged access which accrue to U.S. franchises and transnational corporations operating abroad.

Unfortunately for the U.S., this commitment to free flow has met with intransigent opposition in many regions of the world community, particularly among small and developing countries, which either do not share the American ideological perspective or see the futility of trying to compete levelly with dominant U.S. industries that are already established in the information field. Indeed, it was mainly the intransigence of this international opposition to free flow that prompted the U.S. to withdraw from UNESCO in 1984 on the pretext that the organization had unfairly politicized communications issues. But rather than abandon the issue altogether, the U.S. simply pursued the same policy ends through other bilateral and multilateral means. In particular, the American government transferred its energies away from the United Nations and toward more congenial surroundings, such as the OECD and GATT, where it began working to identify communication, information, and culture as purely economic issues that should properly be encompassed under the umbrella of trade.[14]

Fundamental to this process is the attempt to synchronize the exchange of cultural products with existing rules on commodities by expanding the provisions of GATT to secure better foreign protection for intellectual property and achieve liberalized trade in a broader range of services, including telecommunications and moving image entertainment. In the case of intellectual property, recent international American policy initiatives on copyright signal a pronounced shift toward greater emphasis on the exclusive rights of owners rather than users in legitimizing access to culture. Estimates made in the early 1980s suggested that annual losses to U.S. holders of copyright resulting from foreign infringements amounted to roughly US$20 billion. These included losses of approximately US$700 million on the sale of books and periodicals; US$250 million on sales of sound recordings; and nearly US$1 billion on film and video sales.[15] Faced with industry pressure to counteract such infringements, the U.S. has subsequently introduced two pieces of legislation that closely bind copyright questions to trade policy. The Caribbean Basin Recovery

Act of 1984 makes receipt of U.S. aid contingent on adequate protection of U.S. copyright holders, while Section 301 of the 1988 Trade Act establishes a watch list to monitor and punish foreign countries that fail to provide "effective protection for intellectual property rights ... and equitable market access for persons that rely on intellectual property."[16] Furthermore, in an attempt to exert greater influence in multilateral negotiations on copyright, the U.S. — long an abstainer from international agreements on these questions for reasons of national sovereignty — joined the Berne Union for the Protection of Literary and Artistic Property (Berne Convention) in 1989.

If recent U.S. initiatives on copyright have the effect of aligning culture with notions of private property and commodity trade, the same is true with respect to U.S. strategy on liberalizing trade in services. In a 1984 submission to the GATT, the American government reviewed the importance of trade and investment in services to the world economy in general and argued, as "the world's largest exporter of services," for clearer recognition of their status as "tangible product(s)."[17] Although the precise meaning of the term services remains vague, much of the service sector is dedicated to exchanging information. Indeed, many of the various service industries specifically targeted for trade liberalization by the Americans are directly located in, or closely related to, the cultural sphere. They include telecommunications; data processing; information services; tourism; advertising; and motion pictures, which are defined to encompass "the production, distribution and exhibition of all forms of moving image entertainment (feature films, television films, video tapes, video cassettes, video discs), intended for either cinematic or television exhibition, and related services."[18]

Seen in the context of recent U.S. commercial and foreign policy, therefore, the cultural achievement of FTA looks remarkably different from the way in which it is usually interpreted by Canadians. However comforted they are by the notion that the U.S. is unhappy with the current agreement, and especially with the partial exemption for culture it contains, Canadians cannot afford to ignore the extent to which FTA nevertheless contributes to removing lingering ambiguities about the status of culture as a trade item. Article 2005 is a case in point. Paradoxically, by applying specifically to cultural "industries" — or "business enterprise(s)," as they are referred to elsewhere in the agreement — and carrying a retaliation clause that links the commercial value of culture to other sectors of the economy, the exemption embodies exactly the definition of culture as commodity that it ostensibly exists to deny. Furthermore, the agreement as a whole, with its separate provisions on telecommunications, intellectual property, and information services, effectively undermines the piety that cultural issues are, or can be, isolated within the cloister of an exemption. For example, Annex 1404C on computer and telecommunications services commits the parties to facilitate "the movement of information across the borders and access to data bases or related information stored, processed or otherwise held within the territory of a Party." Hailed as a "trail blazing effort ... that could lay the foundation for further work [on services] multilaterally," this section of the agreement specifically cites several occupations — architects, educators, graphic artists, computer and enhanced telecommunications workers, photographers, and educational researchers — that have roots in the cultural sphere. In addition, FTA contains a binding commitment on both parties to work co-operatively on achieving multilateral progress regarding expanded intellectual property rights now embodied in the NAFTA agreement. Significantly, the U.S. government interprets the FTA requirement that Canadian cable companies pay copyright fees for cross-border retransmission rights as an example of real progress toward guaranteeing "fair and equitable market access [in Canada] to United States persons that rely upon copyright."[19]

Admittedly, the full implications stemming from FTA's definition of culture as an industry, or from its provisions on information services, copyright, and telecommunications, are impossible to predict. But set against the backdrop of U.S. foreign and commercial policy as a whole, the very existence of such provisions exposes the self-deceptive fallacy inherent in Canadian efforts to avoid further discussion of cultural issues in relation to free trade. Indeed, Canadians would be better served by coming to the realization that culture is already part of FTA and that American interests in the topic are deep-rooted, broad, and strong. There may be a consensus in Canada that something called culture is vital to national sovereignty and must be protected and promoted. But an intelligent response to incessant U.S. pressure for liberalization clearly requires systematic deliberation about the meaning and conceptual sovereignty of culture itself. At this juncture, it is not apparent that Canadians are well-equipped to discuss this issue. Although many government studies have been published in the past decade on cultural industries, the information economy, telecommunications technologies, and intellectual property rights, some of the thinking that informs these works has been criticized for its mythologizing, while in other cases — such as copyright — much has been lost in the translation to public policy.[20] Still, these topics must somehow be incorporated within the national debate on free trade and culture. American aggressiveness on cultural issues is not going to go away. But no strategy for effectively responding to it can succeed unless it is based on a better understanding of U.S. motives in the first place.

Chapter 14

Intellectual Property

Roy Davidson

Under NAFTA, intellectual property rights become part of a comprehensive international trade agreement for the first time anywhere. While the American attempt to include this subject in the FTA failed, many of the U.S. bargaining interests were accepted by Canada in off-the-table arrangements.

In this chapter, Roy Davidson shows that as a large importer of U.S. copyrighted works, Canada is likely to pay heavily for according U.S. producers strengthened monopoly rights. Though intellectual property conventions are designed to be incentives for creativity, Canadian producers often find it difficult to break into our domestic market without government intervention of some kind. The effort of NAFTA will be to limit the ability of Canadians to compete with U.S. patent and copyright holders. The impact of this chapter is wide-ranging, from cultural products, to computer software, to plant breeders' rights, and to general research and development.

One of the most surprising things about Canada–U.S. trade negotiations in recent years is that the U.S. somehow managed to persuade Canadians that free trade would be promoted by strengthening private monopoly. Of course, the U.S. task was made easier because it faced a pliant Canadian government, a naive Canadian press, and a far from disinterested Canada business lobby.

During the course of negotiations of the Canada–U.S. Free Trade Agreement (FTA), the U.S. insisted upon a number of measures (some of which required Canada to amend its legislation on intellectual property rights) that the Canadian government preferred to handle as off-the-table or under-the-table arrangements. The amendments that resulted from the FTA will now be entrenched by the terms of NAFTA. Under Article 1721 of NAFTA, intellectual property rights are defined to include copyright and related rights, trademark rights, patent rights, rights in layout designs of semiconductor integrated circuits, trade secret rights, plant breeders' rights, rights in geographical indications, and industrial design rights.

In Canada's circumstances, grounds for concern are greatest in the case of copyright (including copyright in computer programmes) and patent rights (including rights in layout designs of integrated circuits, trade secret rights, and plant breeders' rights).

There are two reasons why a stronger copyright system entrenched in NAFTA — which essentially means more protection for the owner of the copyrights — will be very costly for Canada. The first is that we are huge net importers of copyrighted works, mainly from the U.S. Moreover, it is quite unlikely that the trade balance will change substantially. The main problem for Canada is that once a decision has been made in the U.S. to produce a book, a magazine, a recording, a radio broadcast, a video, a T.V. broadcast, or a movie, for the American market, the marginal cost of making the creation available in the Canadian market is very low. Roughly the same principle applies in other industries, but its impact in the cultural sector is unique because the additional cost is generally so small. Indeed, in the case of radio and T.V. broadcasting in border areas and all T.V. broadcasting by satellite, the additional cost is zero. This situation makes it extremely difficult for Canadian productions in English to find any market at all, even in Canada, without government intervention of some kind. As things stand, depending on the cultural field considered, anywhere from 75 to 95 per cent of the copyright incentive is paid abroad, mostly to the U.S.

Annex 2106 of NAFTA says that any measures adopted or maintained with respect to "cultural industries," as between the U.S. and Canada, shall be governed in accordance with the terms of the FTA. Under the FTA, Canada is allowed to adopt measures to protect "cultural industries" that do not conform with the FTA's normal provisions. However, it is also provided that if Canada introduces a measure under the cultural industries clause that injures the U.S., we either have to pay compensation or face retaliatory measures of equivalent commercial effect.

It is not surprising that an "exemption" that is so constrained has little visible effect. Indeed, we are moving in the opposite direction. Postal rates that favoured Canadian magazines have been dropped. The requirement that magazines or newspapers be printed in Canada so advertisers could deduct the cost of advertising as a business expense has been eliminated. The policy has been terminated that required that book publishers put up for sale should be first offered to Canadian buyers. Proposed legislation to increase the film distribution activities of Canadian film companies so that they would have greater cash flow to finance the production of Canadian movies has been abandoned. The budget of the CBC has been steadily reduced.

Though copyright is intended to provide an incentive for creativity in all these fields, an essential part of Article 1703 in the Intellectual Property Chapter of NAFTA, and of some of the international conventions on copyright, is that each party must accord to nationals of another party treatment no less favourable than it accords to its own nationals. In other words, countries are not permitted to discriminate in favour of native talent. This requirement represents a second reason why a strengthened copyright system will be costly to Canada. The system will handicap, where it does not preclude, badly needed government initiatives that might give Canadians a stronger voice in their own country.

In like manner, one reason why patent rights are such an issue in Canada is that 95 per cent of Canadian patents are owned abroad. Patent rights are intended to provide an incentive for research and development. But a high proportion of Canadian industry is also owned abroad, and in the real world, unfortunately, multinational corporations understandably tend to concentrate their R & D (research and development) either in their home territory or in their largest market because economies of scale are involved.

Canadians pay a high price in granting patent monopolies, but as the record over many years shows, we have had the worst record for R & D among all major countries. In Canada, R & D must be encouraged in other ways if it is to be significant. It must be promoted, for example, by tax incentives, by the establishment of government research organizations, by government funding of university research, or by the promotion of joint ventures among governments, universities, and private organizations. Under the patent system, successful innovators in Canada are given a patent monopoly whether production takes place in Canada or abroad. As in the case of copyright, the cost of the incentive is very high, but the payoff that is attributable to the incentive is extremely modest.

When the FTA was being negotiated, Prime Minister Mulroney, Finance Minister Wilson, members of the negotiating team, and others assured Canadians that cultural industries "were not on the table." What they did not say was that there were under-the-table deals in preparation. We are now asked to believe that bills providing for radical changes in Canadian copyright law and for the virtual abolition of compulsory licensing of drug patents — measures that the U.S. had been pressing for, for many years — just happened to be introduced in Parliament immediately before the signing of the FTA.

One thing NAFTA has done is unmask this high-level piece of deception. At the same time as NAFTA entrenches in Canada the under-the-table deals associated with the FTA, NAFTA imposes the same U.S.-style laws on Mexico.

The U.S. gains twice from the strengthening of the monopolies conferred by copyright and patents in Canada. On the one hand, Canadian users lose ground to their American rivals. On the other hand, there is on important addition to the already substantial transfer of income we make to the U.S. for intellectual property rights.

Under NAFTA, Canada faces a permanent renunciation of the effective measures we had begun to adopt in order to moderate the high cost of intellectual property monopolies. Article 1701 of NAFTA provides that each party shall, at a minimum, give effect to the Intellectual Property Chapter of NAFTA and to the substantive provisions of four of the principal international conventions for the protection of intellectual property.

Article 1705 deals, among other things, with computer programmes. Copyright protection in Canada was first extended to computer programmes, just months before the FTA was signed. The amended Copyright Act was passed in June 1988. In this legislation, computer programmes were included as a category of "literary works." This somewhat improbable classification was necessary if Canadian law and policy was to be harmonized with that of the U.S. Article 1705 now brings Mexico, too, on side. It is thus apparent here and in what follows that in the case of NAFTA, unlike in the FTA, there is no pretence that cultural industries are not "on the table" or that copyright is not part of trade negotiation bargaining.

Article 1706 deals with sound recordings. Paragraph 1706:3 says that each party shall confine limitations or exceptions to the rights provided for in the article to certain special cases that do not conflict with a normal exploitation of the sound recording. This mirrors the new policy that was embodied in the Canadian Copyright Act of 1988, which abolished compulsory licensing of copyright for the making of sound recordings.

Rather than rely on an appropriate level of royalties under compulsory licensing as the reward for creativity, as it had in the past, under U.S. pressure, the government chose in 1988 to strengthen the monopoly conferred on the holders of intellectual property. The new Copyright Act encourages the formation of additional copyright collectives. These will have much more bargaining power than individuals have in negotiating with Canadian users.

Before the passage of the new Copyright Act, the only significant copyright collectives in Canada were two performing rights societies called CAPAC and PROCAN. The last time any precise disclosure was made by these societies about the distribution to authors and composers of performing rights revenues they received was in 1956. At that time the Ilsley Royal Commission indicated that Canadian authors and composers received only 8 per cent of the total distribution. No doubt embarrassed by the facts, both societies have steadfastly refused since 1956 to disclose any similarly precise information. It therefore seems obvious that the government's objective in promoting copyright collectives was not to increase rewards to Canadian creativity. Otherwise, it would not have chosen an instrument that guarantees that most of the increased revenues will go to non-Canadians.

Article 1707 covers the protection of encrypted programme-carrying satellite signals. It provides that within one year from the entry into force of NAFTA, each party shall make it a civil offence to engage in the commercial reception and distribution of any encrypted programme-carrying satellite signal that has been decoded without the authorization of the lawful distributor. This article effectively blocks the reintroduction of one government policy that promised to redress the balance in Canada somewhat. That policy permitted Canadian cable T.V. companies to relay to their subscribers uninvited signals from the U.S. and to substitute Canadian advertising for the advertising on the American broadcasts. The cable T.V. companies were expected to spend a significant part of the revenue from the Canadian advertising to produce Canadian programming. This policy was dropped in the run-up to the FTA under pressure from American broadcasters and the U.S. government. Under NAFTA, no similar policy can ever be reintroduced.

Article 1717 deals with criminal procedures and penalties. Paragraph 1717:1 reads: "Each Party shall provide criminal procedures and penalties to be applied at least in cases of wilful trademark counterfeiting or copyright piracy [sic] on a commercial scale. Each Party shall provide that penalties available include imprisonment or monetary fines, or both, sufficient to provide a deterrent, consistent with the level of penalties applied for crimes of corresponding gravity."

It is important to note that in the run-up to the FTA, the Canadian government had already tugged its forelock. Until 1988, the maximum penalties for copyright infringement in a criminal prosecution in Canada were $10 per copy up to a maximum of $200 per transaction. Under the new Copyright Act passed just months before the FTA was signed, the maximum fine was raised to $1 million, and the maximum jail sentence was raised to five years. No doubt inflation had eroded the deterrent effect of the maximum penalties in the old act. But the harshness of the new penalties — and the draconian nature of the change — can only reflect the American agenda and the interest of the U.S. as the world's biggest exporter of copyrighted works.

Article 1709 covers patents. Several of its provisions ensure that the compulsory licensing of drug patents in Canada will never be reintroduced. Compulsory licensing lowered the price of prescription drugs and paid moderate royalties to patent owners over a period of almost twenty years before the policy became a casualty of the FTA negotiations.

Article 1709:5 says that each party shall provide, where the subject matter of a patent is a product, that the patent owner may prevent other persons from making, using, or selling the product, and where the subject matter of a patent is a process, that the patent owner may prevent other persons from using the process or *importing* the product produced by that process without his consent. Under the programme of compulsory licensing of drug products in Canada, Canadian licensees generally purchased the pharmaceutically active ingredients from *licensed* producers located in low-cost markets abroad and processed the ingredients into dosage forms here. NAFTA thus creates a double obstacle to the reintroduction of any such compulsory licensing programme.

This result is reinforced by Article 1711, which deals with trade secrets. Paragraphs 1711:5 and 1711:6 were clearly inspired by the Canadian experience with the compulsory licensing of drug patents. What happened in Canada was that licensees, in making a "new drug submission" to the federal Department of Health (Drug Directorate), successfully argued that they should have to prove only that their version of a given drug had exactly the same characteristics, based on bio-equivalence and bio-availability studies, as the drug produced by the patent owner. They should not, they argued, have to duplicate all the clinical testing that the directorate already had on file as a result of the patent owner's original application. Paragraphs 1711:5 and 1711:6 provide that if a party requires, as a condition for approving the marketing of pharmaceutical or agricultural chemical products that utilize new chemical entities, the submission of test or other data necessary to determine whether the use of such products is safe and effective, then no person other than the person that submitted them may, without the latter's permission, rely on such data in support of an application for product approval during a reasonable period of time after their submission. A reasonable period, according to NAFTA, will normally mean not less than five years!

Note that contrary to what is implied by the heading of Article 1711, that is, trade secrets, no disclosure of any secret is involved here. The second person simply says to the government agency, "I can prove that my product is exactly the same as that of the first person, and you have already determined that his product is safe and effective."

The least that can be said about this move to extend patent monopoly into the new field of unpatented know-how is that it promises to be a bonanza for lawyers and an additional cost for net importers of technology like Canada.

Article 1709:12 says that each party shall provide a term of protection for patents of a least twenty years from the date of filing. In keeping with what has become the established pattern, the Canadian government did not wait for NAFTA to be signed but introduced legislation in June 1992 extending the period of protection in Canada to provide for a minimum term of twenty years. This replaced a revision introduced in 1987 that had also extended the period of protection to twenty years but only for drugs invented and developed in Canada — a class of drugs that, ironically, is almost non-existent. The 1992 legislation effectively eliminates what was left of the program for the compulsory licensing of drug patents.

Article 1709:3 says that each party shall provide for the protection of plant varieties through patents or a special scheme of protection or both. For many years the U.S. had granted patents on the development of new varieties of plants, and Canada had never done so. However, the Canadian government was persuaded to introduce legislation on plant breeders' rights in January 1988 while the FTA negotiations were underway. Probably, this under-the-table deal was flawed in American eyes because it contained effective compulsory licensing provisions. In any event, a new bill was introduced in May 1989, after the FTA was signed, which contained much weaker compulsory licensing provisions.

There is great irony in the decision to grant patents on plants in order to stimulate research in Canada. The record is clear. Decades of monopoly grants in the form of industrial patents have failed to stimulate much industrial R & D. For example, most of the research that the multinational drug companies claim to do in Canada is clinical research. Much of this clinical research is required by the Drug Directorate before marketing is permitted and is not at all dependent on the Canadian patent system. Much of the rest of the clinical research that is done in Canada has nothing to do with Canadian patents either, but it does reflect the good reputation of Canadians doctors. It is often convenient for U.S. parents to have their subsidiaries in Canada arrange some clinical testing of U.S. discoveries here. But the most important incentive of all for research by the drug companies or anyone else in Canada is the generous tax treatment they receive.

We are dead last among major industrial countries ranked by research spending per capita or by the proportions of patent grants that are of domestic origin. The one shining exception to our mediocrity in research, at least historically, was the experimental farms administration of the Department of Agriculture. These farms, of course, were government funded and did not rely at all on the patent system to stimulate research.

The problem is always the same. Canada's market is small, and much of it is dominated by multinational enterprises owned abroad. It is no surprise, therefore, that press reports at the time that the plant breeders' legislation was introduced indicated that pharmaceutical/agrochemical multinationals like CIBA-Geigy, Dupont, ICI, Monsanto, Pfizer, Sandoz, Shell, and Upjohn had moved, or were expected to move, into seed research. Canada is unlikely to become an important centre of R & D for any of these companies.

What matters most for any country is not whether it invented the new technology but whether it uses the new technology. Here, too, Canada is likely to get shortchanged. The multinationals will not likely focus much attention on crop varieties that are designed to meet the local needs of a diversified Canadian geography and economy. In the case of varieties for which there is a general demand, the grant of a monopoly to a single firm is likely to raise the price and impede the diffusion of the new technology in the country at large. It is wrong to adopt a policy that can be expected to generate substantial research only in a far different market, like the U.S., for instance.

Article 1710 provides that each party shall protect layout designs (topographies) of integrated circuits in accordance with specified articles of the new Treaty on Intellectual Property in Respect of Integrated Circuits as opened for signature on 26 May 1989. This treaty is another extension of monopoly into a field not previously covered by intellectual property laws. NAFTA states flatly in paragraph 1710:5 that "No Party may permit the compulsory licensing of layout designs of integrated circuits." It is worth noting that a generalized system of compulsory licensing, corresponding to what was introduced for drug patents, was precisely what was recommended in a major study by the Economic Council of Canada as a means of more nearly balancing the costs and benefits of the international patent system for a country like Canada. NAFTA pre-empts any consideration of such a government initiative in the future.

Those who defend strong monopolies based on intellectual property rights often argue that Canada should not take a free ride on other people's research. But this position ignores the fact that the Canadian subsidiaries of foreign parents are often explicitly charged a fee as their contribution to R & D. If not, they make a contribution indirectly through management fees, the repatriation of profits, or the higher transfer prices when they buy from affiliates. With respect to copyright, far from being free riders, even before the screws were tightened by the FTA and frozen by NAFTA, Canadians almost certainly paid far more abroad per capita than do the citizens of any other major country. This reflects our wealth, close proximity to the U.S., similar tastes, common language, economic integration, U.S. direct investment, and so forth.

The laws that define intellectual property rights are a useful economic device where they promote creativity. Attempts to justify these laws by an appeal to some notion of natural justice are unconvincing. Intellectual property laws cover different fields in different ways in different countries. The most important common characteristic of intellectual property rights is that they are everywhere of limited duration. Limited duration is compatible with a role as an economic device, but it is not compatible with a role as a fulfilment of natural justice.

Canada's real interest requires that we assume the least onerous obligations that are allowable under the international copyright and patent conventions while we introduce other incentives to creativity that will be much more effective in Canada's special circumstances. In other words, if a country like Canada wants to increase substantially the incomes of its creative people and the resources devoted to R & D, without paying a king's ransom abroad, it will have to do so outside the international copyright and patent conventions.

Chapter 15

Financial Services

Bruce Campbell

Canadian banks have been enthusiastic supporters of NAFTA. They see important business advantages in increased access to the Mexican financial sector.

In this chapter, Bruce Campbell outlines some of the costs to Canada of the financial deregulation approach embedded in NAFTA. The ability to use public financial enterprises for non-commercial purposes is circumscribed, provincial regulatory authority is weakened, and the right to transfer and process information outside Canada is guaranteed.

NAFTA replicates the basic provisions of the FTA and extends them to Mexico — measures such as those exempting U.S. companies from the foreign ownership restrictions on Canadian financial institutions, from the restrictions on Canadian financial institutions, and from the restriction that foreign financial institutions collectively cannot hold more than 16 per cent of the total financial assets of the Canadian banking system.

Moreover, NAFTA goes well beyond the FTA in widening and deepening the scope of financial services deregulation and limiting the power of governments. It is clear that the FTA was the floor from which further deregulation has been negotiated. It deepens the ability of U.S. financial corporations to set up and operate in Canada, take over Canadian companies, process and transfer information abroad, and access and transfer the savings of Canadians in accordance with their own global corporate priorities, regardless of whether they coincide with national or provincial objectives.

NAFTA represents the further entrenchment and advancement of the financial deregulation agenda that the Mulroney government has been pursuing since it came to power. The fact that Canada has allowed its financial system to become increasingly integrated with unregulated private global markets has encouraged an increase in net foreign public and private indebtedness, with an increased portion of this debt being of a short-term nature and, thus, highly sensitive to changed expectations on the part of foreign money managers. Ballooning Canadian current account deficits have been propped up by the inflow of capital maintained by high interest rates.

Governments are increasingly hostage to the logic of these markets. Monetary and fiscal polices are constrained. Political accountability to electorates is superseded by accountability to foreign creditors. Should they defy market expectations — for example, by increasing government spending or lowering interest rates — they risk large-scale capital flight and reductions in their credit ratings, as well as in those of public and private corporations that also depend on global financial markets.

The key new provision of the chapter is the extension of *national treatment* to U.S. (and Mexican) financial corporations with respect to the "establishment, acquisition, expansion, management, conduct, operation and sale of investments."[1] National treatment is defined to mean treatment no less favourable than for domestic financial services providers or financial institutions and encompasses the concept of *"equal competitive opportunities."*[2] Financial services obligations of NAFTA, unlike the FTA, expressly apply to provincial jurisdictions and self-regulatory bodies, such as securities exchanges. There is a limited and not clearly defined exception to the national treatment requirement if governments can justify it for "prudential reasons." Furthermore, any U.S. (or Mexican) company that currently does not have a presence in Canada has the legal right to establish a banking, insurance, or other financial subsidiary in Canada.

Each country can have a public pension plan or social security system or a public entity conducting activities using government resources or guarantees,[3] for example, a national investment fund. However, to the extent that their activities compete with other institutions, they would be affected by the provisions of the agreement: for example, the requirement of compensation for a measure "tantamount to expropriation."

In the case of a new investment fund, its activities would have to comply with the provisions of the agreement. For example, it would have to, as a state enterprise, comply with the terms of Article 1502, which prevent state enterprises from engaging in activities that are seen to discriminate against U.S. investors, and with the obligation to "act solely in accordance with commercial considerations." This would appear to greatly circumscribe the goals of such a fund — for example, to favour Canadian-owned business or to achieve goals, such as regional development or environment protection, that are seen as non-commercial.

A major expansion of the FTA in NAFTA is the intrusion into *provincial jurisdiction*. Under the FTA, provinces were excluded from the application of provisions regarding financial services, with the exception of insurance. Under the NAFTA, provincially regulated entities, such as trust companies, mortgage companies, and loan companies, are exposed to its terms and conditions. Provinces are required to give U.S. investors national treatment, which means treatment as favourable as that given to provincially owned companies.

Existing non-conforming measures may be grandparented, provided that they are explicitly listed in a reservations schedule by 1 January 1994. Any new measures must comply with the provisions of the agreement. They can only be treated differently to the extent that this is justified for "prudential reasons."

Although NAFTA establishes broad new dispute-settlement mechanisms for financial services including those regulated provincially (see below) it provides no consultative or appeal mechanism for provincial governments.

Other measures that deregulate the financial services industry and enhance the ability of corporations to move throughout the continent free from government interference include the following:

- Article 1407 guarantees U.S. (and Mexican) financial institutions based in Canada *the right to transfer and process information outside Canada*. This guarantee has major implications for data-processing jobs in Canada, but it also raises important privacy questions — for example, medical insurance records. It requires changes to the Bank Act and will have to apply to Canadian institutions as well. It is an important precedent, preventing regulation of cross-border information flows. Combined with the removal of restrictions on all types of cross-border financial transfers, this provision has major implications for the Canadian economy, given the growing tradeability of services internationally and the increased knowledge component of production.

• Financial institutions and service providers are free from requirements to hire Canadians for their boards or for senior management positions or to ensure that all board members be permanently resident in Canada (just a simple majority is required). The provisions under the temporary entry chapter make it much easier to move senior staff freely across borders.

• They are able under Article 1109 to make any kind of financial transfer, from dividends and capital gains to management fees, without interference, in convertible currency, at market rates of exchange.

• Finally, financial services are affected by the expansion of the scope of the NAFTA investment provisions, which (unlike the FTA applied only to corporations) are extended to include all investments: portfolio, debt, real and intangible property.

The provisions of this chapter, unlike the FTA, are subject to the NAFTA Chapter 20 dispute-settlement mechanisms. In a major concession to the U.S., NAFTA has an *investor-state arbitration mechanism*,[4] through which all U.S. investors, including financial services corporations, have the right to challenge Canadian legislation directly through international arbitration panels. (Financial services companies have some restrictions on their use of these panels; i.e. they can be used with respect to cross-border financial transfers, expropriation, denial of benefits, and environmental measures). This mechanism is a major new weapon at the disposal of transnational capital which will have a chilling effect on new policy initiatives that affect corporate interests.

The definition of financial services has been vastly broadened. In the FTA, it was restricted to federally regulated financial services provided by financial institutions (excluding underwriting and insurance policies). In NAFTA, a financial service is "a service of a financial nature including insurance, and a service incidental or auxiliary to a service of a financial nature."[5]

Chapter 16

Provincial Powers

Scott Sinclair

Many of the subjects covered by the free trade deals lie within provincial jurisdiction. Services industries, energy and resources, agriculture, aspects of investment, technical standards, government procurement, and provincial crown corporations are all affected.

In this chapter, Scott Sinclair examines the implications of free trade for the exercise of provincial authority. He shows how the capacity of provincial governments to act within their own constitutional spheres is constrained by the FTA and NAFTA and how the federal government, charged with ensuring the compliance of the provinces with the free trade agreements, effectively ends up policing areas of provincial constitutional jurisdiction it has surrendered in signing and implementing the trade deals.

Since the signing of the Free Trade Agreement, the ability of both levels of government, federal and provincial, to respond effectively to the needs of Canadian citizens has been significantly eroded. NAFTA threatens to impair these abilities further. Moreover, the federal government assumes power to limit provincial activities in order to make them consistent with the free trade agreements. The federal government is committed to enforce the trade deals even in areas of provincial jurisdiction. Foreign governments and the private sector also now have the ability to challenge provincial policies and programmes under dispute-settlement provisions. These new constraints are overwhelmingly biased against policies and programmes that enforce or promote social, economic, and environmental rights.

It is this shift of power away from the provinces that gives the free trade agreements their constitutional dimension.[1] The federal government has traded away significant provincial powers and usurped authority to police this surrender. The attorney general of Ontario argued in a 1988 analysis that the assumption of these rights is tantamount to a federal invasion of provincial jurisdiction.[2] It has been carried out without meaningful provincial consultation or consent and over the opposition of several provincial governments. Many existing provincial measures will need to be changed to comply with NAFTA. More importantly, NAFTA further restricts provincial policy development, reducing the flexibility required to respond to a rapidly changing economy and society.

Enforcement

As a matter of law, only the federal governments of Canada, the U.S., and Mexico are "parties" to the NAFTA. States and provinces are not bound by the agreement. However, the federal governments make commitments to enforce the agreements on subnational governments. If a provincial government does something that is not in accord with the NAFTA, the U.S. or Mexico may complain that Ottawa has not met its NAFTA obligations. The federal government is then obliged to bring the provincial measure into compliance. NAFTA, like the FTA, obliges the federal government to "ensure that all necessary measures" are taken to enforce the rules of the agreement.

As the Ontario attorney general pointed out, under the GATT the federal government has the less intrusive obligation to take "such reasonable measures as may be available" to achieve provincial compliance with the GATT rules. Canada has argued before the GATT that certain powers, technically "available" to the federal government, would not be "reasonable" in the Canadian constitutional climate.[3] The stronger provisions of the FTA and NAFTA commit the federal government to use all its powers to compel compliance, even in areas of exclusive provincial jurisdiction and without provincial consent.

The legal and political powers technically available to the federal government to enforce the FTA and NAFTA are formidable. In recent decisions, the courts have taken a broad view of the federal power to regulate international, interprovincial, and general trade affecting the whole of Canada. Where an issue is deemed essentially a matter of federally regulated trade, the federal power may absorb parts normally under provincial jurisdiction. On the other hand, although the federal government has the authority to make treaties, it has no explicit constitutional authority to implement them. In the Labour Conventions Case of 1937, the Judicial Committee of the Privy Council limited the federal power to implement treaties in areas of provincial jurisdiction. The federal government might also exercise its power of disallowance, even though this power has not been used for more than forty years. Finally, the federal government could resort to its spending power, punishing a province through fiscal measures until it agreed to comply.

With respect to standards-related measures covered under Chapter 9, Technical Barriers to Trade, NAFTA obliges federal governments to "seek, through appropriate measures, to ensure observance ... by provincial or state governments." The definitive meaning of these words will likely be established through dispute settlement. It appears to be a less intrusive obligation than "all necessary measures." Nonetheless, NAFTA goes far beyond the FTA, which excludes provinces from its technical standards provisions.[4]

National Treatment

National treatment requires that imported goods, foreign investors, and non-resident service-providers must be treated no less favourably than domestic products, investor, and service-providers. Under NAFTA Article 102, which corresponds to FTA Article 105, national treatment applies to trade in goods, services, and investment. This requirement goes well beyond current GATT rules, which apply national treatment only to trade in goods.

The obligation to provide national treatment explicitly applies to provincial measures. NAFTA Article 301 spells it out for goods; NAFTA Article 1202.2, for services; and NAFTA Article 1102.3, for investment. The wording of these articles is basically the same as FTA Article 502 for goods; FTA Article 1402.2, for services; and FTA Article 1602.4, for investment. NAFTA Article 301.2, for example, reads "The provisions ... regarding national treatment shall mean, with respect to a province or state, treatment no less favourable than the most favourable treatment accorded by such province or state to any like, directly competitive or substitutable goods, as the case may be of the Party of which it forms a part."

These provisions create the anomaly that provincial regulations may discriminate against goods, services, or investment from another province but not against those from the U.S. or Mexico. If a province treats its own residents preferentially in any matter covered by the agreement, it must give the same preference to Americans and Mexicans. In effect, American and Mexicans must be treated better than Canadians from other provinces.

The extraordinary scope of national treatment rules creates much uncertainty. It remains to be seen how these new rights for private investors and service providers will be interpreted. Since its rules generally did not apply to services and investment, the GATT provides little guidance. The definitive meaning of these provisions must await litigation and dispute settlement under NAFTA. These new rights will compel provincial governments to bargain with Canadian, American, and Mexican federal governments as well as private parties and investors over whether measures that are clearly within provincial jurisdiction conform to NAFTA rules. New provincial policy measures in areas governed by NAFTA will be inhibited by the prospect of litigation, dispute settlement, and controversy.

Dispute Settlement and Institutional Provisions

The extensive new rights created for corporations and investors are a formula for litigation and dispute settlement. This prospect alone will have a chilling effect on new provincial policy initiatives. Many specific policies are limited or prohibited by the free trade agreements. Additionally, any provincial measure may be subject to complaint under NAFTA's nullification and impairment provisions,[5] which requires that compensation be paid to those who could have reasonably expected to benefit if a government had not acted to limit their opportunity for profit.

Even though provincial measures are subject to dispute settlement and possible retaliation, neither NAFTA nor the FTA provide for provincial participation in the dispute-settlement process. Provinces do not have the right to make submissions to dispute-settlement panels, to make complaints before the North American Free Trade Commission, to request consultations with U.S. or Mexican officials, or to negotiate compliance or retaliation. Only the federal government, as party to the agreements, enjoys these rights.

Through dispute settlement, the U.S., and to a lesser extent Mexico, acquires a seat at provincial cabinet tables. New economic and social policy initiatives, arguably at odds with the trade agreements, will be subject to negotiation and arbitration with Washington, with Ottawa serving as enforcer. Ottawa's constitutional powers will be available to ensure provincial compliance to dispute-settlement decisions. Meanwhile, Ottawa's power to ensure Washington's or a state capital's compliance through retaliation against the U.S. is negligible. At the end of the day, American power to enforce panel decisions through retaliation overwhelms Canadian power.

Services

The bulk of obligations imposed in trade in services bear on provincial governments since most services fall within their jurisdiction. The basic obligation of provincial governments is to provide national treatment to U.S. and Mexican providers of covered services, which will have a significant impact on provincial ability to regulate services, including those in the social sector.

More services are covered in NAFTA than in the FTA. Certain services, "such as law enforcement, correctional services, income security or insurance, social security or insurance, social welfare, public education, public training, health and child care" may be provided by governments "in a manner that is not inconsistent with this chapter."[6] The consistency requirement qualifies this exemption. Foreign investments, even in non-covered services, are entitled to national treatment in their "establishment."

NAFTA prohibits requiring a service-provider to establish a "local presence." Since services can be provided entirely from outside the country, serious job losses may occur in sectors like data processing. This rule may also impair the ability of provincial governments to regulate services provided from offshore by non-residents. For example, the extent to which a province may require "local presence" for consumer protection or other reasons is unclear.

Under the FTA, non-resident service-providers could be treated differently if the difference was no greater than necessary for "prudential, fiduciary, health and safety and consumer protection" reasons.[7] In NAFTA, this specific exemption has been dropped. Cross-border trade in services falls under the general exemption of NAFTA Article 2101.2: "provided that such measures are not applied in a manner that would constitute a means of arbitrary or unjustifiable discrimination between countries where the same conditions prevail or a disguised restriction on trade between the Parties nothing in the [provisions applying to services] shall be construed to prevent the adoption or enforcement by any party of measures necessary to secure compliance with laws or regulations that are not inconsistent with the provisions of this Agreement, including those relating to health and safety and consumer protection." It is questionable whether this narrow and highly qualified exemption will preserve provincial capability to enforce health and safety and consumer protection.

Environmental protection is not a ground for exceptions to NAFTA in rules on services, despite the environmental importance of many service industries. For example, hazardous waste (goods) and waste management and disposal (services) are treated differently in terms of exceptions, although the environmental issues pertaining to the service and corresponding goods are virtually the same. (Similarly, pesticides are goods, but the application of pesticides is a service; lumber is a good, but forest management and reforestation are services; and so on.) The general exception applying to goods and technical barriers to trade incorporates GATT Article XX, which is clarified to include "environmental measures necessary to protect human, animal or plant life or health" and "measures relating to the conservation of non-living exhaustible natural resources."[8] Services are not covered by this general exception; they fall under the narrower exception referring only to health and safety and consumer protection.[9] This anomaly is a further example of NAFTA's failure to address environmental concerns adequately.

In another change from the FTA, the services chapter of NAFTA explicitly applies to "actions of any non-governmental body in the exercise of any regulatory, administrative or other governmental authority delegated to it" by federal, provincial, or local governments.[10] Licensing and certification, mainly provincial responsibilities, are also covered by NAFTA Article 1210.

Existing measures that do not conform to national treatment, most-favoured nation, or non-discriminatory treatment are not automatically grandparented (i.e., exempted) as they are under the FTA. Instead, the federal government must submit a list of non-conforming provincial measures to the North American Free Trade Commission within two years.[11] A list of provincial quantitative restrictions must be submitted within one year.[12] These non-conforming measures may be continued only so long as they are not made more restrictive and are promptly renewed.[13] The lists must also spell out how governments intend to bring non-conforming measures into conformity.[14] All new government measures must, of course, conform to NAFTA provisions.

Service industries are now the major source of wealth and employment in all industrialized countries. Policy flexibility is an es-

sential ingredient of successful innovation. NAFTA seriously reduces the ability of provincial governments to manage change in
these rapidly developing sectors.

Investment

Again, the basic obligation of the provinces is to accord national
treatment to American and Mexican investors, including the "establishment, acquisition, expansion, management, conduct, operation,
and sale or other disposition of investment" located within the province.[15] This provision broadens the coverage compared to FTA Article 1602, which covered only establishment, acquisition, conduct,
operation, and sale of a business.

There are additional prohibitions on performance requirements in
NAFTA beyond those already in the FTA. Regulations requiring the
export of a given level of goods, the substitution of local for imported
goods, the local sourcing of supplies, and local content rules are
precluded in the FTA. NAFTA prohibitions extend to balancing
imports and exports, foreign exchange, technology transfer, regional
trade, and world product mandating.[16] Investments may be required
to "use a technology to meet generally applicable health, safety, or
environmental standards-related measures" subject to national, most-
favoured nation, and non-discriminatory treatment.[17]

Expropriation and compensation measures have been expanded.
Rules for compensation, with respect to "direct" or "indirect" expropriation or measures "tantamount to expropriation," have been
spelled out in great detail.[18] These requirements may substantially
increase the costs to provincial governments of new public investment or public provision of services currently provided by the private
sector, for example, automobile insurance or child care.

The investment chapter provides foreign investors with direct
recourse to dispute settlement under the International Convention on
the Settlement of Investment Disputes (ICSID) and commits the
parties to respecting resulting judgements made. Individual private
investors would be able to challenge provincial policies and practices. Under GATT and the FTA, only national governments now
have that right.

The review and approval of foreign investments has been the
responsibility of the federal government. However, provincial governments are usually consulted on major investments and acquisitions within the province. Any weakening of federal powers to
review foreign investments diminishes provincial influence.

Agricultural Supply Management

Canadian dairy, egg, and poultry farmers operate under a national supply management system. Supply-managed industries produce mainly for the domestic market. Farmers produce under quota, sell through marketing boards, and receive prices based on the cost of production of an efficient operation. So long as excess production is not dumped onto the world market, supply management stabilizes world food markets otherwise characterized by high export subsidies, dumping, and cut-throat competition. This system is administered by provincial boards, and, as yet, quotas cannot be sold interprovincially. Consequently, the supply-managed industries are important components of most provincial economies.

The viability of marketing boards depends on protection from imports of both basic supply-managed commodities and food products processed from these basic inputs. NAFTA expressly permits Canada to maintain quantitative restrictions in respect of dairy, poultry, and eggs.[19] This nominal protection, however, is ineffective. The Canada–U.S. FTA left import quotas on basic commodities intact, but by removing all tariffs on primary products and processed foods, it sealed the fate of the supply-management system.

The downward spiral has already begun. As tariffs are eliminated, Canadian food processors are unable to compete with U.S. operations that purchase cheaper inputs. They either move their plants to the U.S. or push for lower prices and the dismantling of supply management. The federal government's attempts to protect supply-managed industries by placing processed food products on an import control list have run afoul of the GATT.

GATT Article XI permits import quotas on primary agricultural products for the purpose of supply management. The current Dunkel draft proposes the elimination of Article XI and the replacement of import quotas by tariffs, which would reduce by 36 per cent over six years.

Even if the proposal to eliminate Article XI can be headed off in the Uruguay Round, competitive pressure under the FTA is already forcing the erosion of supply management. Vertically integrated U.S. agribusiness and food corporations, such as Kentucky Fried Chicken and Hagen Daz, are attacking Canada's orderly marketing systems under the GATT and in continental trade negotiations. Domestic food processors are demanding changes so that they can compete with U.S. companies able to purchase cheaper U.S. inputs. While U.S.

factory farms stand to benefit from the opening of the Canadian market, the U.S. administration is resisting demands from American sugar and dairy farmers for their own form of supply management.

Supply management is vital to the viability of smaller family farms and the vitality of many rural communities. The system works reasonably well, and it is within Canada's power to maintain and strengthen it. It is a model for other countries: it could help stabilize world agricultural markets and promote staples self-sufficiency in developing countries. A diversified and viable farm community is also integral to promote environmentally sustainable farming practices. This model system is being sacrificed needlessly. U.S. agribusiness stands to gain from its destruction. Family farmers and rural communities will pay a high price.

Energy and Natural Resources

The FTA and NAFTA undermine the 1982 addition of section 92A to the constitution, which gave the provinces power to control the development, conservation, and management of natural resources. The powers of provinces under section 92A yield to paramount federal laws because a province, acting as regulator of an energy good or natural resource, is subject to federal legislation requiring it to comply with the trade agreements.

The energy chapter's proportional sharing provisions limit the ability of provinces to reserve domestic production of energy goods for local consumption. As under the FTA, if exports are restricted for conservation purposes, the U.S. and Mexico must be guaranteed the same proportion of total Canadian supply as they used in the most recent thirty-six-month period. For example, many provinces have long-term export contracts with the U.S. If domestic demand grows by the end of these contracts, the ability of provinces to cut back exports to serve the increased domestic demand will be restricted. The growth in domestic demand will have to be met by increasing production or outbidding the Americans for our own energy. Ironically, Mexico gained an exemption from these proportional sharing provisions.[20]

The proportional sharing provisions, together with restrictions on export quotas, minimum export prices,[21] and export taxes,[22] trap Canadians on an export treadmill. The financial and environmental costs of energy production are a mounting concern in most provinces. Provincial governments could not impose a minimum price or an extraction fee in order to internalize the environmental or social costs of energy production. Under NAFTA rules, these costs and the environmental damage accompanying energy production must be borne by provincial utilities, local residents, and Canadian taxpayers, while U.S. consumers reap the benefits.

Many provinces require that provincial energy needs be satisfied before export sales are permitted. In a period of energy shortage or of renewed conservation efforts, such requirements could be challenged as a quantitative restriction under the FTA or NAFTA.

National treatment prevents Canadian governments from requiring preferential treatment for Canadian resources over American or Mexican. Unlike the FTA, which was based on GATT Article III and does not apply to government purchases, NAFTA rules extend to crown corporations. NAFTA Article 1502, Monopolies and State Enterprises, goes beyond the corresponding FTA Article 2010, constraining the activities of provincial crown corporations. NAFTA Annex 1505.1 specifically includes provincial crown corporations in the definition of state enterprises. So, for example, a provincial public utility would be prevented from buying Canadian resources in preference to American or Mexican.

NAFTA restrictions pose the same difficulties for conserving non-renewable, or potentially renewable, natural resources as for conserving energy. Chapter 3, National Treatment and Market Access for Goods, prohibits export taxes[23] and minimum prices and applies proportional sharing provisions to trade in goods, including resources.[24] These restrictions, and the parallel provisions governing energy, severely constrain the ability of Canadian governments to conserve natural resources or relieve domestic shortages. Even in an emergency, Canadian policy will be unable to favour Canadian over other North American consumers. The FTA was expected, by phasing out U.S. tariffs on processed goods, to encourage higher value-added processing of Canadian resources prior to export. U.S. trade actions, however, have produced the opposite effect. (See Chapter 10, this volume.)

In the 1992 softwood lumber countervailing duty case, the U.S. Department of Commerce (DOC) ruled that British Columbia's restrictions on raw log exports were a countervailable subsidy. The DOC held that federal and provincial log export restrictions artificially inflate domestic supply, lowering the price.

Applying U.S. countervailing duty law to export restrictions greatly broadens the U.S. definition of subsidy. The DOC, by its own admission, overturned a longstanding and consistent administrative practice that export restrictions did not confer countervailable benefits. The legal reversal confirms that U.S. trading partners cannot rely upon past practice as a guide to future rulings. U.S. trade remedies are flexible enough to provide import relief, as required, to powerful domestic interests.

Furthermore, Article 1203(b) of the FTA explicitly exempts "controls by Canada on the export of logs of all species" from the general prohibition of export restrictions and taxes in the agreement. Even this specific exemption, directly negotiated with the U.S., did not prevent the countervail of B.C.'s log export controls. In a brief footnote, the DOC dismissed the clause, stating that "the Department's determination to countervail B.C.'s log export restrictions does not prohibit B.C. from continuing to implement and enforce these restrictions; the Department is merely imposing a countervailing duty to offset the countervailable benefit enjoyed by the B.C. softwood lumber producers."

The countervailing of log export controls shows that even express and specific FTA safeguards are of limited value. Under the agreement, U.S. trade laws, "including relevant statutes, legislative history, regulations, administrative practices, and judicial precedents," continue to apply to Canadian exports. The U.S. can amend its trade remedy laws without Canada's consent. If a new trade law or amendment specifies Canada, then it will apply.[25] Moreover, section 102 of the U.S. implementing act states that the laws of the U.S. are to prevail in a conflict with the FTA. As the DOC concluded in the 1992 softwood lumber ruling, "nothing in the FTA precludes the Department from applying the U.S. countervailing duty law against a countervailable [Canadian] program."

Conclusions

NAFTA seriously weakens the ability of provincial governments to meet the needs of their residents. The FTA and NAFTA give the federal governments of Canada, the U.S., and now Mexico, as well as the North American corporate sector, new levers to influence Canadian provincial governments. This influence will ratchet down policies and programmes that enforce and promote social, economic, and environmental rights.

Although NAFTA has been negotiated without meaningful provincial involvement and over the objections of several provincial governments and although provincial governments are also excluded from the dispute-settlement process (which will be crucial in defining the exact meaning and extent of NAFTA's provisions), the provinces do have options. Provincial governments can make it clear to the U.S. and Mexico that they will not be bound by an agreement to which they were not a party, that they will not implement NAFTA obligations, and that they will strenuously resist federal efforts to force provincial compliance. The U.S. has repeatedly stated that provincial compliance is crucial to the gains it hopes to secure through free trade deals. If several provincial governments, representing a significant portion of Canadian economic activity, were to take these actions, the U.S. and Mexico might reconsider their support for the agreement. Furthermore, if provincial governments were to implement measures, for example, trade-related industrial policy measures, that did not conform to NAFTA, they would send a strong message that the provinces would not be bound by the agreement.

Section IV
The Continental Outlook

_____

Chapter 17

Why Mexico?

Bob White

*For Canada, NAFTA mainly represents a major renegotiation
of the FTA. But the inclusion of Mexico in a new trilateral
accord will also have an impact on the Canadian economy.*

*In this chapter, Bob White shows that for the corporations
that pushed for the agreement, Mexico is attractive as a site for
low-wage production of standardized industrial goods. In addition to the Canadian and U.S. job losses that will result from
production shifts to Mexico, the potential for such shifts will
exert a downward pressure on wages. Indeed, the prospects are
that wages and working conditions in all three countries could
be adversely affected. This chapter is adapted from a brief
presented by Bob White on behalf of the Canadian Labour
Congress to the Sub-Committee on International Trade of the
House of Commons Standing Committee on External Affairs
and International Trade.*

From the perspective of the mainly U.S.-based transnationals and the
Bush administration, by far the dominant forces in the shaping of the
agreement, NAFTA is more about increasing the international competitiveness of U.S. corporations than it is about trade. Expanded
access to the Mexican market is *not* the major concern.

To be sure, NAFTA does dismantle some significant Mexican
trade barriers, such as the trade-balancing auto decree, and some U.S.
and even Canadian companies will certainly gain from the further
"opening up" of the Mexican market provided by NAFTA. However,
trade between Mexico, on the one hand, and the U.S. and Canada,

on the other, is already largely "free" of trade barriers. (The average Mexican tariff has been cut from 24 per cent in 1986 to less than 10 per cent today, Mexico has recently joined GATT, and it has eliminated a previously comprehensive system of import licensing and import quotas.)

Even if there were significant problems in terms of access, the fact of the matter is that the Mexican domestic market is small. Mexico has almost one-quarter of the North American population, but it accounts for just one twenty-fifth of the North American market — about the same share as Ontario. Income per person is about one-eighth of the Canadian level, and huge inequalities in the distribution of income mean that the market for many consumer goods is even smaller than that figure would suggest.

The real business objective is not to sell in the Mexican market but to take advantage of low Mexican wages and weak Mexican social and environmental standards to become more cost competitive in the U.S. and Canadian market and in global markets.

First, and most importantly, transnational corporations (TNCs) want to "lock in" the economic "liberalization" that has taken place under President Salinas. NAFTA guarantees U.S. companies "national treatment" in Mexico (i.e., guarantees of non-discrimination), prohibits any return to close regulation of foreign investment and foreign trade, and would provide effective security against any threat of future nationalization.

Second, U.S. TNCs want NAFTA to ensure continued secure access to the U.S. market from production facilities relocated to Mexico. Seen from this perspective, the NAFTA would allow more U.S. productive capacity to be relocated to Mexico without fear of restrictive trade measures being taken by the U.S. Congress. It is precisely for this reason that NAFTA, quite unlike the FTA, is such a contentious domestic issue in the U.S.

The central argument of U.S. manufacturing companies engaged in standardized mass production is that they need to relocate production to Mexico and take advantage of the major cost savings to be found there to maintain and increase their share of U.S. and global markets, recapturing markets lost to low-wage-based imports from the newly industrializing countries (NICs). U.S. TNCs are generally oriented towards regaining international competitiveness through cost reduction strategies as opposed to heavy investment in skills training and technological innovation.

Certainly, many U.S. companies have decided that low wages are essential to the achievement of competitiveness in the production of standardized industrial goods. NAFTA — the formal annexation of Mexico as a low-wage production zone for U.S. business — can thus be seen as the culmination of the longstanding tendency of U.S. TNCs to relocate standardized, relatively low-skill production to less developed countries.

The relocation of U.S. production to Mexico until now has mainly taken place under the special terms and conditions of the "maquiladora" programme. Under this programme, U.S. components imported into Mexico for assembly, or sub-assembly, in maquiladora plants are admitted duty free, and U.S. tariffs are imposed only on the value added in Mexico when the assembled product is subsequently exported from the Mexican plants to the U.S.[1] In many cases, products assembled in Mexico are shipped to twin U.S. plants for further assembly. Introduced in the 1960s, the maquiladora programme expanded very rapidly from the mid-1980s and led to major industrialization of the border region. As of 1990, there were almost 2,000 maquiladora plants employing 470,000 workers. These plants accounted for $12 billion of exports to the U.S. in 1989, concentrated in textiles and apparel, electronic components, and autos and auto parts. Maquiladora plants account for 80 per cent of Mexican manufactured exports to the U.S. and 40 per cent of total Mexican exports to the U.S.[2] The majority of maquiladora plants are U.S. owned or controlled, and most of the largest U.S. industrial corporations have a substantial presence in the maquiladora. There is also a significant Mexican-owned presence.

Between 1985 and 1990, foreign direct investment in Mexico doubled to $30 billion, with about two-thirds of the increase coming from the U.S. Employment in the maquiladora plants grew by about 50,000 jobs per year over this period, and the original maquiladora base, centred on low-skill, labour-intensive operations, has grown to include more sophisticated industrial activities. There has been particularly strong growth in the production of auto parts, and GM has become the largest employer in Mexico. Export-oriented non-maquiladora plants have also grown, particularly in the auto sector. The most prominent example is the Ford assembly plant in Hermosillo, which exports Escorts and Tracers. There are also several export-oriented modern auto engine plants in northern Mexico.

Canadian direct investment in Mexico has been modest to date, totalling $486 million, or less than 2 per cent of total foreign direct

Table 17–1

**EMPLOYMENT OF MANUFACTURING PRODUCTION
WORKERS IN NORTH AMERICA BY U.S.-OWNED
CORPORATIONS (Thousands)**

	Canada	Mexico	United States
1988	483	397	13,221
1989	476	444	13,269
1990	452	463	12,974
Change 1988-90	-6.4%	+16.6%	-1.9%

Source: R. Blecker and W. Spriggs, *Manufacturing Employment in North America* Economic Policy Institute. Washington D.C., 1992

investment in Mexico.[3] Such investment appears to be increasing. For example, Magna International has a plant operating in Mexico.

In a growing number of cases, Canadian layoffs can be directly linked to production shifts to Mexico, particularly in relatively low-value-added auto parts production (e.g., Bendix Safety Restraints, Fleck, Custom Trim, the Woodbridge Group, Sheller Globe). In other cases, the linkage to Canadian job losses is more indirect. For example, the pending closure of Ford Canada's Niagara Glass Plant is not unrelated to the opening of a plant in Juarez, Mexico.

As shown in Table 17–1, total employment of manufacturing production workers in Mexico by U.S. affiliates grew by 66,000 or 16.6 per cent between 1986 and 1990 alone. This increase does not include workers in Mexican companies doing work effectively contracted out by U.S.-based parent companies. Over this same period, U.S. affiliate employment in Canada was cut by 31,000, or 6.4 per cent, and U.S. industrial employment fell by 1.9 per cent. Expansion of the maquiladora has been driven primarily by the needs of U.S. TNCs and their junior business partners in Mexico and has contributed little to the development of the Mexican economy. Since few inputs are purchased in Mexico and since most of the production is exported after crude assembly, the major "benefit" to Mexico is employment at very low wages. Often this employment is of short duration. Appalling working conditions, lack of enforcement of health and safety standards, and environmental contamination result in high rates of labour turnover. Until very recently, there was little or no beneficial transfer of technology and skills to Mexico.

Production Shifts

By removing any underlying fears of a return to economic nationalism, NAFTA would lead to an even greater shift of U.S. and, to a lesser extent, Canadian production to Mexico.

The attraction of Mexico as a production site for at least relatively low-skill, relatively labour-intensive manufacturing boils down to low wages — although low taxes, nonenforcement of environmental standards, and other factors also play a role. As of 1990, average wages in manufacturing in Mexico were just US$1.80 per hour compared to $14.77 per hour in the U.S. and $16.02 in Canada (U.S. Bureau of Labor Statistics). Curiously, the Canadian Department of Finance economic assessment of NAFTA uses 1989 data and exchange rates — understating the wage gap considerably.

Proponents of NAFTA argue that U.S. and Canadian workers should not worry about the huge gap because Mexican levels of labour productivity are quite low. While it is true that high labour productivity in the U.S. and Canada can offset the competitive advantage of low wages, it is nonetheless the case that more and more production is likely to shift to Mexico under the terms and conditions of NAFTA, looking at the issue solely from the point of view of production costs.

The Department of Finance economic study of NAFTA is particularly misleading.[4] While it notes that Canadian wages in manufacturing are 7.5 times higher than in Mexico, it argues that this gap is largely offset by the fact that a Canadian worker's productivity — output per hour worked — is 6.5 times greater. Combining the two factors, we are told that wages adjusted for productivity are "just" 18 per cent higher. This 18 per cent is itself a significant figure. But it understates the true position considerably. The appropriate comparison is clearly not between the productivity of the Mexican economy as a whole and the productivity of the Canadian economy as a whole, the measure used by the department. After all, a very large proportion of the Mexican labour force is engaged in very low productivity sectors (subsistence agriculture and the so-called informal sector in the cities), which have absolutely nothing to do with foreign trade. Nor is the appropriate comparison even between manufacturing sectors, given the fact that Mexican industry outside the maquiladoras is overwhelmingly oriented to the domestic market.

The comparison that has to be made is that between actual and potential productivity levels in those sectors that are in direct competition. Here the picture is very different.

Data in the 1992 U.S. Economic Policy Institute study by Blecker and Spriggs show that as long ago as 1984, Mexican productivity (value added per worker) was 83 per cent of U.S. levels in electronic equipment assembly and 57 per cent of the U.S. level in transportation equipment. Background studies for the U.S. Congress by Harley Shaiken of the University of California found that productivity levels in export-oriented auto engine plants in Mexico approach U.S. levels, and the Ford assembly plant in Hermosillo is generally deemed to be at least as efficient as modern U.S. and Canadian auto assembly plants. Ford, Chrysler, and Volkswagen are significant exporters of vehicles from Mexico to the U.S. and Canada.

Summarizing the situation, the 1992 study by the U.S. Congress Office of Technology Assessment *U.S.–Mexico Trade* noted that "over the past decade new plants operated by multinational corporations have demonstrated levels of productivity and quality equal to those in the United States. High performance islands of excellence in Mexico's largely inefficient manufacturing sector span significantly more than simple assembly operations. They include, for example, world-class auto engine and stamping plants."[5]

The fact of the matter is that there is no compelling reason why increasingly sophisticated manufacturing operations cannot be shifted to Mexico, over at least the medium term. To be sure, the major production shifts will continue to be in relatively labour-intensive activities, such as apparel and electronic assembly, but the rapid growth of Mexican auto assembly and auto engine production demonstrates the potential for the shift of more sophisticated, higher value added operations.

Astonishingly, the standard economic assessments of the impacts of NAFTA upon Canada (and the U.S.) exclude even the possibility of a significant shift in investment and production. These studies look only at the effects of the removal of tariffs, which means that they always come up with comforting "win win" outcomes. Yet, the reality of the past few years has clearly been one of major job gains in the export-oriented manufacturing industries of Mexico at the more or less direct expense of more labour-intensive manufacturing operations in the U.S. and Canada.

The standard studies also conjure away the potential for job losses — as opposed to job shifts between industries — because they simply assume full employment, notwithstanding the high unemployment rates in all three countries.

It is no simple matter to judge the potential for direct job shifts from Canada to Mexico, and any quantitative estimate should be treated with scepticism. That said, it can be noted that the available U.S. studies that have attempted to quantify the impacts on the basis of modelling the impacts of likely shifts of investment come up with an estimated potential U.S. job loss of about 500,000 high-wage jobs over the next decade. (Studies have been surveyed by W.E. Spriggs of the Economic Policy Institute.)

It is not unreasonable to believe that Canadian manufacturing job losses could be roughly proportional, given the close integration of many manufacturing sectors, particularly the auto sector, and given that job losses in U.S. industries would have important second round spillover effects upon Canadian industries. In terms of specific sectors, the most immediately threatened are auto parts — because of the growing presence of the Big Three and suppliers in Mexico — electronic assembly, and apparel. In the last, Canada will be at a particular disadvantage because the NAFTA will further speed up the loss of labour-intensive operations and, simultaneously, because the U.S.-biased "yarn forward" rules of origin will erode the competitive position of Canadian manufacturers producing high quality goods from imported fabrics.

Nevertheless, putting the focus on job losses risks misses the nature of the economic impacts of the addition of a very low-wage region on an integrated free trade area. Even in sectors where jobs may not be lost in large numbers, the potential for production to move to Mexico will exert a major downward effect upon wages. Again, this issue has been all but unexplored in Canada, but in the U.S. even the studies of NAFTA produced by the administration conceded that workers with less than a high school education would suffer wage losses.

Even the most optimistic scenarios of the economic impacts of NAFTA anticipate job losses and wage erosion for relatively unskilled workers, further increasing the tremendous inequalities in the distribution of income that developed in the 1980s in both the U.S. and Canada, partly as a consequence of increased exposure to international trade. In both countries, workers displaced from industries vulnerable to competition from low-wage countries have suffered large income losses even when they have found new jobs, and labour adjustment and training programmes have been grossly inadequate to the task of moving displaced workers to such new jobs as have been created.

"Win Win"

Honest advocates of NAFTA concede that it will lead to significant job losses in industries vulnerable to low-wage competition. However, they say that these job losses will be offset by job gains. In the first place, as certain kinds of production are moved to Mexico, the Mexican demand for sophisticated capital goods and equipment will increase, which will lead to an increase in Mexican imports from the U.S. and Canada. In the second place, an expanding Mexican economy will increase the size of the whole North American market.

The first argument is true to a point. Despite a major net shift of U.S. and Canadian manufacturing jobs to Mexico in recent years, American companies have indeed been exporting a lot of capital machinery and equipment and a range of services to Mexico, with the result that the balance of trade is running heavily in favour of the U.S. That said, at some point the balance can be expected to change as the new machinery and equipment being installed in Mexico is used to produce goods for export back to the U.S. and as the Mexican ability to compete in more sophisticated sectors increases.

Even more disturbing, this argument for "win win" outcomes from complementary "win win" trade does not hold true for Canada. The merest glance at the trade data shows that Canada's "comparative advantage" overall is not in capital goods and sophisticated services. We run a huge trade deficit with the U.S. and with Mexico in such areas. Indeed, Mexico exports to Canada six times the value of machinery and equipment exported by Canada to Mexico (1990 data).[6] Therefore, any increase in Mexican demand for sophisticated goods and services brought about by NAFTA will be disproportionately result in an increase in U.S. rather than Canadian exports. Some Canadian companies, such as Northern Telecom and Bombardier, both now active in Mexico, may benefit, but the overwhelming probability is that any job gains will not begin to offset the likely job losses. This scenario is all the more likely to come true because Canada and Mexico are in direct competition to serve the U.S. market in some key sectors, notably auto.

With respect to the second argument, it is unlikely that even a major shift of standardized industrial production to Mexico will result in a major increase in Mexican wages and living standards, given the nature of the NAFTA agreement.

Low Mexican wages are the result of massive unemployment, itself partly the product of the debt crisis of the 1980s, and of a deliberate development strategy. Mexican "restructuring" in response to that crisis — which remains far from resolved with the post-Brady Plan foreign debt still totalling in excess of $100 billion — led to real wage cuts of 40 per cent in the 1980s. Low wages were in turn used to attract the maquiladora industries serving the U.S. and Canadian market.

Given that the whole Mexican "liberal" development strategy is built upon low-wage-based exports, it is highly unlikely that the Mexican authorities would welcome significant improvements in wages in the export sector, even though they are more than justified by productivity. In fact, the Mexican government has strongly resisted the growth of independent unions and has used the "official" trade union movement, an integral part of the governing party, to control wages in line with national policy. In the summer of 1992, the government sanctioned a threat by Volkswagen of Mexico to fire all of its workers at the Puebla plant if they did not repudiate an independent union.

NAFTA does absolutely nothing to secure recognition of basic labour and democratic rights in Mexico. Yet, such rights are essential if Mexican workers are to gain from increased economic integration. Labour rights — which exist on paper but are largely denied in practice — must be respected if a free and independent trade union movement is to develop to deal with often grossly exploitative employers. Democratic rights — effectively denied under the quasi-dictatorship of the PRI, which is widely recognized to rig elections — are needed if social conditions and the quality of the environment are to be improved.

NAFTA works against the improvement of Mexican labour and social standards in other critical ways. The "free market" model embodied in NAFTA demands of the Mexicans that they dismantle trade and investment "barriers" that currently maintain jobs and incomes, albeit at low levels. For example, the U.S. successfully demanded that Mexico progressively dismantle barriers to U.S. agricultural exports, a measure that will ultimately result in the displacement of as many as two million Mexican farmers growing wheat and corn on small, very labour-intensive landholdings. The transfer of agricultural production from labour-intensive Mexico to hugely capital-intensive U.S. agribusiness will result in a massive rural exodus, swelling the huge numbers of unemployed and underemployed Mexican workers in the cities. A similar process will play itself out in the hitherto quite highly protected domestic-market-oriented manufacturing sector, which is labour intensive and ill placed to compete with much more capital-intensive production in the U.S. For example, huge layoffs are now taking place in the Mexican textile industry.

The key point is that the scenario of job shifts from the U.S. and Canada to Mexico in some sectors does not add up to net gains for Mexico. Indeed, the prospect is for a "lose lose lose" outcome in which wages and working conditions are lowered in the U.S. and Canada, while wages and working conditions continue to deteriorate in Mexico as the domestic economy is dramatically restructured under NAFTA rules. As this happens, the North American market as a whole — the market sustained by the wages of working people — could shrink rather than expand.

The underlying contradiction of the "free market" international competitiveness model embodied in NAFTA is that socially unregulated competition between high-wage and low-wage countries will drive down the wages needed to sustain the market in the high-wage country, which is itself needed to drive the productive capacity transferred to the low-wage country. The unregulated ability of business to shift production to take advantage of lower wages thus ultimately rebounds back on business as a loss of the market.

Chapter 18

The Enterprise for the Americas

John Dillon

NAFTA is part of a wider U.S. initiative for the Americas. Eventually, most of the hemisphere could be included under the NAFTA umbrella.

In this chapter, John Dillon outlines the origins of the Enterprise for the Americas project. He examines progress to date in the light of a change of administration in the U.S. and shows the implications of the initiative for countries that eventually join NAFTA under the accession clause.

President George Bush announced the Enterprise for the Americas Initiative (EAI) on 27 June 1990. The announcement came just two weeks after President Bush and President Salinas de Gortari of Mexico initiated the process of negotiating a North American Free Trade Agreement (NAFTA). The EAI was the product of a comprehensive review of U.S. economic policy towards Latin America and the Caribbean under the leadership of U.S. Treasury Secretary Nicholas Brady.

President Bill Clinton reiterated his support for the EAI on several occasions, both before and after his election.[1]

The EAI has three parts:

1. creation of a hemispheric free trade zone;
2. promotion of private investment; and
3. renegotiation of official debts owed to the U.S. government, including provisions for "debt-for-nature" swaps.

Hemispheric Free Trade Zone

Extending the terms of the NAFTA to other countries of the Americas is, without doubt, the most significant part of the EAI. However, it is a misnomer to think of NAFTA or the EAI as primarily trade initiatives. NAFTA provisions affecting investment policy, intellectual property rights, natural resource exploitation, and other aspects of national sovereignty are far more significant than the lowering of trade barriers. U.S. tariffs on most Latin American exports are not significant. The average tariff faced by Latin exporters to the U.S. is only 2 per cent, since many raw materials enter duty free.[2]

President Bush's speech combined rhetoric about looking forward to "a free trade zone stretching from the port of Anchorage to the Tierra del Fuego" with realism: "changes so far-reaching may take years of preparation and tough negotiations."[3]

The speech mentioned only some of the steps on the road towards a continental free trade zone:

* completion of the multilateral Uruguay Round of negotiations under the GATT;
* negotiation of a free trade agreement with Mexico; and
* negotiation of bilateral framework agreements between the United States and Latin American and Caribbean nations that are not yet ready to participate in a full free trade agreement.

Not explicitly mentioned in the Bush speech, but central to the EAI, is the fact that NAFTA and all future trade agreements are designed to extend precedents set in the Canada–U.S. Free Trade Agreement. Similarly, Bush did not say that before other countries are deemed eligible for membership in a Pan-American trade zone, they must first comply with significant preconditions, including changes to investment and intellectual property laws.

Promotion of Private Investment

The EAI proposes two new funds administered by the Inter-American Development Bank (IDB). The first is a *loan fund* for nations that take significant steps to remove impediments to foreign direct investment.

The second is a five-year US$1.5 billion *Multilateral Investment Fund* (MIF) that would provide up to US$300 million a year in grants to countries undertaking market-oriented investment reforms and privatization. The grants would be allocated for technical assistance, human resource development, and enterprise development. President Bush pledged to contribute US$100 million a year to the MIF and to seek matching amounts from Japan and the European Community (EC). As of October 1992, the U.S. Congress had not approved any funds for the MIF. Japan has pledged US$500 million over five years conditional on U.S. congressional approval.[4] The U.S. is also seeking funds from South Korea and Taiwan. The EC has pledged half the amount requested. In June 1991, the Canadian ambassador to the Organization of American States said Canada would contribute an unspecified amount.

Debt Relief

The EAI builds on the March 1989 initiative sponsored by Treasury Secretary Nicholas Brady to relieve less developed countries' external debts. The "Brady Plan" involves the voluntary renegotiation of commercial debts between private banks and debtor country governments willing to undertake strict Structural Adjustment Programs (SAPs) monitored by the International Monetary Fund (IMF) or the World Bank.

Like the Brady Plan, eligibility for debt relief under the EAI is conditional. Beneficiaries must either have in place or be making significant progress towards SAPs. In addition, countries must also have in place major investment reforms or be in the process of adopting an open investment regime. Countries with large commercial debts must also have "a satisfactory financing program" negotiated with their private creditors.

The EAI complements the Brady Plan by offering some relief on official debts owed to U.S. government agencies. As of June 1990 Official Development Assistance loans to the region were worth US$5.3 billion and Public Law 480, "Food for Peace," loans totalled US$1.7 billion. Thus, total concessional loans eligible for reduction amounted to US$7 billion, which is equivalent to only 2 per cent of the total debts owed by Latin American and Caribbean governments. Commercial loans worth US$4.7 billion owed to the Commodity Credit Corporation and the Export-Import Bank may become eligible for debt-for-equity or debt-for-nature swaps under a separate EAI facility.

For the larger Latin countries, the amounts eligible for debt relief are insignificant compared to their substantial debts to private lending institutions. However, for some smaller countries, such as Honduras, El Salvador, and Jamaica, official loans from the U.S. government account for a large proportion of their total foreign debts.

Debt-for-Nature Swaps

The EAI goes beyond the Brady Plan by including provisions for converting some debts into funding for environmental programmes, popularly know as "debt-for-nature swaps." In these cases, debts would be owed in U.S. dollars. Interest payments at concessional rates would be paid in local currency into an "Environmental Fund" if the country has negotiated an Environmental Framework Agreement with the U.S. government. If a country has not signed such an agreement, interest must be paid in U.S. dollars into a U.S. government account.

These agreements establish *local "administrating bodies"* that would allocate grants that link environmental protection with local community development. These bodies are to be composed of:

* one or more U.S. government nominees;
* one or more beneficiary country government nominees; and
* a majority grouping composed of citizens of the beneficiary country representing nongovernmental organizations involved in environmental and community development projects and scientific or academic institutions.

An *Enterprise for the Americas Board*, composed of nine members appointed by the president, is also to be established. Five members will be officers or employees of the U.S. government, and four will be representatives of "private, non-governmental, environmental, scientific, and academic organizations with experience and expertise" in the region. The principal responsibilities of the board would be to advise the secretary of state on negotiations for environmental framework agreements, identify potential candidates for administrating bodies, and review programmes, operations, and audits of each administrating body.

Some U.S. environmental organizations have contended that the debt-for-nature swaps are a device to divide the environmental movement by offering financing for projects in return for support for the administration's policies. *A top official of the U.S. Environmental Protection Agency candidly told a group of ecologists that they should understand that the EAI is geared foremost to the leveraging of changes in macro-economic management rather than to environmental protection.*[5]

Awaiting Congressional Approval

The Bush administration had difficulty obtaining approval from Congress for portions of the EAI. Some measures, such as the establishment of the first Inter-American Development Bank loan fund mentioned above, can be set up without congressional approval since they do not require any new fiscal appropriations. Of the measures requiring congressional approval for new spending, only debt reduction for loans made under the "Food for Peace" programme were approved by Congress in 1991. The legislation allows for the reduction of debts and payment of interest on the remainder in local currencies into environmental trust funds. Chile, Bolivia, and Jamaica have signed agreements to reduce their PL-480 debts by the following amounts:

Chile: US$16 million of US$39 million PL-480 debts

Bolivia: US$30 million of US$38 million PL-480 debts

Jamaica: US$217 million of US$271 million PL-480 debts

Important parts of the EAI have been held up by Congress. A bill authorizing reduction of U.S. A.I.D. loans passed the House of Representatives, but it did not pass the Senate Foreign Relations Committee because it was preoccupied with the Persian Gulf War.

Under the U.S. Federal Credit Reform Act, any official debt relief programme established after fiscal year 1991 must include appropriated funds to cover foregone debt payments. The House Foreign Affairs Committee authorized US$242 million to fund EAI debt relief programmes in fiscal 1992, but the House Appropriations Committee tried to reduce the amount to only $65 million. The Bush administration then reapplied for the full amount as part of its 1993 budget submission.

In October 1992, the House of Representatives approved a bill authorizing Latin American debtors to repurchase up to 40 per cent of their debts owed under the export credit guarantee programme of the Commodity Credit Corporation (CCC).[6] The debt would be bought back at discounted rates prevailing on the secondary market. For example, Brazilian debt owed to the CCC was selling for 37 cents on the dollar in mid-1992, while Mexican debt fetched 80 per cent of its face value. US$500 million of the $1.4 billion owed by nine Latin American and Caribbean countries to the CCC would be eligible for the programme.

Beneficiaries are required to spend either the equivalent of 40 per cent of the repurchased debt in local currency or the difference between the repurchased price of the loan and the total face value of the loan on approved environmental projects. The programme would only be available to countries signing environmental framework agreements with the United States. In the case of Mexico, the government would have to give priority to environmental and infrastructure projects along the Mexico–U.S. border.

Parallel Accords

During the election campaign, Bill Clinton said he would not seek to renegotiate NAFTA.[7] But he did pledge action on three parallel agreements. One would set up "an environmental protection commission with substantial powers ... to stop pollution." A second commission would cover what Clinton calls "worker standards and safety." A third agreement would enable countries to take action against sudden surges in imports. Clinton's October 4, 1992 campaign speech in North Carolina skated over the difficulties involved in negotiating parallel agreements on these matters without changing the wording of NAFTA, which already includes some environmental and emergency safeguard measures.

Given the need to first negotiate the parallel accords, the process of submitting NAFTA implementing legislation for approval in the U.S. is more complicated than it was for the FTA. Congress must engage in a series of hearings, mock mark-ups of draft implementing legislation, and a House-Senate conference before Clinton formally presents the legislation for a "fast track" vote.[8]

Preconditions for Joining NAFTA

As of January 1992, the United States had signed thirty framework agreements with Latin American and Caribbean governments. Only Cuba, Haiti, and Surinam have not been included. Six similar agreements have also been signed with members of the Association of South East Asian Nations. ASEAN is comprised of Brunei, Malaysia, Indonesia, the Philippines, Singapore, and Thailand. At ASEAN meetings held in July 1992, both U.S. and Canadian officials "floated the idea of future linkages" with NAFTA.[9] These framework treaties are more declarations of intent than actual agreements. They make no binding commitments, but they do signal an intention to pursue further negotiations. The Latin American Economic System (SELA — a research and advisory body set up by Latin American governments) characterizes the framework agreements as "essentially consultative mechanisms that do not imply or oblige a trade agreement."[10] The first of these framework agreements was signed with Mexico on November 6, 1987, just one month after the preliminary transcript of the Canada–U.S. FTA was initialled by trade ministers. The framework agreement was immediately followed by a Mexico–U.S. understanding on subsidies and countervailing duties. The Mexican framework agreement set the tone for the other agreements that followed.

Although they differ in detail, each framework agreement typically follows a common three-part format:

- A lengthy preamble lists principles, such as mutual friendship, co-operation within GATT, intent to lower tariff and non-tariff barriers to trade, recognition of the role of private investment, importance of adequate protection for intellectual property rights, and respect for labour rights.
- Each establishes a bilateral Council on Trade and Investment composed of trade ministers with participation from the private sector.
- Each deals with other outstanding bilateral issues or with issues of particular bilateral interest in an annex. For example, the Colombian and Honduran annexes refer to the International Coffee Agreement, and the Chilean annex refers to trade in minerals.

There are unique elements in some of the agreements. For example, the U.S.–Chile Framework Agreement explicitly refers to extracting natural resources in a manner consistent with environmental protection. While this agreement was a diplomatic step on the way towards opening up of negotiations for accession to NAFTA, much more significant were the commitments Chile made to change its foreign investment laws. Chile pledged to open its copper and transportation sectors to foreign investment, to sign international tax and investment agreements, and to pass a law ratifying the use of an international dispute mechanism to arbitrate disputes involving foreign investors.[11] These changes made Chile eligible for a loan from the IDB and reduction of its PL-480 loans from the U.S. government.

Bilateral Investment Treaties and Intellectual Property Rights

Although framework agreements may have a formal symbolic value, various spokespersons for the Bush and Clinton administrations have made it clear that eligibility for accession to NAFTA is dependent on countries meeting other, more concrete criteria. Former U.S. Trade Representative Carla Hills insisted that bilateral investment treaties that formalize and make binding commitments with respect to investment and intellectual property rights are necessary steps before countries can progress toward free trade negotiations.[12] *Inside U.S. Trade* (2 October 1992) reports that "The U.S. already requires a commitment to intellectual property protection as a condition for trade preferences offered under the GSP [General System of Preferences] and CBI [Caribbean Basin Initiative] and the Administration is pressing for similar commitments under the EAI."

With regard to intellectual property rights, the U.S. is proposing bilateral treaties that go beyond Chapter 17 of NAFTA in several respects. For example, the U.S. wants all kinds of life forms — including biological processes, plants, animals, genetic material, and even discoveries derived from the human body — to be treated as patentable private property. Furthermore, the U.S. wants to restrict the licensing of generic medicines to national emergencies or to remedying adjudicated violations of competition laws. The draft bilateral treaties seek concessions the U.S. did not win from Canada and Mexico in NAFTA.

On November 20, 1992, Argentina became the first country to sign a comprehensive bilateral investment treaty with the United States as part of the EAI. The treaty allows for international arbitration of investment disputes, sets standards for compensation in the event of the expropriation of private investments, and allows profits to be taken freely out of the country.

Former U.S. Deputy Assistant Secretary of Commerce for East Asia and the Pacific, Franklin Lavin, identified three criteria countries will have to meet if they wish to join "a U.S. led free trade area":

- opening markets in goods and services
- removing barriers to investment, and
- safeguarding intellectual property.[13]

Lavin spoke about eventually incorporating countries engaging in 40 per cent of world trade in a "GATT-plus" U.S.-led free trade area. He said that the idea of extending NAFTA to Asian countries has not been formally broached with Canada and Mexico and that Australia, Hong Kong, New Zealand, Singapore, and Taiwan are the most likely candidates for joining NAFTA. He also held out the possibility of an agreement linking ASEAN as a whole to NAFTA.

When the Lavin speech aroused concern in Japan, Deputy U.S. Trade Representative Michael Moskow hastily denied that the Bush administration had identified any Latin American or Asian countries, other than Chile, as candidates for accession.[14] Moskow did say, however, that the U.S. would likely use five criteria in deciding whether to enter into new free trade negotiations. Prospective partners must be willing to open markets in goods, and in services, to open investment regimes, to protect intellectual property rights, and to make transparent any informal barriers to trade. Moskow said that while NAFTA would provide the basic "structure and framework" for future agreements, it still remains to be worked out whether elements of the NAFTA would be renegotiated or whether other countries would simply dock on to the NAFTA.[15]

In a May 1993 speech to the Council of the Americas, an influential business group chaired by David Rockefeller, the new U.S. trade representative, Mickey Kantor, revealed how the Clinton administration is pursuing a two-track strategy in its dealings with other Latin American countries. "We will proceed by expanding the NAFTA through accession or bilateral agreements [with] the countries of Central and South America," Kantor pledged. He affirmed that the U.S. is already committed to negotiations with Chile.

For other countries Kantor offered to negotiate "mini-agreements" as "stepping stones" towards an eventual hemispheric free trade area. Kantor said these agreements would involve bilateral investment treaties and bilateral intellectual property agreements. He also held open the door to eventual accession by Asian countries when he said that NAFTA could be used by the U.S. to "provide the hub between the two fastest growing regions in the world" — Asia and Latin America.[16]

Politics of the NAFTA Accession Clause

The accession clause in NAFTA reads as follows:

> 1. Any country or group of countries may accede to this Agreement subject to such terms and conditions as may be agreed between such country or countries and the Commission[17] and following approval in accordance with the applicable approval procedures of each country.

2. This Agreement shall not apply as between any Party and any acceding country or group of countries if, at the time of accession, either does not consent to such application.

Several observations are in order. The clause does not limit potential candidates for accession to any geographic region.

The accession clause gives Canada and Mexico a say in the terms and conditions under which other countries may join the pact. As with any international trade agreement, the clause must be read not only for what it says but also with the actual bargaining power of the parties kept in mind. Unilateral U.S. actions setting preconditions for commencing negotiations are not precluded.

The second part of the accession clause leaves open the possibility that another country might join the pact over Canadian objections. The Canadian government could then exempt Canada from application of NAFTA provisions between Canada and that country. The *Globe and Mail* of 24 September 1992 (p. C3) cites Canadian Deputy Negotiator Bob Clark as saying Canada wanted the accession clause that appears in the NAFTA text "because without such a clause the Americans would have an opportunity to reopen and change the deal whenever a new applicant came along — to Canada's detriment." But the accession clause, as written, does not preclude efforts to rewrite NAFTA provisions on the occasion of other countries joining the pact. In fact, Article 2202 allows for modifications and additions to the agreement at any time, subject to legal approval "in accordance with the applicable legal procedures of each Party."

How many of NAFTA's provisions might be up for renegotiation each time a new country joins is open to speculation. Some U.S. business lobbies, such as the Iron and Steel Institute, maintain that other countries should not be allowed to accede to NAFTA unless they accept obligations that are no less stringent than those that apply to Canada and Mexico.[18] In others words, they want NAFTA to be a floor not a ceiling, leaving open the possibility of extracting new concessions from member countries whenever the treaty is reopened. The existence of long annexes allowing Canada, the U.S., and Mexico to grandparent certain derogations sets a precedent for other countries wishing to negotiate particular exemptions as part of their protocols of accession. But the ability of individual countries to win significant exemptions will very much depend on their bargaining power. Chile will be an important test case.

How far and how fast the Clinton administration will move in expanding NAFTA remains to be seen. In his major campaign address on trade issues, Clinton signalled his intention to extend NAFTA at least to other Latin American countries when he said, "If we can make this agreement work with Canada and Mexico, then we can reach down into the other market-oriented economies of Central and South America to expand even further."[19] After his election, Clinton signalled his intention to proceed with negotiations with Chile.

Chapter 19

The Future of Trading Blocs

Daniel Drache

As a member of a new North American trading bloc, Canada would find itself subject to a set of forces requiring analysis that goes beyond the usual estimates of benefits and costs from participation in a textbook-model free trade area.

In this chapter, Daniel Drache shows that there is a political dynamic at work within the NAFTA trading bloc that could lead to major dissatisfaction on the part of all participants. Unless the partners deal with the asymmetry of power, and the problems caused by enlarged access, through explicit adjustment programmes, internal pressures may well develop that could force a reconsideration of NAFTA.

The principal responsibility of governments used to be to shield their population from the periodic downturns of the global business cycle. Capital formation was encouraged, and, in return, investment decisions were subject to public scrutiny and state regulation. This is no longer the basis on which governments and the private sector interact. Everywhere, states are rushing to internationalize their activities. Joining a trade bloc has become one of the most powerful levers that global capital possesses to alter, in a fundamental way, the relations between the state and the market. More and more, governments want to act with private corporations, while corporations seek to blunt the power of states. The Mulroney government's record shows this powershift; in a little less than ten years, it has forced the Canadian economy to adapt in an unplanned way to the demands of the world economy.

If Canadians are to learn to cope with the global economy, they must see whether NAFTA has long-term potential to promote hemispheric co-operation and, further, whether it is a viable welfare-maximizing agreement. As nations try to find security and increased access through trade blocs, the answers to the previous questions are not straightforward.

A post-national state is one in which countries face losing their national identities in a world without traditional frontiers. In the past, nations were seen as communities of peoples sharing responsibility for their mutual well-being. This is becoming less and less so. What defines the post-national nation state are two characteristics: first, a weakened national economy, since a country's well-being is *externally* determined by its export and trade bloc performance, and secondly, a substantial reduction in the ability of the state to engage in day-to-day *internal* economic management. Many of the states' traditional powers are being surrendered as their economies come to rely on global price movements.

NAFTA is the primary instrument of this kind of market-driven integration. What makes it a high-risk project is that countries themselves do not trade — corporations do. Corporations are actors using the national economy for private gain. And what is striking is the way NAFTA empowers the private sector. This continental initiative marks a fundamental break with the past; it is much more than an investment opportunity to kickstart the troubled economies of North America. It is a different kind of trade agreement, broadening the investment frontier.

Trade liberalization has been a prominent feature of the postwar order. For a trade bloc to be viable it has to meet a "Triple-A" test. First, a way has to be found to neutralize the *asymmetry* of power between the partners.[1] This is crucial. Countries will not participate in a regional trading relationship for very long if there is no means to ensure that benefits from larger and more open markets are not shared between all parties fairly. The question remains, however: Who pays for the adjustment costs when workers lose their jobs and firms close their doors? For small and medium-size countries, neutralizing the asymmetry of power requires that the trade bloc have an institutional means to distribute benefits from the dominant to the smaller members.

Secondly, a way has to be found to ensure that *access* to each other's markets is in fact enhanced. This, too, is a major issue and, potentially, an explosive one. In an abstract sense, increased access normally occurs when countries lower tariff barriers and restructure their industries. But markets left to their own devices do not necessarily ensure that countries with structurally weak industries will diversify and that their firms will take a larger share of the market. Unless such firms have prepared themselves over a long period for free trade, they will find themselves overwhelmed by competition from industries that are better financed, more technologically advanced, and better situated to increase market share. With imperfect markets, wide-open trade liberalization is not always the optimal policy for industries. What matters for firms are not the abstract rules of trade liberalization but the results obtained from such a system. If firms do not directly benefit, they will prefer industrial support and strategic trade measures to maximize their chances of obtaining a bigger share of international markets.

Finally, trade-led *adjustment* is one of the most difficult issues that NAFTA faces. It touches a raw nerve. As countries trade more, factories close and workers lose their jobs. How is this process to be managed? Again, state policy is crucial to ensuring that such a situation is properly handled. A case in point is the way France has coped with the trade adjustment of its coal industry. Seventy-five thousand jobs have been phased out in Alsace and Lorraine since 1975 at a total cost of $1.5 billion. This money was spent by the French government on retraining and income maintenance programmes for those who lost employment. By contrast, the British government recently decided to close its coal pits, thus putting thirty thousand British miners on the streets.[2] Britain had no means of addressing the real costs of adjustment. Not surprisingly, threatened with massive public protests, John Major's government was forced for the time being to back down on this issue, which shows that labour adjustment has to be managed by state intervention. This is what renders trade liberalization problematic: it is only sustainable as long as the complexities of the adjustment process are confronted. From this perspective, how sustainable is NAFTA as a trade bloc?

The Post-war Growth Model

In the 1950s and 1960s, trade was not seen as the new frontier promising unparalleled growth. For much of the post-war period, most industrial countries regarded their export performance primarily as a way to increase the strength of their domestic economies and to support higher wage levels. The potential bonus was that a well-managed economy stood a fair chance of making gains in foreign markets provided that it had a core group of national firms large and powerful enough to win market share. Thus, the pursuit of export opportunities was just *part* of a growth model, never a growth model in itself. Countries stressed countercyclical Keynesian policy measures to protect themselves against the ever-present business cycle. Currency devaluation was an option that countries used as a trade weapon. A proactive industrial policy was another. Faced with unexpected difficulties, a country could invoke "contingent" ad hoc protection authorized by GATT to protect itself against import surges or other short-term difficulties.

In the 1960s and 1970s, it was natural that all countries looked outward as barriers to trade fell. But growth was not premised principally on success in export markets. A high standard of living and rising productivity depended on deepening domestic demand and on supporting economies of scale in mass production industries. States were largely free to control their national economies. Labour was a partner in the process. Some industries were given special status and protected from international competition. Social safety nets were not on the table. Collective bargaining forced firms to become efficient by competing on productivity gains rather than by driving down wages. Because consumers had more to spend, diversification of a country's industrial structure was as important as the drive to specialize in order to be internationally competitive in a few sectors. The idea of shielding social programmes from competitive pressures was seen neither as a particularly radical innovation nor as a worrisome departure from the precepts of trade liberalization. These established practices made sense because they helped guarantee social peace. Working-class gains at the plant or the national level could not easily be attacked through GATT.

Growth through Free Trade

The rules governing global trade are being rewritten. Almost every sector and most aspects of society are to be opened to international competition. Once the rules are established, market processes dominate. Government's role is to maintain a trade-friendly environment and accept the symmetric rights and obligations to open their markets regardless of the costs and consequences. As Jagdish Bhagwati put it in his book entitled *Protectionism:*[3] "the logic of efficiency has to determine the allocation of activity among all trading nations." In practical terms, what kind of dynamic is unleashed?

The logic of NAFTA rules requires Canada and Mexico to adopt less of a national trade strategy and more of a hemispheric approach. The idea behind all regional trading arrangements is that the nation state can no longer satisfy the growth needs of transnational corporate players. Doing so requires enlarging markets by integrating national markets into larger trading areas.

In terms of production organization, NAFTA imposes a very different model of workplace practice and principles. The dominant model of production throughout the industrial world used to be "Fordist"; now lean production replaces mass production. Inherent in this paradigm shift is the fact that trade is no longer employment-friendly but a powerful stimulant to shed labour.

In terms of government priorities, the differences are also marked. Full employment was the priority and objective of most industrialized governments, but this is no longer true. Deficit reduction, price stability, and trade competitiveness are the principal objectives of capitalist economies. National economies experience fiscal restraint, slow growth, high levels of unemployment, and spending cuts. Those active in the labour market have to stay active longer, often look after their own welfare needs, and pay more of the costs of whatever services they consume. Social welfare is no longer a right but a consumer entitlement, like a private insurance scheme. No longer are states to rely on tariffs or other measures of protection against the uncertainty of free trade. They have to have a tough-minded commitment to opening markets even when it means job loss and factory closings. What has caused this profound change in the trade regime?

Classic Trade Liberalization

The global trading system post-1945 was founded on the principles of liberal internationalism — multilateralism, nondiscrimination, and the economic theory of comparative advantage. Good performance depended on technology and investment inflows, the effectiveness of the industrial relations system, state macro-economic management of the economy, and the success of industrial policy. There was a commitment to gradual trade liberalization and the opening of markets; tariffs were to be eliminated over a long period. GATT ensured that commerce, broadly defined, was subject to state policy and regulation. Countries were free to manage their economies, while the international economy was left to market forces within a system of rules and obligations.

Table 19–1

FREE TRADE REGIMES COMPARED

Institutional Forms	*Cold War Free Trade Regime 1945–1985*	*Free Trade Bloc 1985–1993*
International Regime	GATT	Single European Act/NAFTA
International Legal Norms and Instruments	Most-favoured-nation; GATT panels; gradual tariff reduction; niche competition	Rules of origin; contingent protection; discrimination against non-members; adversarial trade
International Finance	Stable exchange rates; Bretton Woods till 1971; longterm low interest rates till mid-1970s	Deregulation of financial institutions; inflation speculation cycle; internationalization of financial markets and increased capital mobility
Capital–Labour Compromise	Fordist–Beveridge State; expanding social wage; wages out of competition in core Fordist male-dominated mass production	Neo-conservative state; downward pressure on wages; competitive labour markets contracting social wage; rise of part-time employment and the feminization of labour markets
Production Model	Mass production of standardized engineered commodities; long production runs; economies of scale in monopolized sectors	Lean flexible production systems; differentiated markets; economies of scope in monopoly and competitive side of the economy; downsizing of the workforce; niche competition; contracting out
Distribution Norm	Static inequality; progressive tax system	Dynamic inequality; regressive tax system; consumer-based taxes

There was a dispute resolution system to referee the game. Under the GATT system, when allegations of trade injury occurred, countries went before third-party panels to resolve their differences. GATT had no way to impose its authority on unwilling governments short of providing for states to retaliate. Parties to trade disputes were sovereign states, and under GATT rules, they were required to settle their differences through negotiation. What was appealing was that countries with very different national practices did not have to fear that GATT would force them to harmonize their programmes with countries having other priorities. In the event of trade disputes, mediation was provided for. Codes were designed to prevent dumping, trade-distorting subsidies, and other contentious practices.

Finally, the post-war liberal international order was underwritten by U.S. hegemonic power. This situation ensured that countries would be rewarded for supporting the principles and the theory of comparative advantage as embedded in the GATT trading system.[4] Those inside the system were more likely to receive U.S. investment and technology flows. Those outside, like the Soviet bloc, were penalized because they could not get access to much-needed investment flows. Developing countries also found much to criticize. They often faced closed markets for their labour-intensive products, such as clothing and shoes. These discriminatory measures kept Third World consumer goods out of the industrial markets of Europe and North America.

Despite these and other shortcomings, on balance, post-war trade liberalization had devised a safeguard solution to the question of competitiveness. Competitive pressures were kept within bounds. Commercial rivalry was not flat-out nor as adversarial as it became by the mid-1980s. Despite all the rhetoric, the best-kept secret of three decades was that the liberal trading regime that grew up after World War II was managed within a set of clearcut parameters, codes, and international norms that respected the rights of countries to shape their economic destinies. This is the reason why GATT survived for as long as it did. National needs and international interests were held in a delicate balance inside its institutional procedures.

New World Trade Regime

An international trading order in which regional trade blocs occupy centre-stage weakens multilateralism and non-discrimination. Regional trading blocs fragment markets rather than open them for all. Access to the trade bloc is controlled through the rules of origin codes. These rules applied by customs are designed to limit entry into the region and divert trade, particularly from Third World countries. Hundreds of pages of NAFTA are designed with this end in mind. Far from being a force for internationalization, NAFTA erects new barriers to trade.

Secondly, regional trading arrangements now politicize trade as never before. Non-economic factors have been given new legitimacy, including asymmetrical terms of trade. Under NAFTA, Canada or Mexico supplies resources to the U.S. at market prices but may buy U.S. goods at higher than average market prices because intra-firm pricing is not regulated. On the industrial side of the economy, U.S. multinationals set up production facilities in Mexico and Canada, and corporate interests can use NAFTA to bargain down taxation levels. In terms of resource management, Canada is prohibited from introducing a two-price system for its oil and gas exports, while Mexico is required to use its energy revenue to retire its external debt.

Thirdly, social policy is on the table to an unprecedented degree. The forces of harmonization work themselves out across borders. Entitlements can be more easily reduced for competitive reasons. No programmes can be taken "out of competition" as previously. Moreover, regionally specific programmes can be scrutinized by U.S. authorities for possible distortions to trade. This power limits the proactive role of member governments to use social policy and other programmes for their immediate national developmental needs.

There is no definition of a subsidy in NAFTA or in the FTA. This judicial oversight serves an important purpose. In a world without borders, the adjustment process has become more volatile and more difficult to manage. The resulting uncertainty means that governments are restricted in the kinds of programmes they can mount for fear that these will be regarded in Washington as potentially causing trade injury and that, therefore, they will be subject to lengthy and costly trade disputes before U.S. judges and legal norms.

Other changes are equally unsettling. Under NAFTA, access is contingent and ad hoc rather than guaranteed or enhanced because Canadian and Mexican exporters are subject to U.S. trade law. Canadian experience under the FTA is relevant in this regard. Since the agreement was signed, there have been more than twenty new trade disputes. Some are minor, but many are major. Indeed, the trend has been toward disputes that are more costly to Canadian producers. U.S. interests are now targeting core Canadian industries, such as steel, agricultural exports, and automobiles, and the new disputes have hurt Canadian exporters. What is equally disturbing is that this form of trade harassment shows no sign of diminishing. Far from broadening access to the U.S. market, juridically guaranteed access thus far has led to *less* access than before the FTA or NAFTA was negotiated.

Finally, it is wrong to think of NAFTA as simply a regional trading alliance. It is more precise to call it a dollar zone disguised as a trade bloc. The U.S. dollar is the region's reserve currency, and Washington has the de facto power to set monetary policy for Canada and Mexico. As a result, the U.S. is the *boss* of NAFTA, with currency fluctuations determining the competitiveness of Canadian and Mexican exporters. Canadian exports surge when the Canadian dollar is weak against the U.S. dollar, and exports drop when the Canadian dollar is upvalued. If anything, under NAFTA Canada and Mexico are more directly subservient to Federal Reserve policy.

Far from stabilizing the post-national nation state, this trade bloc is likely to be a destabilizing force for two principal reasons. First, the U.S. remains better positioned than its Canadian and Mexican counterparts to address the footloose nature of U.S. business. Second, asymmetry means that NAFTA does not inhibit Washington from addressing its long-term problems, but it does restrict what Canada and Mexico can do.

When Clinton decides to encourage American corporations to stay at home as a better solution to rising U.S. unemployment rather than move to Mexico, no U.S. official will be required to look at NAFTA before deciding whether these kinds of measures are contrary to the agreement. If necessary, Clinton can also rely on a variety of U.S. subsidies at both the state and national levels to restrict access to the U.S. market. But if Mexican and Canadian authorities try to take the same measures, the Clinton administration will play hardball with them. Why are two different standards envisaged, tolerated, and juridically acceptable?

Legally, NAFTA offers no means to force U.S. authorities to amend U.S. trade practices to prevent them from harassing Canadian and Mexican exporters. On the other hand, it has plenty of muscle to limit Mexican and Canadian governments from tackling basic economic issues that are structural and not trade driven. The kind of specialization envisaged by NAFTA will accentuate many of the existing structural weaknesses confronting Mexico and Canada.

Michael Porter of Harvard recently completed a major study on the state of Canadian competitiveness.[5] He warned that Canada's economy is at the crossroads and has fallen dramatically behind other industrialized countries. Canada's share of world exports has fallen from 5.3 per cent in 1971 to 4.0 per cent in 1989. He found that the country is overspecialized in resource exports and that Canadian manufacturers are weaker than ever and more dependent on high-tech imports than at any other time in recent history. The problem, in a nutshell, is that Canada's private sector does not invest sufficiently in technology, manpower skill-training, or long-term planning. Even if Canada exporters experience some success, the long-term trend is far from bright. Ontario has been shedding manufacturing employment at a record pace.

Canada is losing ground to industrial growth poles located in the U.S. sunbelt and northern Mexico. With capital more mobile than ever, no Canadian manufacturing sector is secure. Yet every major expert in the field, including Porter and Robert Reich,[6] underlines the importance of long-term stability to a good economic performance. For these experts, control of the home market is crucial to building industries and firms that can hold their own in global markets. In Porter's words, "nations gain competitive advantage in industries where the home demand gives their companies a clearer or earlier picture of emerging buyer needs ... than their foreign rivals." The character of home demand is the critical variable that stands between success and failure, and it is precisely this dynamic that is not sustained by a trade bloc. Therefore, planning and restructuring are next to impossible. Governments are constrained from giving any overall direction to the building of stronger industries.

An open economy empowers the financial sector to move across national boundaries and creates new kinds of competitive pressures from international investors and foreign direct investment inflows. The working assumption is that the multinational giants are to be the motor of growth. According to the United Nations, 35,000 transnational and 156,000 subsidiaries now control foreign direct investment flows worldwide.[7] Trade blocs are essential to this sector. What they offer the TNCs are new rights to invest and divest with the minimum of restriction. Now, wages are directly subject to competitive pressures on a continual basis. This is not a one-time external shock like a wage freeze imposed for a specific period.

With weakened unions in all three countries, real wages in the pockets of workers have barely changed for more than a decade. While there are significant differences between Canada, the U.S., and Mexico and between the different sectors of the labour market, the overall pressures on wage movement is downwards. Wages are much more vulnerable to competitive pressures than ever before. And the social wage is also shrinking. The entire industrial wage-setting mechanism has to incorporate wage pressures that are no longer primarily local but are now starkly global. In these circumstances, a social wage for all Canadians is seen as an impediment to competitiveness rather than as a benefit integral to a society with a high performing economy. What then is the future of Canada and Mexico as post-national states in a borderless world and handcuffed by NAFTA?

Conclusion

In the short term, trade blocs are not viable because there is no redistributing mechanism to ensure that the benefits from open economies are shared. This is problematic for countries like Canada and Mexico; their weak economies cannot benefit sufficiently in terms of increased market share *or* job creation. As well, the amount of access actually diminishes under the norms and practices of a trade bloc like NAFTA because access is essentially transformed into a juridical question. No country can expect enhanced access via this means. Not only is it an artificial and unrealistic way of securing market entrance, but also there is no exemption from U.S. trade law under its terms and conditions. By design, access under NAFTA is contingent, ad hoc, and arbitrary. Finally, a trade bloc promises larger markets, but with larger markets come even larger problems of adjustment. These are not manageable in a market-driven system. Countries that want to join a trade bloc require the state to organize the market. Without the state, markets function poorly and the adjustment costs get out of hand. So, NAFTA will need to find a different rationale for its existence, or it will eventually collapse because it is too narrowly conceived. As the child of the neo-conservative Reagan, Thatcher, and Mulroney revolution, it is unlikely that it will survive for very long in its present form. Assuming that globalization is a permanent feature of the international order, the challenge is to give the trade bloc a different direction. Canada and Mexico are not world powers, but they are significant regional actors nonetheless. What choices do they have?

In a globalized world, the role of the state has to be rethought. Governments face two immediate dangers: the first is from financial capital, which is highly mobile, and the second is from lean production systems. If countries expect to delimit the power of foreign capital, they will have to put in place strategies that do not rely on competing on wages. For many sectors, trade is a double-edged threat. On the one hand, trade has become uncoupled from employment creation, and, on the other, the kind of specialization promoted by trade blocs frequently promotes structurally weak economies. The only way to escape a low-productivity growth trajectory is to discourage it. In the post-national era, doing so requires the state to be an affirmative agent, nationally and internationally, in its approach to global markets. The state must take a "hands on" approach to building strong and effective industries. Learning by doing in production requires governments to favour interventionist policies over "hands off" ones.

A strategic trade policy means adopting programmes that create employment rather than shed jobs. Building a high-wage/high-productivity economy requires governments to see that market access cannot be artificially guaranteed by a trade deal. Countries cannot look to a hemispheric trade deal for an economic miracle. They will only acquire strong industries when they have their own indigenous technological capacity. By contrast, foreign investors are more likely to drive out local competitors and diminish any such capability from arising.

At a time when tariffs are at an all-time low, a comprehensive trade agreement establishes too many structural impediments to creating new industries. It gives the dominant member of the bloc too much of an advantage, and it offers too little to the others. The competitive struggle for markets can only produce winners and losers. Trade adjustment requires that what one nation gains, others lose. In these circumstance, the difference between success and failure ultimately depends on how countries nurture their local industries. Because knowledge about production tends to be local in character, every particular national setting needs to reinforce its technological capacity. Regaining control over the economy becomes an issue of the highest priority. Until this happens, people will be held hostage to the speculative needs of global finance, and countries will be denied the technological knowledge to build strong dynamic industries.

As presently conceived, NAFTA is much too crude an instrument of economic integration to be a viable hemispheric force to co-operation in the long term. The Clinton administration has taken the unilateral decision to reshape NAFTA to reflect its needs and objectives in the area of labour standards and environmental protection.

This change in policy should not go unnoticed. NAFTA cannot be permitted to constrain Mexico and Canada from rebuilding their industrial bases. If it does, then both governments need to take seriously the abrogation option and leave NAFTA.

Canada and Mexico need to find ways to use international fora to address the real developmental needs of peoples. More and more trade blocs divide the world. They erect barriers rather than tear them down. They are protectionist in concept and undermine any broader and revitalized form of internationalism. In short, they are backward-looking because they prevent countries from developing new forms of sustainable development. They polarize wages and force countries to adopt out-of-date, short-term solutions to deeply rooted structural problems. In the end, it would not be a great loss if NAFTA fell apart. Other more equitable multilateral agreements are not only possible but preferable.

Chapter 20

Renegotiation and Termination

Duncan Cameron
with the assistance of Mel Clark

The major political issue surrounding the FTA and NAFTA is whether a new Canadian government could renegotiate the terms of the trade deals to Canadian advantage.

In this chapter, prepared with the assistance of Mel Clark, Duncan Cameron outlines the reasons renegotiation would fail to produce a satisfactory conclusion for Canada. He estimates that the costs of terminating the agreements are easily exaggerated and judges that termination is a viable option for Canada.

Renegotiating either the FTA or NAFTA to buy back powers ceded (as proposed by the Liberal Party of Canada) will not work for three reasons. First, U.S. power greatly exceeds Canada's in bilateral negotiations. Second, the agreement gives the U.S. most of the concessions it sought, and there are not many left to concede. Further concessions would be counterproductive because they would buy back only a small fraction of powers relinquished while further damaging Canadian interests (e.g., privatization of grain marketing in the Prairies and Ontario). Third, the agreement has accelerated the process of integration, and if it is patient, the U.S. will fully dominate Canada.

The reality of the enormous power the U.S. possesses in bilateral negotiations with Canada means that the U.S. would not give Canada a free ride in negotiations relating to the FTA or anything else. The Americans would begin negotiations from the position that the FTA reflects a balance of rights and obligations and that they must be paid for any changes that benefit Canada. There is no evidence that the U.S. has ever made unrequited concessions to Canada in the FTA or any other bilateral or multilateral negotiation. But in the FTA Canada makes many unrequited concessions to the U.S. For example, Canadian concessions on water, energy, export taxes, subsidies and countervailing duties, forest products, and marketing boards are not balanced by concessions of equivalent importance by the U.S.

Since the U.S. market is ten times larger than Canada's, the U.S. would take the position in negotiations that a symmetrical exchange of concessions relating to normal trade barriers, such as countervailing duties, would not provide reciprocity, and they would therefore request additional concessions.

Before the FTA negotiations began, Simon Reisman said, "A major difficulty" in negotiating a bilateral agreement with the U.S. "is that the economic benefits from free trade are likely to be asymmetrical," and the "Americans would ... have to see concrete benefits in other areas, if they were to accept the terms and conditions that Canadians would justifiably request in negotiations." In an article published in *The Canadian Business Review* (Fall, 1985), Mr. Reisman illustrated this fundamental point by proposing that the Grand Canal project would "provide bargaining leverage to Canada." The FTA gave the U.S. national treatment rights to all of Canada's water — not just the waters of James Bay — as well as "concrete benefits in other areas," and the most important benefit Canada obtained was the removal of U.S. tariffs, which was not a big gain. The average U.S. tariff has been reduced in multilateral negotiations from 50 per cent in the early 1930s to around 4 per cent on dutiable industrial goods and 1 per cent on all industrial goods, including goods that enter duty free.

The FTA changes that Canada would request would adversely affect powerful U.S. private-sector interests — who would therefore oppose them. They would, for example, refuse to return to Canada any substantive rights the FTA gave them in the parts the Liberal Party wishes to renegotiate. Thus, these private-sector interests alone could make non-negotiable most, if not all, the changes sought by a Chrétien government.

Any substantive change in the FTA would have to be approved by Congress. There is a high risk, therefore, that Canada would be required to pay twice: first, by the administration and, second, by the Congress. The cost of negotiating under double jeopardy is best illustrated by what happened to U.S. subsidies following the FTA negotiations. Chapter 19 sets out the rights and obligations negotiated by Canada and the U.S. relating to anti-dumping and countervailing duties. After the negotiations concluded, Congress decided to amend the agreement, acting unilaterally under Section 409 of the U.S. Implementation Act (to amend Chapter 19). Section 409 establishes a new track for U.S. industry to petition for non-tariff measures to gain an advantage over Canadian exports. It is unique because it applies only to Canada. The adverse implications for Canada can be illustrated by two examples: first, Section 409 circumvents the injury test (i.e., the U.S. does not have to prove that so-called subsidies caused damage to U.S. industry) and establishes easier criteria for action against perceived subsidized Canadian exports than previously applied; second, U.S. law previously limited countersubsidy action to a countervailing duty equal to the subsidy, but Section 409 permits the use of a range of non-tariff measures that could provide much more protection than a duty equal to the subsidy.

The main source of U.S. power in bilateral negotiations with Canada — its huge market — does not operate in GATT (General Agreement on Tariffs and Trade) because countries assess reciprocity primarily on a multilateral basis. The power the U.S. derives from private-sector and congressional interests is substantially reduced in GATT negotiations by its export interests in third countries. And Canadian interests vis-à-vis the U.S., especially in eliminating non-tariff measures or their trade-distorting effects, are shared by other countries. During the Tokyo Round of GATT, the U.S. made a number of concessions of value to Canada, which Canada either could not have obtained on a bilateral basis or for which we would have had to pay an exorbitant price. These U.S. concessions related to subsidies, countervailing duties, "buy American," and valuation.

Canada's weakness in bilateral negotiations with the U.S. is illustrated by this summary of the bilateral FTA negotiations on subsidies and countervailing duties:

The Canadian objective was to obtain "security of access to the biggest, richest market in the world," especially by exempting Canada's exports from U.S. countervailing duties. The prime minister said, "Our biggest priority is to have an agreement that ends threat to Canadian industry from U.S. protectionists who harass and restrict exports through misuse of trade laws."

The result was to make Canadian exporters much more vulnerable to U.S. harassment than they were under GATT and inevitably to induce Canadian companies (as well as overseas companies) to move to the U.S. because:

- The legality of U.S. countervailing and dumping duties will be judged on the basis of U.S. law and not GATT law, and FTA panels are limited to deciding whether the U.S. government applied U.S. law correctly.
- In a process controlled by the Americans the U.S. can change its laws and it has already done so twice since the FTA was implemented.
- From the time an American trade action is initiated, it can take eighteen months or more to obtain an FTA panel ruling. This compares to six months for a GATT panel decision.
- FTA legal fees will be substantial: for example, the $10 million paid in less than a year by Canadian lumber producers in the 1986 case, whereas GATT is free of such fees.
- There is no corrective recourse to GATT because the FTA states that U.S. law applies.

What concessions would we offer the U.S. to pay for requested FTA changes? Since the U.S. would possess much greater power than Canada in the proposed negotiations, U.S. demands would control the result. Further U.S. negotiating aims are outlined in public U.S. papers, including the *President's Statement of Administrative Action on the FTA,* correspondence between the president and congressional representatives relating to the FTA, and known U.S. requests in the GATT Uruguay Round. When these are compared with the further concessions made by Canada under the NAFTA — which amounts to a renegotiation of the FTA — it can be seen that the U.S. has already been able to extend the list of its bargaining gains. There is no reason to believe it would back off from these gains, and they provide ample evidence that the U.S. would seek further advantage in new negotiations.

Termination

Termination of the FTA and refusing to proceed with NAFTA will work. Article 2106 states: "This Agreement" can be "terminated by either Party upon six-months notice to the other Party," that is, without conditions.

If the FTA is terminated, Canada's trade with the U.S. would again be covered by GATT. Tariffs could not be raised above GATT-bound levels, non-tariff measures (NTMs) would be subject to GATT provisions, and disputes would be settled on the basis of GATT rights and obligations. The result would be substantially better total access to the U.S. — that is, the access derived from four variable factors: tariffs, NTMs, dispute settlement, and the covering agreement. Since U.S. GATT tariffs are already very low and will be reduced further in the Uruguay Round, increases would be limited and more than offset by GATT's superior NTM and dispute-settlement provisions — for example, U.S. interests could no longer obtain countervailing duties (CVDs) on demand. The prospects of obtaining even better total access to the U.S. in the future are greater in GATT than the FTA because Canadian interests are shared by most other countries, which substantially increases our negotiating power. GATT's forty-year track record is evidence that it provides effective collective security against U.S. beggar-your-neighbour measures as well as those of other members.

Termination of the FTA would return to the federal government powers the Mulroney government ceded and permit it to act again to ensure the survival and development of Canada as an independent and humane nation. For example, all ceded powers itemized in Chapter Three of this book would be recovered, and federal governments could again act to preserve and strengthen the national policies listed in that chapter.

Would termination reverse business decisions caused by the FTA that have benefited Canada? FTA provisions most likely to affect business decisions relate to CVDs, national treatment, minimum export prices, export taxes, investment, and tariffs. All these provisions — with the exception of certain tariffs — are likely to result in decisions to make processed and manufactured goods in the U.S. instead of Canada. More often than not, elimination of Canadian tariffs is also likely to result in decisions to produce in the U.S. (e.g., food products and motor vehicles and parts), although in certain cases, it could increase production in Canada by reducing costs of imports. Elimination of most U.S. tariffs is unlikely to increase Canadian production because they are already very low, and reductions will be more than offset by CVD and possibly by other provisions, although, again in certain cases, it could work to our advantage (e.g., zinc castings). During the first four years of the FTA, Canada lost more than 500,000 full-time jobs. These considerations suggest any costs that accrued from termination would not be very onerous. The prospect of regaining powers ceded by the FTA far outweigh the costs of termination.

Since the elimination of tariffs could provide benefits for Canada, it is suggested termination be combined with two proposals: first, that both countries continue to eliminate all industrial tariffs except those relating to motor vehicles; and second, in GATT, they ask other industrialized and newly industrialized countries also to eliminate remaining industrial tariffs. The U.S. might well agree to at least the first proposal because Canada's tariffs on dutiable industrial products are more than double U.S. tariffs — 9 per cent as opposed to 4 per cent. If the U.S. did not agree to either proposal, Canada could proceed to reduce its own tariffs and ask other GATT countries to take equivalent action. Bargaining power would be retained providing free entry was not bound in GATT until the other countries matched it. Such actions would not only retain the most important advantage Canada obtained from the FTA and virtually eliminate termination costs, but also they would help defuse any initial U.S. annoyance.

The main obstacle to termination will probably be the corporate establishment represented by the BCNI (Business Council on National Issues), including the media it controls directly or influences through its lobbying activities and its spear-carriers in think-tanks and in the universities. The BCNI will use every means available, unfair as well as fair, to retain a neutered federal government. Despite the BCNI, however, a majority of Canadians voted against the FTA in 1988, and the Charlottetown referendum appears to have raised their level of resistance to manipulation. Moreover, it is well recognized that the corporate establishment is not always right and does not always win.

Afterword:
The NAFTA Side-Deals

Mel Watkins

Negotiators for Canada, Mexico and the U.S. struck a tentative deal on NAFTA in Washington at the infamous Watergate Hotel on the August 12, 1992. On December 17 of the same year, the three leaders — Brian Mulroney, Carlos Salinas and George Bush — affixed their signatures. But Bush was already a lame-duck president, and president-elect Bill Clinton was prepared to honour the deal only if "side-deals" were added on environmental and labour standards. Talks to that effect began in mid-March of 1993. By June, though no side-bar agreements had been finalized, the Mulroney government had pushed legislation approving NAFTA through the House of Commons and the Senate.

Side-deals were announced on August 13, though there would be no final text for several weeks. Meanwhile, on June 30 a U.S. federal court held that NAFTA could not proceed until an environmental impact statement had been prepared; the Clinton administration, while insisting that it truly cares about the environment, has appealed. NAFTA plus the side-deals will now go as a package to the U.S. Congress; if Congress moves expeditiously, NAFTA kicks in as intended on January 1, 1994.

Within an hour of the August 13 announcement, however, Richard Gephardt, the Democratic leader in the House of Representatives, said the side-deals, particularly the one on labour standards, were not enough for him. Ross Perot, who continues to command the support of 20 per cent of the American electorate, was likewise unmoved in his opposition to NAFTA. Ominously for Clinton, none of the groups opposing NAFTA — trade unions, environmentalists, and so on — were sufficiently persuaded by the side-agreements to switch sides. But none of NAFTA's supporters — big business and most Republicans in the House and the Senate — saw the side-agreements as gutting the deal proper, either. The side-deals seem pretty much like a non-event, the substance of NAFTA not having been altered. Much depends on Clinton and where he throws whatever weight he has in a crowded political agenda; will he push harder for health care or for NAFTA?

The outcome is uncertain. But there is no doubt as to where power lies in the "new" emerging North America, regardless of the media spin here and in Mexico. As befits both the Canadian-American and the Mexican-American relationships, at the end of the road it will be America that has decided, keeping in mind that the American business class tends to get its way when it comes to foreign policy. It could be otherwise only if publics (such as the Canadian public, which polls consistently show does not want NAFTA) were heeded.

A dab of deconstruction is in order. Why *side*-deals? Why is trade a deal unto itself, but the quality of the environment and the nature of working conditions merely side-bars? One could easily argue that *they* should get the priority, that trade is not an end in itself but a means to higher "goods"; at minimum, there might be parity.

Of what do the deals consist? Presumably, new and tougher standards to protect the environment and improve the lot of workers. But in fact, the three governments have committed themselves only to enforcing their own existing laws and to setting up cumbersome bureaucratic machinery, well removed from democratic public accountability, to make themselves do that. Even within the two areas in question, the range of the laws subject to enforcement is constrained; on labour standards, the rights excluded include such fundamental matters as the right to free and independent unions (independent, that is, of the state, which is clearly not the case in Mexico) and the right to bargain collectively (a right which is severely abridged in the right-to-work states of the American South). For Canada, the side deals automatically apply to labour and environmental laws under federal jurisdiction, but in fact these matters fall substantially under provincial purview. There they will apply only if enough provinces ratify them and that seems unlikely.

Why, in the light of there being so little in these agenda, did the Canadian government and Canadian business make such a fuss about fighting them, and then claim a great victory in the end? The U.S. wanted to apply trade sanctions to force governments to enforce their laws. Canadian negotiators adamantly refused, properly making the point that this would simply give the U.S. more clubs with which to harass Canadian exporters — who are being constantly harassed already in spite of a free trade agreement which was supposed to put an end to that.

Setting aside the possibility that sanctions might well be warranted, say, to protect the environment from the externalities generated by the Canadian forest products industry, what is being begged is the question of the point of a further free trade agreement with the U.S. when the existing one has proven itself unable to disarm the U.S. The contradiction is neatly encapsulated in a *Globe and Mail* editorial of August 13, 1993. We are told, within the same paragraph, that "Canadian industries — from forestry to steel — already have enough trouble dealing with frivolous American trade complaints" and that "NAFTA was supposed to build on the gains Ottawa made in the Free Trade Accord, which gives Canada significant protection against unfounded U.S. trade actions."

With much windy rhetoric on our part, the American negotiators gave us our way on sanctions (perhaps feeling that they were doing enough to us already in that regard) and we agreed instead to fines paid by governments. Canadian taxpayers may have trouble seeing the gain. The Mexican government, desperate for any deal to salvage its credibility, was stuck with sanctions. A headline in the *New York Times* said it all: "Mexico Opts for the Sanctions It Bitterly Opposed." It's all a bit reminiscent of how the Mulroney government caved in on getting any genuine exemption from American protectionism in order to get a deal in 1988.

All of this discussion regarding sanctions was accompanied by much ballyhoo about sovereignty — fending off theirs (American) and preventing the diminution of ours — from corporate spokespersons like Tom d'Aquino of the Business Council for National Issues. Their hypocrisy is manifest, these being the same people who otherwise devote their time to rendering Canadian governments impotent in the face of transnational capital on economic and social policies that would serve the public and national interest. As for Prime Minister Kim Campbell's sham fight against the U.S. on the NAFTA sanctions as part of her overall gambit of distinguishing herself from Mulroney, Wayne Roberts captured the "difference" brilliantly in *NOW* magazine: "In stark contrast with former prime minister Brian Mulroney, she has shown her ability to cloak social and environmental degradation with assertive nationalism, not abject continentalism."

As multinational arrangements go, what is the nature of NAFTA that remains, untouched and untouchable, by these side-deals? A free trade agreement like the FTA or NAFTA, while comprehensive in terms of the corporate agenda, creates a free trade area, not a common market. The textbooks tell us the distinction between these is that commodities move in the first case and commodities and factors of production in the second. But, in fact, capital has great freedom to move in both cases and only labour is constrained in the case of a free trade area. This means labour can be stranded to its detriment. But nothing can be done to permit labour to follow capital without moving to a common market. There is slight evidence of a willingness, on the part of the Americans (who see free trade with Mexico as an alternative to yet more Mexicans migrating to the U.S.) or of Canadians, to go that route.

The alternative way to offer some protection to labour is to imbed an agreement on labour standards — not a side-deal but a full-ledged social charter — into the trade agreement. But then how is it to be made effective without an institution, democratically constituted with real power, that stands above the participant governments, thus necessarily and properly threatening their sovereignty — and that might actually have more muscle to hold mobile transnational capital to account? The same question, of course, dogs the issues of environmental protection.

There is a profound paradox here that makes NAFTA unacceptable with or without the side-deals that are on offer. NAFTA could only make sense as part of a much larger arrangement that took the powers national governments are losing to the companies and gave them to a higher government that was directly accountable to a newly constituted North American public. But there is no real constituency in North America for such a transnational structure, and it is not the project presently of the governments or the corporations or the people.

What we get instead is the unacceptable half-way house of NAFTA. As the project of corporate capital, it risks disempowering, even impoverishing, people in all three countries. Better no deal at all than this one.

Selected Plant Closures and Production Relocations: January 1989–June 1992, Ontario

Theresa Healy

Some indication of the extent of the free trade adjustment process can be gained from this table prepared for the Canadian Centre for Policy Alternatives *by Theresa Healy. It shows the strong tendency of small, medium, and large manufacturing concerns to close operations in Ontario and relocate to the U.S. or Mexico under free trade. This industrial "rationalization" was widely predicted by both opponents and supporters of free trade. What has not occurred to offset job losses is the new investment in Canada foretold by free trade supporters, though not by opponents.*

Company/ Ownership	Community	Products	Relocation	Job Losses	Date
Advanced Gibson Canada Ltd. (US)	Windsor	circuit breakers /electrical switch components	US	36	August 1989
Allied-Signal Canada Inc. (US)	Mississauga; London	brake plants	Charlotte, NC / Frankfurt, KY	670	February 1992
AM International Canada Inc. (US)	Scarborough	coating and blue print paper	US	10	December 1990
Amerock Inc. (US)	Meaford	household cabinet hardware	Chicago, IL	140	September 1990
Andrew Malcolm Furniture	Listowel	furniture	Atlanta, GA	137	June 1990

Company/ Ownership	Community	Products	Relocation	Job Losses	Date
Arnold Manufacturing	Windsor	restaurant furnishings	Louisville, KY	100	?
B.F. Goodrich Tires (US)	Kitchener	tires	Cleveland, OH	70	1991
Ball Packaging Products Inc.	Simcoe	paint cans	Philadelphia, PA	210	January 1991
BASF (US and Germany)	Cornwall	chemicals	NJ; Germany	250	January 1990
BASF Coatings and Inks Canada (US and Germany)	Toronto	liquid inks container coatings	Ohio	60	December 1990
Beckman Industrial Corp. (US)	Toronto	electronic temperature, voltage components	Fullerton, CA	80	April 1990
Bendix Corp. (US)	Collingwood	seatbelts	Alabama; Mexico	459	April 1990
BIC Inc. (US)	Downsview	assembly & packing consumer products	US	45	August 1991
Bilt-Rite Upholstr. Co. Ltd.	Toronto manufacturing	furniture Tupelo, MS	Bauhaus;	450	March 1990
Black and Decker (US)	Trenton	lock assembly	Berlin, CN	264	1991
Borden Co. Ltd. (US)	Ingersoll	dairy products	New York	79	November 1991
Burlington Carpets (US)	Brampton	carpets	Georgia, Virginia	450	May 1990
C & D Charter Power Systems (US)	Perth	industrial batteries, battery chargers, power systems	US plants	120	April 1992
Canadian Coleman (US)	Etobicoke	camping equipment, heating	Kansas, Texas	214	1991
Canron Inc. (US)	Etobicoke	railroad maintenance equip.	Columbia, SC	20	1991
Carter Automotive (US)	Bramalea	auto parts	Lafayette, TN	230	?
Caterpillar of Canada Ltd. (US)	Brampton	tractors	Raleigh, NC; Peoria, IL	430	April 1991

Company/ Ownership	Community	Products	Relocation	Job Losses	Date
CCL Custom Mfg.	Toronto	consumer/ packing products	US locations	205	1991
Celanese Canada Inc. Hoechst (Germany)	Millhaven	heavy decitex industrial yarn	Queretaro, Mexico	160	April 1992
Champion Spark Plug (Texas)	Windsor	premium gold plugs	Burlington	75	June 1992
Clevite Elastomer (US)	St. Thomas	auto parts, shock absorbers	Napoleon, OH	50	1991
Cobi Foods Inc. (US)	Whitby	packing plant/ canned/froz. vegetables	Picton, Ont.	250	December 1989
Colgate-Palmolive Canada (US)	Toronto	cleaners, toothpaste, detergents	US	250	September 1991
Commander Electrical Equipment Inc.	Scarborough	electrical equipment	Jackson, MS	175-190	March 1991
Consumers Glass	Hamilton	glass containers, molds	Washington, PA	95	September 1991
Cooper Canada	Rexdale	sports equipment	US/Mexico	600	October 1990
Croydon	Cambridge	furniture	Chicago, IL	360	1991
D.G. Trim	Petrolia	door panels, auto parts	Kentucky	32	January 1989
Dixon Ticonderoga Inc.	Newmarket	pens, typewriter correction fluid	Versailles MO.; Deer Lake, PA; Actonvale, PQ	60	June 1990
Dominion Fabrics	Long Sault	weaving plant, cloth for work wear	Malaysia, Tunisia	365	February 1992
Dow Chemical Canada Inc. (US)	Sarnia	chlorinated solvents	?	40	October 1991
Dylex Ltd.	Toronto	garment manufacturing	New Jersey	45	November 1991
Echlin Canada (US)	Rexdale	auto parts	US plants	100	March 1989
Electro Porcelain/ Leviton (US)	Waterloo	lamps, fixtures, appliance receptacles	US/Mexico	200	?

Company/ Ownership	Community	Products	Relocation	Job Losses	Date
Emblematic Jewelry Product	Rodney	lapel pins	Mexico	40	?
Fedders Inc. (US)	Orangeville	air conditioners	New Jersey	140	November 1990
Ford Motor Co. (US)	Windsor	engines	Mexico	900	?
Ford Motor Co. (US)	St. Thomas	auto parts	Mexico	140	1991
Ford Export/Office (US)	Windsor	auto	US	45	November 1989
Freedland Industries	Kingsville	auto parts	Dearborn, MI	45	March 1989
Freudenber Nonwovens	Cornwall	textiles	New Jersey; Massachusetts	57	July 1991
Friskies Pet Products (US)	Mississauga	pet food	US	121	September 1990
Galtaco	Paris, Orillia, Brantford	auto parts	Grand Rapids, MI; Dover/ Greenfield, TN	400	?
General Tire Cda. Ltd. (US/Germany)	Barrie	radial and tire trucks, replacements	Mount Vernon, IL; Mayfield, KY; Charlotte, NC	950	July 1991
General Motors (US)	Scarborough	vans	Flint, MI	2,700	May 1993
General Motors of Canada Ltd. (US)	Windsor	auto trim	Findlay, OH	255	June 1990
Gerber (Canada) Inc.	Niagara	baby food manufacturing	Fremont, MI	?	April 1990
Gilles Mill (US)	Braeside	pine lumber	Chicago	103	May 1992
Glidden Paints Canada (UK)	Bramalea	paint	Boucherville, PQ; US plants	90	April 1990
Greb Inc.	Kitchener	workboots and casual footwear	Quebec; US; Asia	230	November 1990
Grolier (US)	Toronto	book distribution	Danbury, CN	171	August 1991
Harding Carpets	Brantford	carpets	Tennessee	470	October 1990
Hartz Canada (US)	St. Thomas	pet foods	US	26	1991

Company/ Ownership	*Community*	*Products*	*Relocation*	*Job Losses*	*Date*
Harvard Industries (US)	Whitby	car mirrors	Tennessee	150	July 1990
Industrial Part Coaters	Windsor	metal plating	Buffalo, NY	50	April 1991
Inglis (US)	Toronto	major appliances	Clyde, OH	650	1991
Inglis Ltd. (US)	Mississauga	refrigerators	Evansville, IN	350	January 1991
International. Playing Card Co.	Windsor	playing cards	Cincinatti, OH	35	September 1989
ITW Shakeproof (US)	Mississauga	fasteners manufacturing	Tennessee	45	July 1989
J.H. Warsh Ltd. US)	Toronto	garment, designer, sportswear	?	30	December 1990
Johnson Controls (US)	Port Perry	seating	US	280	February 1992
Johnson Controls Ltd. (US)	St. Thomas	automotive batteries	US	170	February 1992
Kandresco (US)	Cambridge	trucks	Peoria, IL	200	?
Kaufman Furniture	Collingwood	furniture	North Carolina	100	?
Kellogg Canada Inc. (US)	Etobicoke	foods	US locations	361	March 1992
Kelsey-Hayes (US)	Windsor	steel wheels	Japan; US	424	June 1990
Komdresco Canada Inc. (US)	Kitchener	mining and construction trucks	Peoria, IL	200	August 1991
Lawson Mardon Packaging (Ireland)	Toronto	soap boxes	Radisson, NY	125-140	March 1992
Melita Canada	Rexdale	filtering production	US	50	April 1991
Mercury Marine	Toronto	outboard motors	US	40	April 1990
Midas	Scarborough	auto parts, mufflers	Hartford, Chicago	140	1991
Modine Canada	Rexdale	auto parts, radiators	?	40	July 1989
Monaco Group	Toronto	garments	?	85	December 1991

Company/ Ownership	Community	Products	Relocation	Job Losses	Date
Motor Wheel Corp Canada Ltd. (US)	Chatham	wheels and brakes	Lansing, MI; Medota, IL	582	January 1991
Murata Erie North America (Japan)	Trenton	electronic systems, radar components aviation communications instruments	Georgia; State College, PA	463	April 1992
Nestle/Dr. Ballards (US)	?	pet food	?	80	March 1990
Newcor Inc. (US)	Windsor	auto parts, custom welding equip.	Michigan	26	1991
Olan Mills (US)	Kingston	photofinishing	US plants	95	August 1990
Outboard Marine	Peterborough	electric motors	US; Mexico; Belgium; Hong Kong	290	?
Peerless Carpet Corp.	Toronto	carpet mill	Acton Vale, Qué.; Georgia	155	May 1990
Phil Carry	North York	garment manufacturing	?	300	November 1987
Philips Electronics (Holland)	Scarborough	computer monitors, electronics	Europe, Italy	253	June 1992
Picker International (US)	Bramalea	X-ray equipment	Cleveland, OH	160	1991
Playtex Ltd (US)	Renfrew	women's underwear	Philippine; Caribbean, Mexico	160	June 1990
PPG Canada Inc.	Etobicoke	paint	US	119	February 1989
Random House (US)	Mississauga	?	Westminster MD	73	December 1991
Redirack Ltd (US)	Toronto	steel racks	Illinois	136	October 1990
Research Development Industries	Etobicoke Mississauga	industrial solvents and cleaners	France	200	January 1991

Company/ Ownership	Community	Products	Relocation	Job Losses	Date
Robertshaw Controls Canada Inc. (US)	Toronto	temperature and industrial control products	Texas	150	October 1990
Rockwell Plastic Products (US)	Cambridge	plastic products	US	74	November 1990
Rubberset Co. Canada (US)	Gravenhurst	paint brushes and rollers	Ohio, Maryland	100	April 1992
Schlegel (US)	Burlington	auto parts, weather stripping	Tennessee; Oklahoma	104	1991
Scholl Plough, Mabelline	Burlington	cosmetics	Little Rock, AR	78	1991
Schwitzers Manufacturing (US)	Stratford	construction vehicle parts	Ackville, NC	80	1991
Sheller-Globe of Canada Ltd. (US)	Kingsville	steering wheel covers	Mexico	419	April 1990
Sklar-Peppler	Hanover	furniture	Mississippi	42	?
Solaray, Sunbeam Corp. Canada Ltd.	Brantford	gas barbecues, electric lawnmowers	US; Mexico; Etobicoke	125	June 1990
Square D Canada (US)	Stratford	electrical panels; industrial safety switches	Lexington, KY	140	December 1990
Standard Products (US)	Etobicoke	auto trim	South Carolina	121	April 1992
Star Suspension Industries (US)	Mississauga	fasteners	US patent plant	32	?
Steel Fabric ating and Welding Co.	Dundas	steel products	Abingdon, VA	23	March 1992
Sterling Drug (US)	Aurora	pharmaceutical	US; Puerto Rico	180	1991
Stevens Controls	Pembroke	thermostats	Norwalk, OH	49	?
Sunar-Hauseman (US)	Waterloo	office furniture	Holland; Michigan	280	1991
Suncor (US)	Toronto	blending and packaging oil and lubricants	US plants	86	September 1990

Company/ Ownership	Community	Products	Relocation	Job Losses	Date
Superior Performance Products (US)	Newmarket	cast aluminum road wheels	Arkansas; Kansas	150	December 1990
T.A.G. Inc.	Cambridge, London, Woodstock	clothing	US	1,250	?
Therm-O-disc Inc. (US)	St. Thomas	thermostats	US; Mexico; Ireland; Netherlands	300	October 1990
Thomson Transportation Company	London	trucking	Detroit, MI	250	?
Tridon Ltd.	Burlington, Oakville	wiper blades, hose clamps, electronic signal flashers	Smyrna, TN	632	September 1990
TRW Canada Inc.	Penetang	seat assembly	?	400	February 1992
TRW	Penetang	seat belts	Mexico	194	October 1992
Uniroyal Goodrich (France)	Kitchener	tires	US, Mexico	1,000	January 1992
United Technologies Automotive (US)	St. Thomas	wire harnesses	US; Mexico	319	April 1991
Vogue Bra Canada	Cambridge	women's underwear	Mexico	50	August 1992
Warnaco Activewear Canada Ltd.; Speedo (US)	Carleton Place	swimwear	Kentucky	70	April 1990
Wayne Canada (US)	Windsor	bus manufacturer	Richmond, IN	145	March 1990
WCI Canada Inc. (US; Sweden)	Cambridge	washers and dryers; refrigerators	Webster City, IA; St. Cloud, MN	325	August 1990
Wilton Grove Bendix	London	auto parts	Kentucky, North Carolina Mexico	46	?
Woodbridge Foam (US)	Tilbury	auto parts	Romulus, MI	140	?

The Exchange Rate: 1988–91

Nate Laurie

The importance of the exchange rate in international trade is well recognized. An increase of 15 per cent in the value of the Canadian dollar, as occurred between 1985 and 1989, is the equivalent to removing an average tariff of 15 per cent on all imports and placing a 15 per cent tax on all exports.

In this appendix, Nate Laurie reconstructs the events surrounding the rise in the Canadian dollar. He shows that the upward move in the exchange rate is compatible both with American objectives in the free trade talks and the type of tough industrial adjustment measures favoured by the Bank of Canada. Though the dollar subsequently declined to below 80 cents U.S., the damage to Canadian industry from the lethal combination of free trade and an appreciating exchange rate had already been extensive.

When Prime Minister Brian Mulroney first raised the prospect of a Canada–U.S. free trade pact in the fall of 1985, the Canadian dollar was trading at 72.8 cents U.S. By the time the trade deal came into effect at the beginning of 1989, the dollar had risen 15 per cent, to almost 84 cents U.S. Towards the end of 1991, it had drifted upward into the 86- to 87-cent range. Some economists attribute the run-up in the Canadian dollar to the Bank of Canada's tough anti-inflationary stance. Others say the high dollar is the unfortunate side-effect of an interest-rate premium Canadians must pay to attract needed

foreign funds. But the chronological overlap between the free trade
timetable and the dollar's rise points to a third possibility — that the
Canada–U.S. exchange rate was, in fact, negotiated as part of the
overall deal.

For a time, this sinister theory was regularly served up to journal-
ists as an "off the record" conversational appetizer at lunch. But it
only attained the status of news briefly in 1990, when a former
member of Mulroney's cabinet announced in the *Toronto Star* that
he was sure it was true. That the ex-minister was Sinclair Stevens
explains why the theory was so quickly and easily dismissed. Having
been thoroughly discredited for breaching Ottawa's conflict-of-inter-
est guidelines, Stevens's credibility with the public was almost nil.
Moreover, he could not really substantiate his claim that Ottawa had
made a secret "gentlemen's agreement" with Washington to boost
the dollar because he had been forced out of cabinet a week before
the preliminary free trade negotiations actually began.

Stevens did have an interesting story to tell. In the 2 December
interview with the *Star,* the former industry minister recalled how
Malcolm Baldrige, then U.S. commerce secretary, "drove it home to
me" late in 1985 that the dollar was the key to a Canada–U.S. free
trade deal. When Stevens asked point-blank what it would take for
Canada to get an agreement, Baldrige is said to have replied: "The
level of your dollar." As Stevens reconstructed the conversation, "I
said, 'What do you mean?' And he said, 'Well, we could never
contemplate a situation where your dollar would be at a level that
would be an inherent advantage that we felt was unfair.' " Baldrige,
who died in a 1987 rodeo accident, reportedly told Stevens that the
dollar "would have to be up towards the 90-cent mark — it has
certainly got to be closer to par with the American dollar." As
Stevens explained it, Baldrige likened a trading agreement with Canada to trade between California and the rest of the U.S. "There's no
way they'd want California to be sitting out there with a 70-cent
dollar. It'd be like giving a 30-per-cent subsidy to anybody who
manufactures in California."

Although Stevens provided the *Star* with a graphic, behind-the-
scenes account of Baldrige's thinking, the colourful U.S. politician
made no secret about how he felt. In a September 2, 1986 appearance
before a U.S. congressional committee, Baldrige said that an increase
in the value of the Canadian dollar would help to ease the U.S. trade
deficit, then Washington's top economic concern. As the *Star*'s
David Crane wrote after the Stevens revelations, Baldrige was far

from alone in this view. During the trade talks, American negotiator Peter Murphy frequently pointed to U.S. congressional concerns over the low Canadian dollar. Senator Max Baucus, an influential Democrat on trade policy, had even called for the dollar to the pegged within a "target zone." The U.S. National Association of Manufacturers emphasized that a deal with Canada had to have "an agreed procedure for consultations" on the dollar "so that trade distortions arising from this cause can be resolved." And when the negotiations commenced in 1986, the *New York Times* reported that American industry was "pressing for a higher Canadian dollar almost as a pre-condition for closer trade arrangements."

Washington's motives for striking a secret deal on the dollar seem to be abundantly clear. Ottawa's motives — beyond its determination to secure a trade deal at almost any cost — will be examined below. But if motive can be readily established, opportunity and means are much more difficult to show. Stevens himself suggested just how difficult it would have been for the dollar to be included in the free trade talks when he told the *Star,* "I would be very surprised if it was on anybody's agenda in a formal way." The risks for Mulroney of tying the dollar directly to the trade deal were simply too great. His government would have toppled like a house of cards had a single shred of evidence of a fix on the dollar ever leaked out. As a practical matter, too many people — decent people — would have had to be involved in cynical negotiations to sell this country out.

In a May 1986 study speculating on "why the exchange rate will be a factor in bilateral trade negotiations between Canada and the United States," the Ontario Ministry of Treasury and Economics set out a plausible scenario providing both the opportunity and means for a deal on the dollar to take place. Recognizing the political imperative for Ottawa to decouple dollar discussions from the trade negotiations, Treasury and Economics stressed that "the only issue, and it is a semantic one, is at which table the exchange rate will be formally discussed." The table identified in the study was, in fact, the same one then U.S. Treasury Secretary James Baker pointed to a week earlier — on 20 May, the day before the preliminary trade talks formally began. Responding to complaints that Canada was deliberately holding down its dollar to sell into the American market, Baker told the U.S. Senate foreign relations committee that a higher dollar was the price Canada might have to pay to join the exclusive club of major industrialized countries, then known as the Group of Five (G-5). The U.S. had already begun to use the G-5 as an instrument for manipulating exchange rates to stem its burgeoning trade deficit. In September 1985, Washington reached agreement with the other G-5 countries — Japan, Germany, Britain, and France — to lower its currency relative to theirs. As the Ontario treasury study noted, in the seven months following the agreement, known as the Plaza Accord, "the U.S. currency declined by roughly 30 per cent against the yen, 23 per cent against the German mark, 12 per cent against sterling and 20 per cent against the French franc." Almost as a warning, the study went on to say that "despite considerable volatility in the intervening period, the Canada–U.S. exchange rate was the same at the end of April [1986] as it was immediately prior to the G-5 accord."

The expansion of the Group of Five into a new Group of Seven to include Canada and Italy effectively set the stage for the Reagan administration to dictate the range in which the Canadian dollar would be allowed to trade. The G-7 provided the perfect cover for Ottawa to make the necessary dollar downpayment to secure a deal on trade. It would be the true gentlemen's agreement, to use Stevens's words, reached as part of a celebrated policy co-ordination exercise by the world's top finance ministers and central bankers — the majority of whom had no direct interest in the Canada–U.S. free trade deal. From this august forum, moreover, there was no risk whatsoever that the agreed range for the Canadian dollar would ever leak out. All that would have been required was for Baker to point out to then Finance Minister Michael Wilson that Japan, Germany, Britain, and France had already made a significant contribution to reducing the U.S. trade deficit and that as a member of the G-7 — and America's largest trading partner — Canada had an obligation to do it is part. The Japanese and the Germans would almost certainly have supported a proposal to boost the Canadian dollar, if only to help relieve continuing U.S. pressures against them. The path of the dollar lends credence to the hypothesis that that is, in fact, what transpired in 1987 when G-7 finance ministers agreed in Paris to set target zones for their currencies in what has become known as the Louvre Accord.

But if the Louvre Accord provided the setting for a secret deal on the dollar, the unanswered question still remains: Why would the government of Canada deliberately set out to damage the country's prospects under a free trade deal? While there can be little doubt about the government's readiness to make side deals to meet an array of specific American sectoral demands — on pharmaceuticals and softwood lumber, to name but two — is it really conceivable that it would subject Canada's entire industrial base to a high-dollar yoke? Not only is it conceivable; it is the logical course of action for those who hold to the view that the threat of economic annihilation is the best spur to boost productivity growth. In the clichés of fashionable lean-and-mean economics, an over-valued dollar makes necessity the mother of invention (and innovation); it is the ultimate "cold shower" to speed industrial restructuring and adaptation; it is a form of shock therapy to promote competitive well-being; it is "short-term pain for long-term gain." As the Bank of Canada would see it, the establishment of a G-7 target zone for the dollar would be little more than a formal affirmation of its chosen instrument for bringing Canada's cost structure into line with that of the United States. Instead of a sinister sell-out of the country, it is indeed possible that Mulroney and his advisers would have rationalized a fix on the dollar as a prerequisite for realizing lasting benefits from the free trade deal.

That's certainly how Stevens saw it: "The last thing I think the Canadian government would want is a Canadian industrial sector constantly wanting an advantage from a declining dollar. In the sense that that's not going to help productivity, it's not going to help competitiveness. It's ... almost like a subsidy to allow you to be more effective in a market that, subject to some restructuring, the theory is, you should be able to compete in." So there it is: motive, opportunity, and means. But the legal burden of proof means little to economists who judge their theories on the basis of how well they predict. By that scientific test, the conspiracy theory of a dollar fix works better than any other theory put forward before the fact to forecast the dollar's rise.

Endnotes

Introduction

1. See Rick Salutin, *Waiting For Democracy* (Toronto: Penguin, 1988). For background, see Duncan Cameron (ed.), *The Free Trade Papers* (Toronto: Lorimer, 1986), and Duncan Cameron (ed.), *The Free Trade Deal* (Toronto: Lorimer, 1988).
2. *The Canada–U.S. Free Trade Agreement: An Economic Assessment* (Ottawa: Department of Finance, 1988).
3. See the publication, *Mergers and Acquisitions Canada*, various issues.

Chapter 1

1. "Predatory" compared to "benevolent" hegemony: Robert Gilpin, *The Political Economy of International Relations* (Princeton: Princeton University Press, 1987), p. 90.
2. Internationalization of the state: Robert W. Cox, "Production and Hegemony: Toward a Political Economy of World Order," in H. K. Jacobson and D. Sidjanski, eds., *The Emerging International Economic Order: Dynamic Processes, Constraints and Opportunities* (Beverly Hills: Sage Publications, 1982), p. 53.
3. Import substitution industrialization: Glen Williams, *Not for Export: Towards a Political Economy of Canada's Arrested Industrialization* (Toronto: McClelland and Stewart, 2nd ed., 1988).
4. National mode of regulation: Stephen Clarkson, "Disjunctions: Free Trade and the Paradox of Canadian Development," in Daniel Drache and Meric S. Gertler, eds., *The New Era of Global Competition: State Policy and Market Power* (Montreal: McGill-Queen's University Press, 1991), pp. 103–26.
5. Folly and ambition: Stephen Clarkson, *Canada and the Reagan Challenge: Crisis and Adjustment, 1981–85* (Toronto: Lorimer, 2nd ed., 1985), chs. 2, 3.
6. Canada, *Report of the Royal Commission on the Economic Union and Development Prospects for Canada, Volume One* (Ottawa: Minister of Supply and Services Canada, 1985).

7. How Washington outnegotiated Ottawa: G. Bruce Doern and Brian W. Tomlin, *Faith & Fear: The Free Trade Story* (Toronto: Stoddart, 1991).

8. See Graham Carr in this volume.

9. Stephen Clarkson, "The Canada–United States Trade Commission," in Duncan Cameron, ed., *The Free Trade Deal* (Toronto: Lorimer, 1988), pp. 26–45.

10. Gary N. Horlick and F. Amanda DeBusk, "The Functioning of FTA Dispute Resolution Panels," in Leonard Waverman, ed., *Negotiating and Implementing a North American Free Trade Agreement* (Vancouver: Fraser Institute, 1991), ch. 1.

11. Richard G. Lipsey, "The Case for Trilateralism," in Steven Globerman, ed., *Continental Accord: North American Economic Integration* (Vancouver: Fraser Institute, 1991).

12. For a masterly comparison of European with North American integration: Bruce W. Wilkinson, "Regional Trading Blocs: Fortress Europe versus Fortress North America," in Drache and Gertler, *The New Era of Global Competition,* pp. 51–82.

13. On the trade-off between reduced sovereignty and increased autonomy: Albert O. Hirschman, *National Power and the Structure of Foreign Trade* (Berkeley: University of California Press, 1980).

14. For the position of the popular forces in Canada: Maude Barlow and Bruce Campbell, *Take Back the Nation* (Toronto: Key Porter, 1991); Mel Hurtig, *The Betrayal of Canada* (Toronto: Stoddart, 1991).

Chapter 2

1. Economic Policy Council–UN Association of the United States, *The Social Implications of a North American Free Trade Agreement,* 1993, p. 11.

2. J.O. Stanford, *Continental Economic Integration: Modelling the Impact on Labour, Annals of the American Academy of Political and Social Science,* March 1993.

3. Attorney General of Ontario, *The Impact of the Canada/U.S. Free Trade Agreement: A Legal Analysis,* May 1988, p.9.

4. Statistics Canada, *National Accounts.*

5. Statistics Canada, *Balance of Payments Quarterly.*

6. United Nations, *World Investment Report 1991*; U.S. Department of Commerce, *Survey of Current Business* (various); Banco Nacional de Mexico, *Basic Statistics 1991.*

7. *Wall Street Journal,* 21 August 1992.

8. Ibid.

9. "What Yankee Traders Think of Free Trade," *Canada Business,* August 1992, pp. 19–20.

10. Cited in *Globe and Mail,* 31 October 1992.

11. S. Krajewski, "Intra-Firm Trade and the New North American Business Dynamic," Conference Board of Canada, September 1992, p. 7.

12. Ibid.

13. Cited D. Crane, *Toronto Star,* 1 April 1993.

14. Cited *Financial Post,* 9 October 1990.

15. Susumi Eto, *Toronto Star,* 2 April 1993.

16. Assessment, *U.S.–Mexico Trade: Pulling Together or Pulling Apart,* U.S. Congressional Office of Technology, October 1992, p. 7.

17. David Conklin, *The FTA and Ongoing Negotiations: Case Studies,* January 1991, mimeo, p. 15.

18. Ibid.

19. *Globe and Mail, Report on Business Magazine,* March 1993, p. 13.

20. *Globe and Mail,* 5 November 1992.

21. See H. Shaiken, *Mexico in the Global Economy* (San Diego: UCLA, 1990), pp. 21–44.

22. Cited in *Toronto Business,* October 1989.

23. H. Daly and R. Goodland, *An Ecological Assessment of Deregulation of International Commerce under GATT,* World Bank, Environmental Department, 1992, mimeo, p. 7.

24. Conference Board of Canada, *Impact of Environmental Measures on International Trade,* 1992, pp. 3–4.

25. G. Klepper, "The Political Economy of Trade and the Environment in Western Europe," in P. Low (ed.), *International Trade and the Environment,* World Bank Discussion paper 159, 1989, p. 252.

26. UN Conference on Trade and Development (UNCTAD), *Environment and International Trade,* July 1991.

27. P. Low, "Trade Measures and Environmental Quality: The Implications for Mexico's Exports" in Low (ed.), *International Trade,* 1992, p. 108.

28. Ibid.

29. R. Sanchez, "Health and Environmental Risks of the Maquiladora in Mexicali," *National Resources Journal* 163 (Winter 1990), p. 185.

30. Cited in L. Kochan *The Maquiladoras and Toxics,* AFL-CIO 1989, p. 2.

31. Development GAP, *Look before You Leap*, Washington, 1991, p. 5.

Chapter 3

1. Much evidence has been published by the American press. The Hon. Ralph Ferguson, M.P. has repeatedly drawn attention to the lowering of U.S. standards (e.g. statements in the House of Commons on May 1, 1992 and May 25, 1993.

Chapter 5

1. *The Canada U.S. Free Trade Agreement: An Economic Assessment* (Ottawa: Department of Finance, 1988).
2. Ibid, p. 37.
3. See Duncan Cameron (ed.), *The Free Trade Deal* (Toronto: Lorimer, 1988), and Ed Finn, Duncan Cameron, and John Calvert, eds., *The Facts on Free Trade* (Toronto: Lorimer, 1988). Detailed sectoral studies — looking at such variables as degree of protection, structure of trade, plant size, and so forth — tended to project much larger job losses than the econometric models, e.g., the study on job impacts on manufacturing completed in 1988 by the Ontario government and the leaked in-house study of the Bank of Nova Scotia.
4. *OECD Historical Statistics,* Table 3.5.
5. Statistics Canada, 15-001, *GDP by Industry.*
6. See in particular the chapters by John Holmes and Anthony Masi in D. Drache and M. Gertler, eds., *The New Era of Global Competition* (Montreal and Kingston: McGill-Queen's University Press, 1991).
7. Data supplied by the Canadian Labour Market and Productivity Centre. Productivity and labour cost data in both Canada and the U.S. are subject to major periodic revisions, making interpretation of relative trends difficult. The U.S. Bureau of Labor Statistics regularly publishes relative cost competitiveness data that similarly show the importance of the exchange rate as a determining factor in the recent major loss of Canadian manufacturing cost competitiveness.

Chapter 8

1. Statistics Canada, Employment, Earnings and Hours, Catalogue 72-002.

Chapter 9

1. For example, Canada's balance of payments may improve somewhat thanks to the ultimate flow back to Canada of interest and profits from the overseas investments. Also, at the same time as they are transferring production jobs abroad, successful Canadian multinationals might hire more highly skilled workers to perform various head-office tasks (such as research or management) in Canada. The net effects, however, of the foreign investment abroad are almost certainly negative.

2. Technological changes are making some of these services tradeable, so that foreign firms in some industries (such as telecommunications, banking, and some types of marketing) are able to choose how best to serve the Canadian market just as manufacturers are currently able to.

3. Other countries also used tariff walls to support the initial development of domestic industry. However, foreign control did not become as dominant in these countries as in Canada for various reasons: they were further away from and culturally distinct from the U.S.; their governments often imposed stricter controls on foreign investment; and their domestic firms were able to develop attributes (such as unique products or technologies) that allowed them to compete successfully with multinationals even after tariffs were gradually reduced.

4. Recent experience has shown that this is even true of oil and gas, long thought to be the exception to this rule.

5. Firms will also minimize transport costs. For certain hard-to-move goods, this may mean that some facilities are located close to the largest population centres even if production costs there are not the lowest. A region that is both high cost and far from the largest markets of the integrated market is uncompetitive on both grounds; this describes most of Canada today.

6. This type of control on capital mobility has proven to be extremely difficult to implement in practice.

7. This is similar, but not exactly equivalent, to "foreign direct investment."

8. The net real effect in this case depends on whether the performance of the firm improves under the foreign owner (which may benefit the Canadian economy) and on whether the former (Canadian) owner decides to reinvest the proceeds of the sale elsewhere in the Canadian economy.

9. Strictly speaking, the FTA does not prevent Canada from carrying out new nationalization programmes, but they would have to meet stringent standards (including the payment of "fair" market value to foreign owners). As the case of the Ontario auto insurance industry revealed, the FTA makes the public takeover of private industry considerably more difficult.

10. Whether or not this increased investment has net benefits for Canada — let alone whether or not those benefits outweigh the potential costs of giving up the policy-making powers that are restricted by the continental treaties — is, of course, a subject for debate.

11. The owners of Power Corporation sold this company at the top of the market. The FTA probably helped them get a better price. Power has moved out of the resource sector.

12. Unit labour costs equal hourly wages divided by the value of hourly productivity. A high-wage economy can still have low unit labour costs if its productivity is high.

13. Private sector union penetration in the U.S. has fallen to about 10 per cent, compared to over 30 per cent in Canada.

14. Of course, labour costs are not the only costs that firms consider when locating their facilities, although they are certainly the most important. Transportation costs, for example, are also relevant. If transport costs (which have also fallen steadily) were included in Figure 9–1, then the erosion of Canada's "landed" unit cost competitiveness would be even more severe. Land expenses, taxes, and other costs should also be included in a more complete analysis. Anecdotal evidence suggests that high land prices have been an important factor contributing to the exodus of manufacturing firms from Ontario; reducing the price of land to manufacturers might thus be a relatively easy way to slightly improve the cost competitiveness of Canadian production locations without attacking Canadian living standards.

15. This seems rather unlikely, given that most Canadian manufacturers are owned by U.S. parents and thus already concentrate their R & D activity in the U.S.

16. Nissan's recently successful campaign to break union-organizing attempts at its new Tennessee facility indicates that even Japanese firms, despite their heralded "co-operative" labour-management relations, will happily take advantage of repressive and conflictual industrial relations institutions.

17. Although if financial capital is borrowed abroad in order to finance real investments by *Canadian* firms or governments, then it

is conceptually similar in its long-run effects to real foreign investment.

18. Actually, Canada's current account deficit generally results not from commodity trade (Canada usually has a trade surplus) but from interest and dividend payments to foreign investors and other payments to foreign firms for services. The latter in particular have increased dramatically since the FTA was implemented (see Figure 9–2).

19. This sparked some speculation that an agreement to appreciate the Canadian dollar was a hidden part of the FTA package itself. The Bank of Canada's misguided monetary policy is probably more deserving of the blame. (See Appendix II.)

20. The net foreign investment position reflects all changes in foreign ownership of real and financial assets in Canada compared to Canadian ownership of all types of assets abroad.

21. This deterioration marks a reversal of the trend prior to the FTA, when much-heralded investments by Canadians in the U.S. (particularly in real estate) served increasingly to offset the longstanding U.S. investment stake in Canada.

22. This inflow of financial capital from the U.S. in 1992, simply offset, to a large degree, capital that was formerly borrowed from investors from outside of North America but who became worried about the outcome of Canada's constitutional negotiations.

23. Indeed, this was the point of the initial maquiladora programme, which was specifically intended to create jobs in the hard-hit northern border region of Mexico after the U.S. barred the use of temporary Mexican labour on U.S. farms.

24. In Mexico's maquiladora, for example, the domestic content of intermediate inputs and supplies is estimated to be as low as 2 per cent. Mexico's government will now have to hope that free market processes will be able to increase this domestic spin-off.

25. It is also important to note that these countries sharply restrict the role of foreign capital in their respective economies.

26. Of course, the often brutal suppression of democratic and labour rights in many of these countries is not an aspect of their development strategies that we would like to see emulated; the point here is merely that strategic government intervention played a crucial role in their successful economic records.

27. The EC agreements also contain many provisions enshrining foreign investors' rights, opening up government procurement processes, and so forth that are similar to those discussed above. How-

ever, the basic principle that governments should be able to regulate investment as part of overall economic development policy has not been questioned in Europe.

28. The same pattern is evident in the treatment of subsidies in trade law; it is only the U.S. government that has paid so much attention to subsidies as a non-tariff trade barrier. Other countries are more receptive to the notion that subsidies are an important element of interventionist industrial policy, but they have been forced (until recently) by the bargaining power of the U.S. (based on its market size) to agree to the regulation of subsidies through the GATT and other fora.

29. So far, of course, the right of human beings to move freely throughout North America has taken a distant back seat to the similar rights of investment capital.

Chapter 10

1. Brian Mulroney quoted in Mel Clark, "Why Renegotiating Free Trade Won't Work," *Canadian Forum*, June 1990, p. 10.

2. The five U.S. trade remedy instruments of most concerns to Canada were the anti-dumping law, the countervailing duty law, Section 301 of the Trade Act of 1974, Section 337 of the Tariff Act of 1930, and emergency safeguard rules. See Duncan Cameron, Stephen Clarkson, and Mel Watkins, "Market Access," chapter 4 in Duncan Cameron, ed., *The Free Trade Deal* (Toronto: Lorimer, 1988).

3. Clark, "Why Negotiating Free Trade Won't Work," p. 11.

4. Cameron, Clarkson and Watkins, "Market Access," p. 53.

5. Andrew Anderson, "Piecemeal Trade Reform Cited as Dangerous," *Report on Free Trade,* 21 May 1990, p. 6.

6. Canadian Labour Congress, Free Trade Briefing Document no. 4.

7. Don Mazankowski, speech to Canadian Meat Council, 9 February 1990, quoted in "Free Trade: The Sellout," NDP, Dave Barrett, May 1990.

8. Quoted in Giles Gherson, "Washington's Agenda," in Duncan Cameron, ed., *The Free Trade Deal,* p. 11.

9. The panel ruled that 10 to 20 per cent of Canadian West Coast salmon and herring could be exported without being landed in Canada. The final settlement agreed to by the Mulroney government inexplicably allowed 20 per cent, increasing to 25 per cent in 1992, to be exported without landing. Similar regulations for the East Coast fishery are also at risk, even though they were nominally protected in the FTA.

10. "Confidential Appraisal of U.S.–Canada Pact Weighs Benefits, Shortfalls," *Inside U.S. Trade,* 9 October 1987, p. 18.

11. Among those programmes found to be countervailable in the fresh Atlantic groundfish case and in the 1986 preliminary ruling against softwood lumber were: Investment Tax Credits, Regional Development Incentive Program, Industrial and Regional Development Program, Agricultural and Rural Development Agreements, P.E.I. Comprehensive Development Plan, General Development Agreements, transitional programmes for the Atlantic Fishery, Community Industrial Adjustment Program, and Economic and Regional Development agreements.

12. Carbon Black from Mexico, *Federal Register* 48, no. 29, (1983), 564, cited in Christian Yoder, "United States Countervailing Duty Law and Canadian Natural Resources: The Evolution of Resource Protectionism in the United States," in *Trading Canada's Natural Resources,* Owen J. Saunders, ed. (Calgary: Carswell, 1987), p. 86.

13. Carla Hills, the Bush administration's trade representative, reiterated the tough U.S. position on regional development subsidies in a dispute with the European Community over steel. "The steel multilateral talks did not come to a conclusion on March 31, as I had hoped. The difference is the desire of the Europeans to have regional subsidies be a permitted category. That's unacceptable from the point of view of the U.S." Reuters transcript of briefing by USTR 3 April 1992, mimeo, News Transcripts, Inc. Washington, D.C.

14. U.S. Dept. of Commerce, International Trade Administration, "Certain Softwood Lumber Products from Canada: Final Affirmative Countervailing Duty Determination; Notice," *Federal Register* 57, no. 103 (28 May 1992), 22610n.

Chapter 11

1. NAFTA, Articles 105 and 201.2.
2. Richard Simeon, "Federalism and Free Trade," in Duncan Cameron ed., *The Free Trade Paper* (Toronto: Lorimer, 1986).
3. NAFTA, Article 1202.
4. NAFTA, Article 1205.1.4
5. NAFTA, Article 1101.4, 1201.3(b).
6. British Columbia Teachers' Federation, presentation to the Parliamentary Committee on the NAFTA, December 1992.
7. NAFTA, Annex II (page II-C-2).
8. NAFTA, Article 1206, 1, c.
9. NAFTA, Article 1208.

10. NAFTA, Articles 1207, 1213.

11. NAFTA, Article 1001.

12. NAFTA, Annex 1101.1b-2.

13. NAFTA, Annex 1001.1.

14. NAFTA, Article 1001.1, Annex 1001.1a-3.

15. NAFTA, Article 1017.

16. NAFTA, Article 1024.1.

17. NAFTA, Article 1019.

18. Ontario Premier's Council, *Competing in the New Global Economy*, 1988.

19. Ontario Hydro, personal communication to CUPE, 19 November 1992.

20. NAFTA, Article 1106.

21. NAFTA, Article 1108.

22. NAFTA, Article 1502.3(b).

23. NAFTA, Article 1505.

24. NAFTA, Article 1503.

25. See: David A. Aschauer, "Public Investment and Private Sector Growth," Economic Policy Institute (Washington, D.C.: 1992; Robert Ford and Pierre Poret, "Infrastructure and Private Sector Productivity," *OECD Economic Studies* 17 (Autumn 1991); and Alice Munnell, ed., *Is There a Shortfall in Public Capital Investment?*, Federal Reserve Bank of Boston, Conference Series no. 34 (June 1990).

26. NAFTA, Article 1502.

Chapter 12

1. *The Canada–U.S. Free Trade Agreement*, Article 409 and Article 904.

2. Ibid., Annex 708.1.

3. The Salmon and Herring Trade Panel Decision, 1989.

4. *The North American Free Trade Agreement*, Article 605, Annex 605, and Article 315.

5. Ibid., Chapter 7 and Chapter 9.

6. Ibid., Article 105.

7. Ibid., Article 711.

8. Ibid., Article 713.

9. Ibid., Article 712.

10. Ibid., Article 712.6.

11. Ibid., Article 718.

12 Ibid., Article 718, Paragraph 2.

13. *Managing Interdependence: The Foreign Policy Framework of External Affairs and International Trade* (Ottawa: October, 1991), p. 11.
14. *The North American Free Trade Agreement*, Article 904.
15. Ibid., Article 904, Paragraph 2.
16. Ibid., Article 907, Paragraph 3 and Paragraph 4
17. Ibid., Annex 2004.
18. Ibid., Article 904, Paragraph 2.
19. Ibid., Article 904, Paragraph 2.
20. Ibid., Article 915.
21. Ibid., Article 905.
22. Ibid., Article 913, Paragraph 5.
23. Ibid., Article 1902.
24. Ibid., Article 2005, Article 2015.
25. Ibid., Article 2012 and 2017.
26. Ibid., Article 1114.

Chapter 13

1. Article 2005 of FTA, entitled "Cultural Industries," states: "(1) Cultural industries are exempt from the provisions of this Agreement, except as specifically provided in Article 401 (Tariff Elimination), paragraph 4 of Articles 1607 (divestiture of an indirect acquisition) and Articles 2006 and 2007 of this Chapter. (2) Notwithstanding any other provision of this Agreement, a Party may take measures of equivalent commercial effect in response to actions that would have been inconsistent with this Agreement but for paragraph 1." Canada, Department of External Affairs, "Free Trade Agreement between Canada and the United States of America: Text, Explanatory Notes," in *Trade: Securing Canada's Future* (Ottawa: Ministry of Supply and Services, 1988).
2. Carla Hills, quoted in: Drew Fagan, "Canada Won't Walk Out on Trade Talks; Hills," in *Globe and Mail*, 23 July 1991, p. B3; Ian Austen, "U.S. Wants Culture in Trade Deal," in *Ottawa Citizen*, 23 July 1991, p. B3; and Drew Fagan, "First Day of Trade Talks Produces Discord," in *Globe and Mail*, 13 June 1991, p. A1.
3. Allen Gotlieb, quoted in Jonathan Ferguson, "Former Envoy Doubts Culture at Risk," in *Toronto Star*, 1 August 1991, p. A10.
4. David Crane, "Lay Off Our Cultural Industries or Else, Canada Should Tell U.S.," in *Toronto Star*, 24 August 1991, p. D2.
5. Susan Crean, "Reading between the Lies: Culture and the Free-Trade Agreement," in *The Free Trade Deal*, ed. Duncan Cameron

(Toronto: Lorimer, 1988); and Colleen Fuller, "Fade to Black: Culture under Free Trade," in *Canadian Forum* (August 1991), pp. 5–10. For example, in 1990 the U.S. trade representative created an interagency committee specifically "to review Canadian compliance with the telecommunications provisions of the U.S.–Canada FTA," Office of the United States Trade Representative, *1991 Trade Policy Agenda and 1990 Annual Report of the President of the United States on the Trade Agreements Program* (Washington: GPO, 1991), p. 20.
6. "Culture Groups Dust off Trade Agreements," in *Gazette* (Montreal), 24 July 1991, p. B1; Gotlieb quoted in Ferguson, p. A10; and Michael Wilson, quoted in John Saunders, "Wilson Defends Culture," in *Globe and Mail,* 17 May 1991, p. B3.
7. U.S. Department of Commerce, International Trade Administration, *1991 U.S. Industrial Outlook* (Washington: GPO, 1991).
8. Jeffrey J. Schott, *More Free Trade Areas?* Policy Analyses in International Economics, no. 27 (Washington: Institute for International Economics, 1989), p. 6; and Government of the United States, "Statement of Administrative Action," in *the United States–Canada Free Trade Agreement Implementation Act* (Washington: GPO, 1988), pp. 132–33.
9. *1991 U.S. Industrial Outlook*, pp. 26–3, 32–4, 26–6, 26–9, and 32–3.
10. *Trade Policy Agenda*, p. 1.
11. Barbara D. Kibbe, "Creative Workers, Cultural Industries and Technology in the United States," in *Cultural Industries: A Challenge for the Future* (Paris: UNESCO, 1982), p. 120.
12. Charles Bray III, quoted in Thomas Guback, "International Circulation of U.S. Theatrical Films and Television Programming," in *World Communications: A Handbook*, eds. George Gerbner and Marsha Siefert (New York: Longman, 1984), p. 155; and Congress of the United States, Office of Technology Assessment, *Critical Connections: Communication for the Future* (Washington: GPO, 1990), p. 182.
13. Congress of the United States, Office of Technology Assessment, *Intellectual Property Rights in an Age of Electronics and Information* (Washington: GPA, 1986), p. 225; and *1991 U.S. Industrial Outlook*, pp. 27–2 and 27–3.
14. *Intellectual Property Rights*, pp. 228–53; and *Critical Connections, pp.* 140–41.
15. *Intellectual Property Rights*, pp. 238–45.
16. *1991 Trade Policy Agenda*, p. 89.

17. Government of the United States, *U.S. National Study on Trade in Services: A Submission by the United States Government to the General Agreement on Tariffs and Trade* (Washington: GPO, 1984), p. 158; and *1991 Trade Policy Agenda*, p. 28.

18. *U.S. National Study on Trade in Services*, p. 154, no. 3.

19. "Statement of Administrative Action," p. 132.

20. Robert E. Babe, *Telecommunications in Canada: Technology, Industry, and Government* (Toronto: University of Toronto Press, 1990), pp. 9–14, 247–58; and "Copyright and Culture," in *The Canadian Forum* (February/March 1988), pp. 26–29. In 1988 the Canadian government passed Bill C-60 as the first of two bits of legislation designed to amend the copyright law. Bill C-60 protects the rights of creators. The second piece of legislation, which is designed to protect the rights of users, has not been passed.

Chapter 15

1. *The North American Free Trade Agreement: Final Text*, 17 December 1992, Article 1405.

2. Ibid., Article 1405.6.

3. Ibid., Article 1401.3.

4. Ibid., Article 1115–39.

5. Ibid., Article 1416.

Chapter 16

1. Attorney General for Ontario, *The Impact of the Canada/U.S. Trade Agreement: A Legal Analysis* (May 1988), p. 2.

2. Op. cit.

3. Ibid., p. 90.

4. *The Canada–U.S. Free Trade Agreement*, Article 601.2

5. *The North American Free Trade Agreement*, Annex 2004.

6. Ibid., Article 1201.3(d).

7. *The Canada–U.S. Free Trade Agreement*, Article 1402.3.

8. *The North American Free Trade Agreement*, Article 2101.1.

9. Ibid., Article 2102.2.

10. Ibid., Article 1213.

11. Ibid., Article 1206.1(b).

12. Ibid., Article 1207.2.

13. Ibid., Article 1206.

14. Ibid., Article 1208.

15. Ibid., Article 1102.2

16. Ibid., Article 1106.

17. Ibid., Article 1106.2.
18. Ibid., Article 1110.
19. Ibid., Chapter 7, Section II, Appendix A,5.
20. Ibid., Annex 316 and Annex 603.6(2).
21. Ibid., Article 603.
22. Ibid., Article 604.
23. Ibid., Article 315.
24. Ibid., Article 316.
25. *The Canada–U.S. Free Trade Agreement*, Article 1903.

Chapter 17

1. Congress of the United States, Office of Technology Assessment, *U.S.–Mexico Trade: Pulling Together or Pulling Apart?* (Washington, D.C., 1992), Chapter 3.
2. Ibid.
3. *The North American Free Trade Agreement: An Economi Assessment from a Canadian Perspective* (Ottawa: Department of Finance, 1992).
4. Ibid.
5. Congress of the United States, Office of Technology Assessment, *U.S.–Mexico Trade.*
6. M. Grant, *Canadian Export Opportunities in Mexico,* (Ottawa: Conference Board of Canada Report 84–92, 1992), p. 16.

Chapter 18

1. "Clinton Signals Support for the Americas Initiatives," *Inside U.S. Trade*, 4 December 1992, p. 13.
2. Comisión Económica para América y el Caribe, "La iniciativa para las Américas: un examen inicial," *Comercio Exterior* 41, no. 2, Mexico City, February 1991.
3. George Bush, "Enterprise for the Americas Initiative," United States Department of State, Bureau of Public Affairs, Washington, D.C., 27 June 1990, p. 2.
4. *Inside U.S. Trade*, 28 June 1991, p. 2.
5. Steve Hellinger, "America for the Enterprises," the Development GAP, Washington, D.C., April 1991, p. 2.
6. "Debt for Environment Swap in Latin America Approved by House AG Committee," *Inside U.S. Trade*, 3 July 1992, pp. 4–5, and "U.S. House Approves Debt-Nature Swap Bill," *EAI News*, Institute for Agriculture and Trade Policy, Minneapolis, 16 October 1992, p. 1.

7. Bill Clinton, "Expanding Trade and Creating American Jobs," North Carolina State University, Raleigh, 4 October 1992. Text released by Clinton-Gore Campaign Headquarters.

8. *Inside U.S. Trade*, 18 December 1992, p. 6.

9. *Wall Street Journal*, 24 September 1992, p. R20.

10. Secretaria Permanente del SELA, "Análisis de los acuerdos marco suscritos entre países de América Latina y los Estados Unidos de América," *SELA Capitulos*, no. 28 (enero-marzo 1991), p. 83.

11. *Inside U.S. Trade*, 28 June 1991, p. 2.

12. Ibid., 20 September 1991, p. 21.

13. "U.S. Will Seek to Extend NAFTA, Create Trade Network with Asia, Official Says," *Inside U.S. Trade*, 9 October 1992, p. 11.

14. *Inside U.S. Trade*, 23 October 1992, p. 15.

15. Ibid., p. 16.

16. *Inside U.S. Trade*, 7 May 1993, p.4.

17. The commission is the oversight body composed of cabinet ministers (or their delegates) set up by Article 2001. Unlike the FTA, NAFTA also has a permanent secretariat.

18. *Inside U.S. Trade*, 10 July 1992, p. 5.

19. Bill Clinton, "Expanding Trade and Creating American Jobs."

Chapter 19

1. Laura D'Andrew Tyson, *Who's Bashing Whom? Trade Conflicts in High-Technology Industries* (Washington D.C.: Institute for International Economics, 1992).

2. *Financial Times of London,* 8 February 1992.

3. Jagdish Bhagwati, *Protectionism* (Boston: MIT Press, 1988).

4. George Friedman and Meredith Lebard, *The Coming War with Japan* (New York: St. Martin's Press, 1991).

5. Michael Porter, *Canada at the Crossroads* (Ottawa: Business Council on National Issues and Supply and Services Canada, 1991).

6. Robert Reich, *The Work of Nations* (New York: Knopf, 1991).

7. United Nations, *World Investment Report 1992: Transnational Corporations as Engines of Growth* (New York: United Nations).

List of Contributors

Jan Borowy is with the International Ladies Garment Workers Union in Toronto.

Duncan Cameron teaches political economy at the University of Ottawa and is president of the Canadian Centre for Policy Alternatives and editor of *The Canadian Forum*.

Bruce Campbell is a research associate with the Canadian Centre for Policy Alternatives and an advisor to the governments of Ontario and British Columbia on international trade.

Graham Carr teaches history at Concordia University.

Mel Clark is a former senior trade negotiator living in Ottawa.

Stephen Clarkson teaches political economy at the University of Toronto.

Roy Davidson is a former senior public servant living in Ottawa.

Linda Diebel is the Washington bureau chief for the *Toronto Star*.

John Dillon is a researcher with the Ecumenical Coalition for Economic Justice in Toronto.

Daniel Drache teaches political science at Atkinson College, York University.

Sam Gindin is assistant to the president, Canadian Auto Workers.

Theresa Healy is a graduate student at Carleton University.

Andrew Jackson is senior economist at the Canadian Labour Congress.

Nate Laurie is an economic journalist with the *Toronto Star*.

Matthew Sanger is a researcher with the Canadian Union of Public Employees.

Michelle Swenarchuk is acting director of the Canadian Environmental Law Association.

Scott Sinclair lectures in political science at the University of Prince Edward Island and is a doctoral candidate at York University.

Jim Stanford is a doctoral candidate at the New School for Social Research in New York and visiting fellow at the Brookings Institution in Washington.

Mel Watkins teaches economics at the University of Toronto.

Bob White is President of the Canadian Labour Congress.

Index